*Ye kitaab aapse baatein karegi :)*

*Koi sapna zyada bada nahi hota, koi lakshya namumkin nahi hota, aur koi background itna chhota nahi hota jo tumhe rok sake.*

# KISKE LIYE HAI YE KITAAB?

1. Harr woh insaan jo Soft Skills seekhna chahta hai
2. Woh insaan jo life me stuck feel kar raha hai
3. Woh jo small town se ya duniya ke kisi bhi kone se apni journey shuru kar raha hai, aur agey ka rasta dikhane ke liye koi nahi hai.
4. Jiske sapne bohot bade hai
5. Jo apne aap ko prove karna chahta hai ki 'main bhi kisi se kamm nahi hu'

Is book ko likhne ka intention hai — aapko clarity dena aur life ki important skills seekhne me help karna.
Apni journey ke zariye main aapko woh sab batana chahta hoon jo agey aapki zindagi mein kaam aane wala hai.
Maine isme apni galtiyan bhi likhi hai taaki aap unse sikhein aur dohraein nahi.

Jab aap iss kitab ko padhenge, aapke paas do raaste honge:

1. **Judge karna** – 'Yeh aisa kyu kiya Jai ne', etc. Ya phir..
2. **Ache se seekhna aur samajhna** – Jo likha hai usme se learnings lena, aur apni life mein apply karna.

Apko is kitaab se ek naya nazariya milega
Agar aapko kitaab padhne ka shokh nahi bhi hai toh bhi aap isey ache se padh paenge kyuki isey maine us tarike se hi likha hai.
Isme stories hai, 50+ Soft Skills hai aur Self Assessments hai.
Padho, samjho, seekho aur use karo.
Mera daava hai ki agar aap ise ache se padhenge, toh yeh kitaab aapki zindagi badalne wali hai.

Aur haa, kyuki is kitaab me bohot saari kahaniya hai toh aapka mann karega padhte jaaye, par aap koshish karein ki aap ek din me 1 ya 2 chapters hi padhein.

# PREFACE

Ek chhote sheher mein bada hote waqt, mere aas-paas na toh mujhe success ke liye bhookh dikhti thi, na self-improvement jaise concepts ka koi zikr. Soft skills jaise zaroori tools ko toh koi jaanta bhi nahi tha, aur agar koi apne upar kaam karna chahta tha toh sab uspar haste the.

Main padhai mein average tha, par andar ek awaaz hamesha kehti thi — "Tu ruk mat, tujhe life me bohot kuch karna hai abhi"

Kai saalon ki struggle aur jobs ke baad mujhe samajh aaya — mera asli purpose hai **khud khush rehna aur doosron ki zindagi behtar karne mein unki madad karna.**

Yeh kitab mera tareeka hai — harr us insaan ke liye kuch karne ka, jiske paas mentorship nahi hai, skills ka exposure nahi hai, clarity nahi hai ki life me karna kya hai par uske sapne bohot bade hain.

Chahe aap student ho, housewife, professional, businessman, athlete ya bas zindagi mein ek nayi direction chahte ho —

**Yeh kitab aapke liye hai.** Yeh aapko inspire karegi, motivate karegi, aur woh Soft Skills sikhaayegi jo aaj ki duniya mein safal rehne ke liye sirf important nahi, necessary hain.

Maine ismein apne personal experiences, real-life lessons, aur practical exercises share kiye hain — ek aisa roadmap diya hai jo agar mujhe shuru mein milta, toh safar aur behtar hota.

Har chapter ke baad aapko kuch actionable skills milengi, jo aapko apni zindagi ki command lene ke liye tayar karegi.

Main na toh ghar ka sabse pasandeeda baccha tha aur na school ka topper. Phir bhi aaj main woh insaan bann raha hu jisse log milna chahte hain, jiske saath waqt bitaana chahte hain ya photos lena chahte hai. Kaise? Ye aap aagey samjhenge aur seekhenge.

Ye kitaab Hinglish mein likhi gai hai taaki hamare Bharat ka harr insaan Soft Skills seekh sake. Mera maksad hai ki har baat tum tak directly pohoche — tum samjho, feel karo, aur apply karo.

Kaafi personal baatein share ki hain... taaki jab tum unhe padho toh tumhe lage — "Main akele nahi hoon."

Kuch topics turant kaam aayenge, kuch baad mein — lekin har chapter ko ache se padhna. Woh ek beej hai. Aaj boyoge, kal yeh beej ek naya mindset ban ke tumhari zindagi badal dega.

# Jai V. Pareek

*A Big Brother to Small-Towners*

Jab main chhota tha aur Rajasthan ke ek chhote se pyaare se town Kishangarh ke ek middle class parivar mein bada ho raha tha, tab education ke alawa koi bhi bada sapna dekhna sirf distraction maana jata tha. Dost kehte the, "Aukaat me reh bhai," aur rishtedaar bolte the, "Zameen se udd mat, padhai kar."

Ab lagta hai, wo log galat nahi the. Wo sirf wahi bol rahe the jo unhone suna tha ya jo unko sikhaya gaya tha.

Unke liye zindagi sirf marksheets tak seemit thi, aur kuch fix career options the jisme se aapko ek career choose karna hota tha.
Ek middle class family mein bacche ki samajhdaari uske EQ aur IQ se nahi balki 'woh ghar ka kitna kaam karta hai aur badon ki kitni sunta hai' usse measure hoti hai. Main samajhdaar nahi tha, kyuki jab sab bacche mango dolly khane ke liye maan jate the tab main Chocobar maangta tha. Jo badon ko acha nahi lagta tha.

Koi nahi tha jo mujhe bole "Beta, alag hona galat nahi hai," ya phir koi yeh keh sake ki "**Agar tere marks average hain, toh iska matlab yeh nahi ki tu zindagi mein kuch bada nahi kar sakta**." Toh maine apne aap ko guide karna shuru kiya. Aur apna bada bhai khud bana.
Aaj, main wahi bada bhai aap logo ke liye is book aur mere videos ke zariye banna chahta hoon.

Mera naam Jai Pareek hai. Ek joint family mein bada hua, jisme 17 log ek saath rehte the. Mummy ek teacher thi, jo ek gaanv me roz paidal chal kar door-door tak parents ko samjhane jaati thi ki apne bachon ko school bhejna zaroori hai. Unki mehnat ne mujhe yeh seekh di ki change aapko chahiye toh khud lana padega.
Aap bethke wait nahi kar sakte.

Mujhe yaad hai, main school me bohot competitions jeeta karta tha. Mujhe yaad hai ek samay aisa tha jab results announce karte waqt Principal ma'am bolti thi '1st prize goes to, **AS USUAL** Jai Pareek' Woh As usual sunne ki na mujhe aadat si thi.
Ek baar maine ek bade dance competition me first prize jeeta tha. Mera naam stage par announce hua, crowd taliyan baja raha tha— aur mujhe laga, "Bas, ab ghar wale mujh par proud feel karegenge!" Main ghar aaya, trophy haath me thi, par jaise hi unko bataya, pehle sawaal aaya, *"Tu phir ye sab karne lag gaya*, padhai bhi karle"

Woh trophy ek pal me ek bojh lagne lagi. Maine chup chaap usse almirah ke peeche rakh di. Parehan toh tha main par andar se mujhe ek cheez pata thi — Main alag tha. Aur mujhe kisi ko yeh decide karne ka haq nahi dena tha ki meri value sirf ek report card se define hogi.

Mujhe ye samajh aa raha tha ki 'Duniya sirf unhi ko yaad rakhti hai jo kuch alag karte hain, jo apni kahani khud likhte hain.
Agar tumhare sapne bade hain, toh ho sakta hai tumhe lage ki duniya tumhe rok rahi hai, lekin ek baat yaad rakhna— **rocket bhi tabhi udta hai jab uske neeche aang lagti hai!**

Har chhota sheher ek nayi kahani likhne ka mauka deta hai. Bas zaroori hai ki kahani likhne wala usse duniya tak pahunchane ka jazba rakhta ho!

Over the years, I've worn many hats: Maine 15 alag-alag jobs ki hain (jo pehle ek galti lagti thi, hum iske baare me baad me baat karenge),
8 countries me travel aur kaam kiya hai, 7 alag alag Industries ko samjha aur 6 businesses banaye— Actually kisi business ko maine banaya aur kisine mujhe. Kabhi struggle kiya, kabhi zor se gira, aur kabhi kaamiyabi mili.

Bohot rejections face kiye, failures ke saath lada, aur apne sapne baar-baar khud se dobara khade kiye.

Mera sabse bada sapna tha ek din International job karna. Jab meri pehli International hotel job ka visa cancel ho gaya, toh aisa laga jaise bachpan ka sapna bikhar gaya ho. Lekin wahi ladka jo ek visa rejection se tut gaya tha, aage chal kar duniya ke sabse bade hotel Burj Al Arab me kaam kar raha tha, international award functions me celebrity manager bankar poora show manage kar raha tha, bus se travel karne wala, mahine ki 3 international flights le raha tha aur jo zyadatar log soch bhi nahi sakte, woh zindagi jee raha tha.

Tab samajh aaya— Jo apne aap par aur apne sapno par believe karta hai, uske liye kuch bhi impossible nahi hai.
Is book me main aapko kaafi cheezein bataunga jo maine experience ki.. uska reason apni badhai karna nahi hoga balki aapko ye feel karwana hoga ki agar main kar sakta hu toh aap bhi kar sakte ho, hum dono me koi farq nahi hai.

Aaj, main yahan hoon tumhe yeh batane ke liye ki tumhare sapne matter karte hain! Tumhe kisi se permission lene ki zaroorat nahi hai unhe chase karne ke liye. Compromise mat karna kyunki tumhe lagega ki log tumhari soch nahi samajh rahe. Tum usse kahin zyada capable ho jitna tum khud ko maante ho! Trust me.

Is book ke zariye, main tumhara bada bhai, dost aur guide hoon—
jo tumhare saath khada hai, jo tumhe guide kar raha hai, aur jo tumhari potential me vishwas rakh raha hai jab poori duniya tumhe underestimate kar rahi ho.

Chalo, milkar seekhte hain aur agey badhte hain.
Let's rewrite the narrative—because your dreams are worth fighting for.

**Welcome to your journey of transformation.**
**Let's together, build The Better You.**

# CONTENT

Aapko lagega kuch topics repeat horahe hai, aap unhe phir bhi padhna.
Aur jo topic acha lage uske baare me aur research karna, videos dekhna, books padhna. Jaise jaise aap is book ko padhoge, waise waise ye aur interesting hone lagegi.

**Dedicated to My Parents (Mere mata pita ji ke liye)**
***Mr. Vijay Kumar Pareek & Mrs. Vishnu Kanta Pareek***

Meri maa, jinhone mujhe समानुभूति (Empathy) ka arth sikhaya. Bachpan me dekhta tha, kaise wo subah jaldi uthti, 17 logon ki joint family sambhalti, khana banati, do bachon ko school bhejne ki tayyari karti, aur phir apni naukri par nikal jaati. Jaisa maine bataya Maa ek Government school ki teacher thi, jo har din ek chhote se gaon me jaakar wahan ke bachon ki zindagi sudharne ka kaam karti thi.

Shaam ko jab ghar laut ti, toh aksar papa ko baith kar batati ki kaise unhe parents ko samjhana padta hai ki "Apne bachon ko school bhejna zaroori hai." Meri maa sirf ek teacher nahi thi— woh gaanv walo ke liye ek margdarshak thi, ek prerna thi, ek vishwas thi ki shiksha zindagi badal sakti hai.

Aaj jo bhi main hoon, jo bhi seekha hai, wo unhi ki wajah se hai. Unhone sikhaya ki asli prabhav tab padta hai jab tum Empathetic bante ho aur duniya se lene me nahi, dene me vishwaas rakhte ho.

Empathy ka matlab sirf kisi ke dukh ko samajhna nahi hota, balki us dukh ko kamm karne ke liye kuch karna hota hai. Agar tumhe kisi ko inspire karna hai, toh pehle unke dukh, unki pareshaani aur unke sapne samjho.
Woh aaj bhi logo ke sath chalti hai, unke saath khadi rehti hai—Wo parivartan maangti nahi hai, Wo logon ke saath chal kar parivartan laati hai.

Mere pitaji—ek shaant vyakti the, par unki baatein hamesha gehri hoti thi. Chaar bhai, ek joint family, dada-dadi sabke saath rehna. Phir bhi, unhone meri har chhoti-badi icchha poori karne ki koshish ki. Computer, travel, skating shoes, laptop—jo bhi zaroori laga, mujh tak pahunchaya, chahe unke liye kitna bhi mushkil ho.

Unki zabardast soch aur sense of humor aaj bhi mujhe unke hone ka ehsaas dilata hai. Kisi insaan ko zarurat hai aur mere papa ko pata chal jaaye.. woh uske maangne se pehle madad kar dete the.
Meri school khatam hone ke baad unhone mujhse sirf ek hi baat kahi — "Teri iccha ho jo kar."

Papa, aaj jo kuch bhi acha chal raha hai, aapki wajah se hai.
Aapne hamare liye sab mumkin banaya aur hamein is laayak banaya uske liye thank you.

## SKILLS KITNE TYPE KI HOTI HAI?

- **Domain Skills / Hard Skills (15% success contribution)**

Technical, degree, diploma.

- **Soft Skills (85% success contribution)**

**Appearance**
Aap apne aap ko dusro ke samne kaise present karte ho - Clothing, grooming, body language,

**Behavior**
Aap din raat kaise behave karte ho - your attitude and habits

**Communication**
Aap apne aap se aur dusro se kaise communicate karte ho

CEOs to underprivileged- sabko ye seekhne ki zarurat hai. Government bhi apne departments me Soft Skills ko zaruri kar rahi hai. Aapke paas choice nahi hai ab.
Aap ye nahi sikhoge toh piche reh jaoge.

Hamari 2/3 population poor self-image and low self-esteem se suffer kar rahi hai. Zyadatar logo ko lagta hai unki communication skills acchi nahi hai

Next page par kuch researches ke baare me likha hai
Unko acche se samjho

# IMPORTANT RESEARCHES

**Harvard University ke research ke anusaar:**
"Career success ka 85% hissa aapke soft skills par depend karta hai aur sirf 15% hissa aapke technical skills ya academics par."

**Carnegie Foundation ke study ke mutabiq:**
"Kisi bhi job ya career mein long-term success ke liye aapki personality, communication aur leadership jaise soft skills, technical knowledge se zyada zaruri hote hain."

**LinkedIn Global Talent Trends Report (2019):**
"92% recruiters, candidates select karte waqt ye maante hain ki Soft skills, technical skills jitne ya usse bhi zyada important hain."

**Stanford Research Institute ke anusaar:**
"75% se zyada career-long success interpersonal skills (logon se achha vyavhaar karna, communication aur emotional intelligence) par depend karti hai."

**World Economic Forum ke Future of Jobs Report (2020):**
"Creativity, problem-solving, aur emotional intelligence jaise soft skills 2025 tak sabse zyada demand mein honge."

**Deloitte ke ek survey ke mutabiq:**
"Employers ke liye top soft skills hain: Teamwork, Communication, Problem-solving, Critical Thinking, aur Adaptability."

**Gallup Organization ki research:**
"Jin logon ke paas strong soft skills hote hain, wo professional aur personal dono life mein zyada khush, zyada productive, aur successful hote hain."

Ye box jis page par hai
waha Soft Skills hai

Chapter 1

# LIFE IN SCHOOL

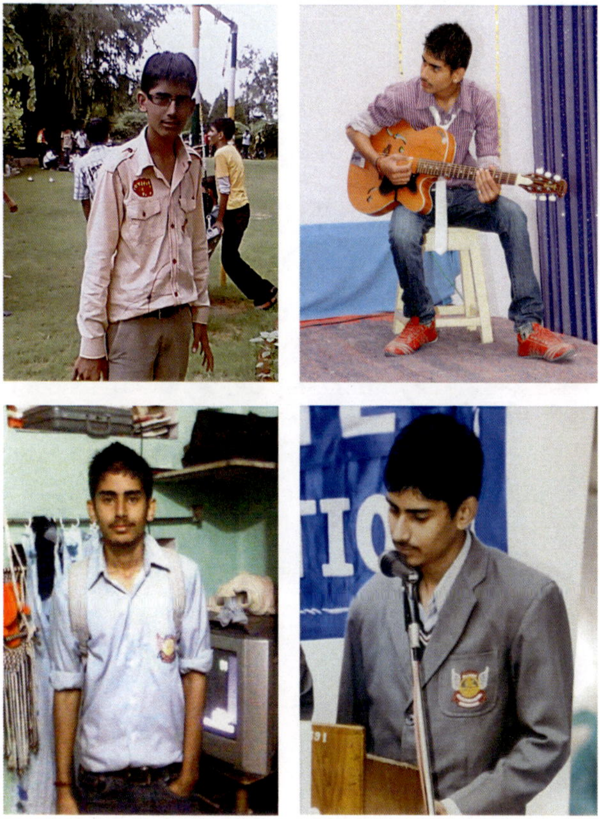

*Meri school time ki kuch pictures*

Mujhe hamesha ek sawaal sataata tha— 'school aur ghar wale mujhe uss cheez par zyada focus karne kyun nahi dete jisme main actually accha hu?'

Jo subjects mujhe samajh nahi aate the, unko padhne me struggle hoti thi. School me supplementary exams diye— isliye nahi kyunki main padh nahi sakta tha, balki isliye kyunki uss knowledge se main zyada connect nahi kar pata tha, mein exams me answers aane ke baad bhi nahi likh pata tha.
Maine kaafi baar English aur computer subjects me top kiya tha,
9th me maths subject me supplementary aane ke baad 10th mein usi maths ke paper me 78/100 marks bhi lekar aaya hoon, bass mujhe aisa lagta tha ki mujhe in subjects me interest nahi hai.
Mujhe baaki activities karni hai jaise dance, music, art, skating, etc.
Agar aapke around bhi aise bacche hai toh ek bar puchna zaroor unse ki 'tera kya karne ka mann hai'?

Jab bhi marks kam aaye, aisa lagta tha jaise har kisi ki nazar sirf meri kamiyon par hai. Parent-teacher meeting meri zindagi ka sabse ganda din hua karta tha. Jis din me beemar hota tha mere mata pita samajh jate the ki school meeting aane wali hai aur iski acting chalu hogai hai. Teachers, relatives, aur family sirf meri weakness par dhyaan dete the, par school bag me meri jeeti hui trophies kabhi kisi ko nahi dikhthi, aur yeh baat mujhe pareshan karti thi.
Unki expectation aur mere sapne—beech ka balance samajhna mushkil ho raha tha.

Aaj jab main peeche mudkar dekhta hoon, toh ek baat samajh aati hai— Apni taqat aur junoon ko pehchanna hi apne asli potential ko unlock karne ka pehla kadam hai.
Har cheez me perfect hone ki zaroorat nahi hai, bas uss cheez pe dhyaan do jo tumhe andar se jeene ka jazba deti hai aur tumhe sabse alag banati hai.
Iss life ke phase se meri kuch learnings aap aagey padhenge.

**Note**: Main kahi kahi aise words bhi use karunga jo aapke liye samajhne me tough ho sakte hai. Par yeh seekhne zaruri hai toh aap uska meaning check karte rahe aur phir aagey badhein.

## Self Awareness – Apne Aap Ko Pehchano

Self-awareness ka matlab hai samajhna ki tum kis cheez ki taraf naturally attract hote ho aur tumhari asli taqat kaha hai.

Yeh ek aisi ability hai jo tumhe yeh pehchanne me madad karti hai ki tumhe jeene ka ehsaas kis cheez se hota hai, chahe duniya abhi uski value samjhe ya na samjhe.
Jab tum apne unique talent ko pehchan lete ho, tabhi tum apni life me ek aisa rasta bana sakte ho jo tumhe tumhare goals tak lekar jaaye.

Mujhe yeh baat bohot baad me samajh aayi—main har cheez me kharab nahi tha, bas apni asli strength par focus nahi kar raha tha.

Jab maine apni taqat pe dhyaan dena shuru kiya, toh maine apna career uske around build karna shuru kiya, aur isse meri puri zindagi badal gayi.

### Log Self Awareness Develop Karne Me Kya Challenges Face Karte Hain?

- **Society ke expectations me fit hone ki koshish** – Hume aksar yeh sikhaya jata hai ki hume kis cheez me accha hona chahiye, par yeh nahi pucha jata ki hume kya karna acha lagta hai.

- **Dusron se compare karna** – Agar koi aur kisi cheez me accha hai, toh hume lagta hai ki hume bhi wahi karna chahiye. Par sach yeh hai ki har insaan ki strength aur journey alag hoti hai. Aap ek machli ko uske ped chadne ki speed se judge nahi kar sakte, woh bandar zyada acha kar paega. Iska matlab ye nahi hai ki machli me potential nahi hai. Usko ekbar paani me daal kar dekho, bandar se acha perform karegi.

- **Apne emotions aur instincts ko ignore karna** – Kabhi-kabhi dil ke andar se ek awaaz aati hai jo batati hai ki tumhe kya karne se sach me khushi milti hai, par hum us awaaz ko sunne se inkaar kar dete hain iss darr se ki kahi fail na hojaye, log kya kahenge. Bacche toh theek hai, Meri trainings me 40-50 age ke log aakar bolte hai ki '***sir kaash woh 18 saal ka baccha apne dil ki sunta toh zindagi me aaj bohot khush hota***'. *Ab woh isiliye career nahi badal sakte kyuki unko lagta hai responsibilities bohot zyada hai aur ab risk lena sahi nahi hoga.*

Zakir khan sahab ki ek baat yaad agai.. *jab aap **manpasand** chhod kar **jo sahi hai** woh karne lag gaye ho toh aapne apna bachpan kho diya hai.*
Agar aap mujhse puchein ki kya karna chahiye toh mujhe lagta hai **25 ya 30 ki umar tak tumhe career option explore karna chahiye**.
Samajhna chahiye ki tumhe kya kaam karne me acha lag raha hai. Kisme tum khush ho. Kya hai woh jo tumhe roz excite kar raha hai. Bass side me ek aisa kaam chalu karlo jisse basic income aati rahe, kisi par depend na hona pade.
Haa, agar apka bachpan se sapna hi doctor banna ya family business karna hai toh aap woh karo.
Main abhi unse baat kar raha hu jinhe pata nahi hai ki karna kya hai aur clueless hokar kuch bhi kar rahe hai.
Aur agar aap us situation me ho ke apne mann ki karne ka time, paisa, freedom nahi hai toh phir jo kar rahe ho usme 100% dedo. Universe aapke liye raste nikal dega.

Main ye isiliye bol pa raha hu kyuki maine 15 jobs aur 6 business try kiye hai uske baad mujhe samajh aaya ki mujhe karna kya hai. Abhi jo kar raha hu usme bohot khush hu. Lekin ye bhi ho sakta hai ki agle saal kuch aur karlu.
Kya main khush hu? Haaaa!
Kya kabhi kabhi lagta hai ki risk kyu li. Haa ek baar laga tha.
But phir laga, agar risk nahi leta, job kar raha hota pehli wali aur usme bhi pareshan rehta toh? Dukh ke sath regret bhi karta.
Aur 50 ka hokar sochta ki explore karta hu toh shayad zyada difficult hota. Regret bohot bada pain hai bro.

2022 tak meri maa kabhi kabhi kehti thi ki Dubai wali job nahi chhodta toh tu manager bann jata aaj teri 3-4 lac rs. income hoti, rehna khana sab tha, kitni saving karleta, ghar leleta, yeh woh!

Haa baat sahi hai. Hota ye sab possible. Par kya us time mujhe mera manager us position par khush nazar araha tha?
Nahi yaar. Woh dukhi tha. Pareshan ghumta tha. Umar se pehle bada lagne lag gaya tha. Gaali deta tha apne aap ko. Parivar se door, bacho se door, akela.
Haa kuch log khush bhi hai, ho sakta hai aapke liye woh life sahi bhi ho. Par main us life se relate nahi kar pa raha tha.

Main abhi Training Business aur Social Media karta hu. Shayad ek manager apne mahine ke 250 ghante dekar jitna kamata hai utna mein 8 ghante me 2 instagram video bana kar ya 5 logo ko train kar ke kama leta hu. #GratefulToGod

Plus, apne mann se sota uthta hu. Ghar me koi pareshan hai toh kisi se chutti nahi maangni padti. Apne bacche ko bada hota dekh raha hu, Wife aur parivar ke sath jab mann hota hai bahar ghumne nikal jata hu. Jo mann karta hai khata hu, 2 crore ka ghar nahi kharida par 2 crore ke ghar me 50,000 mahine ka rent dekar khushi se rehta hu. Duniya ke best hotels aur accommodations ko explore kiya hai. Jab mann hota dusra ghar rent par leleta hu jisme amenities behtar ho aur Kanha ji ko thank you bolta rehta hu.
Shayad kuch time me mann hojaye apna ghar lene ka, par abhi toh aise hi jeena acha lagta hai. Free like a bird.

Ye aapko isiliye bata raha hu kyunki humein na 'society' ko kya accha lagega woh karne ki aadat hogai hai. Aap apne bache ko college ke baad 7-8 saal explore karne ke liye nahi doge aapka mann bhi hoga toh. Pata hai kyu?

Kyuki sharma ji ka ladka CA bann gaya hoga aur Sharma ji aapse puchlenge 'haanji, beta kya kar raha hai aajkal'
Toh aapko society ke against jaake bolna pad jaega 'abhi toh woh samajh raha hai ki usko karna kya hai'.

Ab aap assume karne lagoge ki woh soch rahe honge 'aapka beta 25 ka hogaya aur kama nahi raha.' Ab woh agar kama bhi raha hoga toh unke ghar jaakar thodi batayega.
Phir ekdin jab woh baccha ghar aega toh usko aas pados me sunne ko milega ki **ye toh 10,000 kamata hai bass. Rent par rahta hai dusre shahar me aur ek chhoti moti bike khareed rakhi hai. Pata nahi kya design wisign karta rehta hai.**
**Dekho sharma ji ka ladka car chalata hai. Savings aur investments bhi karta hai suna hai.**
Acha ye bhi ho sakta hai Sharma ji ka ladka 20,000 kamata ho, papa ke ghar me rehta ho, wahin khana khata ho, papa ki car chalata ho aur ghar se paisa leta ho. Lekin koi uske baare me baat nahi karega kyuki woh toh set rules par chal raha hai galat kaise ho sakta hai?
Kuch log kehte hai - **Baap se paise leta hai?**
Arey leta hoga yaar uska apna personal baap hai. Tujhe kya?

Aise logon ke kaaran pata nahi kitne bacche pressure mein hai, ghut ghut ke jee rahe hai, suicide kar rahe hai.
Aapne stories toh suni hi hoga.

Mere parents ne bhi ye sab khoob face kiya. Kuch log toh abhi bhi ye hi bolte hai mere baare me ki main abhi bhi kuch nahi karta
Aur maze ki baat ye hai ki mujhe pata hai woh log kaun hai. :D
Mujhe bohot samjhaya tha ki bhai job karle wapas, umar nikal rahi hai. Koi ladki nahi dega.
Khair, woh bhi galat nahi haina, pure din ye sab sunke aap influence ho hi jate ho.

**Anyway ye sab hota rahega.. par humein isse kya seekhna hai?**
Jo free hota hai woh waise bhi kuch na kuch bolta rahega
Dikkat unme nahi aapme hai ki aap apna keemti samay nikal kar unko sunn rahe hai. Busy hojao apni growth me aur unko apna kaam karne do.

Ek cheez yaad rakhna, kisi ke haath me agar coffee ka cup hai aur aap usse takra gaye toh aap par kya girega? Coffee.
Waise hi aapko choose karna hai ki aapko kisse takrana hai
Jiske paas pyar aur izzat dene ko hai. Ya jealosy, anger, hatred.

Ab samjho ki

## Self-Awareness Kaise Develop Karein?

- **Apne Happy Moments ko yaad karo** – Woh kaunse moments the jab tum sach me khush aur productive feel kar rahe the?
- **Feedback Par Dhyaan Do** – Dusre log tumhari kis quality ki tarif karte hain? Kabhi-kabhi jo taqat hume khud nahi dikhti, wo dusre log clearly dekh sakte hain. (hum agey aur baat karenge is bare me)
- **Nayi Cheezein Try Karo** – Alag-alag activities me apne aapko involve karo. Jisme tum naturally accha kar rahe ho, wahi tumhari asli strength hai.
- **Journal Likho** – Apne thoughts/vichaar aur experiences likhna shuru karo. Dheere-dheere patterns samajh aayenge jo tumhe dikhayenge ki tum asal me kaun ho.
- **Apne Emotions Ko Suno** – Agar koi cheez tumhe excite karti hai ya andar se us kaam ko poora karne ka ehsaas deti hai, toh samajh lo tum sahi raste par ho.

**Activity:**

- 10 min nikalo aur socho ki tumhe sabse zyada kya karne me maza aata hai? Aisi kaunsi cheezein hain jisme tum time ka track kho dete ho aur bilkul best self feel karte ho?
- Unhe likho aur dekho kaise tum unhe apni daily routine me aur zyada include kar sakte ho.

Iss QR code ko scan karne se aapko 'SELF ASSESSMENT' aur baaki Soft Skills related resources milenge.
*aap ye link ko bhi type kar sakte hai.*
**bento.me/shutupandlevelup**
Aur same data website par bhi mil jaega book section me
**www.jaivpareek.com**

*Duniya tumse kya chahti hai yeh mat socho.*
*Yeh socho ki woh kya cheez hai jo tumhe feel karati hai ki tum zinda ho. Kyuki duniya ko zaroorat unhi logon ki hai jo jeene ki asli wajah khoj lete hain.*

## Aise hui meri Self Help Journey Ki Shuruat

Main sapne toh bohot bade dekhta tha par life me agey kya karna hai, videsh kaise jaana hai, ye sab ka kuch idea nahi tha.
2007 me mere haath ek self help book lagi. Achi toh lag rahi thi, kaafi kuch seekh bhi raha tha main par itni bhaari english mujhe ache se samajh nahi arahi thi. Toh interest loose horaha tha.
English seekhta bhi kaise? Agar main English bolne ka try karta tha toh saath wale ek dusre ko koni marne lag jate hai. Haste the sab.

Phir 2008 me mere dost Chetan ne ek din mere paas aakar bola, "***Bhai ek documentary dekh... tera dimag hil jaega. Bas ek baar poori dekh le. Yeh teri life badal degi***."
Woh itna serious tha, jaise uske paas koi life-changing formula ho.

Phir usne ek pen drive mere haath mein di aur bola, "***Promise kar, ek baar mein poori dekhega, bina ruke.***"
Maine haan bol diya. Raat ko video chalayi, lekin main thaka hua tha... video start hui, aur mujhe neend aa gayi. Main so gaya.

Agle din woh aaya same seriousness ke sath aur pucha,
"**Dekhi tune**?"
Maine bola, "**Haan**."
Usne kaha, "**Jhoot bol raha hai tu. Itni badi cheez dekh kar tu aise shaant nahi reh sakta. Abhi dekh**."
Woh maan nahi raha tha aur itna force karne laga toh main finally baith gaya us documentary ko dekhne.

Woh 90 minutes me... mera life ko dekhne ka nazariya badal gaya.
Usne meri soch ko completely shift kardiya.
Aur us documentary ka naam tha – **The Secret**.
Aur wahi se meri self-help journey properly shuru hui...

Yeh documentary aapko YouTube par 'The Secret Movie In Hindi' mil jaegi. Maine Hindi version dekha tha. Netflix par bhi hai.

# The Secret
## Law of Attraction

Ye ek book and documentary hai by Rhonda Byrne.
Law of Attraction ka matlab hai – aapka mindset, aapki reality banata hai. **Vichaar banaye zindagi.**
Jo energy aap universe ko dete hai—positive ya negative—waise hi experiences aapke paas wapas aate hain. Like Boomerang.
Aap jo sochte ho, jo mehsoos karte ho, wahi aap apni zindagi mein attract karte ho.
Matlab agar aap positive sochte ho, gratitude mehsoos karte ho, to aapke paas zyada achhi cheezein aayengi. Aur agar aap hamesha negative sochoge – darr, gussa, shikayatein – to wahi cheezein aapke paas aur aaengi.
Sochke dekho, jab aap khush hote ho toh kaise sab kuch sahi hone lag jata hai. Ache log milte hai, aap best dressed nahi ho toh bhi aapko tareefein sunai deti hai, opportunities aati hai aapke paas.

**The Secret ka ek 3 steps process hai..**

- **Ask** – Jo chahiye, usse clearly maango. Apne dimaag mein uski tasveer/image banao.
- **Believe** – Yeh maan lo ki woh cheez aapke paas aa rahi hai. Doubt mat karo. Visualize karo aur kaam karo uske liye.
- **Receive** – Apne aap ko uss cheez ko paane ke liye ready rakho, feel karo jaise ki woh aapke paas aa chuki hai. Aur phir use paao.

**Kaise Use Karein Law of Attraction?:**

- **Visualize Your Goals** – Start me difficult hoga par aap aankh band karke apne dimag me woh sab dekho jo aapko chahiye. Har detail mehsoos karo. Direct visualize karne se pehle aap aankh khol kar apne around cheezon ko dekho phir aankh band karke unhe visualize karo. Jaise aapke haath ki lakirein. Practice hone lagegi.

- **Gratitude Practice Karo** – Jo hai, uske liye thank you bolo. Zindagi aapko aur degi.
- **Positive Affirmations Bolo** – Khud se roz kaho, “Main kar sakta hoon”, “Success meri hai”, ”Main khush insaan hu” etc.
- **Actions Lo** – Sirf sochne se nahi hota. Kaam karna zaruri hai. Universe actions ke upar response deta hai.
- **Negative Self-Talk Band Kardo** – “Mujhse nahi hoga” hatao. “Main kar ke dikhaunga/dikhaungi” lagao.

**Law of Attraction koi jaadu nahi hai—it’s a mindset.**

The Secret kehta hai ki humari soch ek magnet hai. Agar humne gratitude aur positivity ko apnaya, to hum apni reality ko change kar sakte hain.

Law of Attraction ek law hai jaisi ki Law of Gravity.
Aap isey maano ya nahi maano, ye kaam karta hai.
Jaise agar aap 12 manzil ki building se kood jaoge toh niche hi giroge, upar nahi jaoge.
Matlab upar toh jaoge par pehle niche aoge, kyuki waha Law of gravity kaam kar raha hai.
Waise hi Law of attraction bhi kaam karta hai.

***“Aapke thoughts hi aapki reality banate hain. Jo aap sochoge, wahi hoga.”***

Aur yaha se meri journey shuru hui...
Is ek soch ne meri zindagi badal di.

Aasha karta hu, yeh kitab **‘Shut Up And Level Up’** bhi aapke liye ek nayi shuruwaat ho...

# MERA MENIFESTATION KA PROCESS :)

Jo chahiye hota hai uska print out hamesha mere samne hota hai. Jo book aap padh rahe ho kuch mahine pehle mere imagination me woh aisi dikhti thi. (3rd Pic)

**AAP BHI YE TARIKA APNA SAKTE HAI JO CHAHIYE USKA PRINT OUT APNE SAAMNE RAKHO AUR FEEL KARO KI WOH AAPKE PAAS ALREADY HAI**

# Success Story from Kishangarh

**Mr. Ashok Patni**
Chairman, R.K. Marble Group

Jab Kishangarh se nikal raha tha tab ek thought aaraha tha ki life toh R. K. Uncle jaisi honi chahiye. Big house, luxury cars, businesses.
Unka ghar mere ghar ke kareeb hai aur jab bann raha tha tab mere dada mujhe andar se dikhane lekar gaye the. Kuch 7 saal ka tha main shayad. Us ghar ko banne me 4 saal lage the.
Pehli baar maine waha ek khaali swimming pool dekha tha aur samajh nahi araha tha ki ye kya hai.

Ye book likhte samay ek iccha thi ki Ashok Uncle se milu aur ek conversation karu, kyunki maine meri life ki shuruaat me koi ultra successful insaan dekha tha toh woh yahi the. Aur main kabhi inse mila nahi tha.
Maine unke official email par meri book ke baare me ek video bana kar bheja aur thankfully unhe woh pasand aaya aur mujhe unse milne ka mauka mila.
So simple, classy and down to earth. Aisa laga hi nahi ki kisi aise insaan se baat horahi hai jinki company ka advertisment
Mr. Amitabh Bacchan karte hai.

Mann tha video banane ka unke saath par woh social media se door rehte hai aur Interviews karna woh pasand nahi karte toh baat baat main kuch unhone mujhe aisi cheezein kahi jinhe me lifetime yaad rakhna chahata hu aur follow karna chahta hu.

Agle page par aapko hamari conversation milegi, ache se samajhna aur koshish karte hai hum hamari life agey inhi values aur learnings ke saath spend karein.

Itne saal travel aur jagah jagah kaam karne ke kaaran successful log toh maine bohot dekhein hain par success ke saath ek itni sorted aur spiritual life jeena harr kisi ke bass ki baat nahi hai.

**Maine unse pucha ki aap mujhe aapki woh skills ke baare me batao jo agar aap ke paas nahi hoti toh aap yaha tak nahi pohoch paate.**

Unhone muskura kar confidently mujhe jawab diya,

**Sapna. Iccha Shakti** aur **Kuch karne ki umang.**
Ek umang thi kuch accha karne ki. Aur sapne dekhenge tab hi toh saakaar honge na. Aise hi thodi honge.
Phir apan ne mehnat ki, aur mehnat ki toh rasta milta gaya agey.
Phir jab raasta niklta gaya toh sacchai se rahe. Honesty.

Kisi ko dhokha nahi diya, mehnat me koi kami nahi rakhi. Kaam kar kar ke itna thakk jaate the ki scooter chalate chalate neend aajati thi.
Khoob kaam kiya, logon ka vishwaas jeeta aur keval apni nahi sochi. Dusre ki bhi sochi jo saath kaam karte the.
Hamesha win win ki position rakhi ki main bhi kamau aur dusra bhi kamaye.
Kisi ko nahi lagna chahiye ki mera fayda nahi ho raha.
Kisi ki jaib nahi kaatni.
Saath me kaam karne walon ke liye margin chhoda taaki sabka kaam agey badh sake aur woh bhi paisa kamaye.

Koi bhi vyakti jo sab ko saath lekar chalta hai
Sirf apna akele ka nahi, sabke faayde ki sochta hai
Dil saaf rakh kar sahi kaam karta hai,
usko koi dikkat nahi aati hai,
saare raaste apne aap milte hai.

## Chapter 2

# OFF TO JAIPUR

**2011 ki baat hai..**
12th khatam hone ke baad, maine Kishangarh chhoda aur Jaipur shift ho gaya, B.sc in Hotel Management padhne ke liye.

Is faisle ke teen bade reason the:
**Pehla**: Koi bhi doosra college mujhe admission dene ko tayar nahi tha kyunki mujhe 12th me ek supplementary exam aai thi.
**Doosra**: Main apne upar kaam karna chahta tha, aur mujhe judgements se door jaakar apne aap ko behtar karna tha. Mujhe pata tha ki agar mujhe apni life badalni hai, toh mujhe khud ko upgrade karna hoga aur woh mein apne hometown me rehkar nahi kar sakta tha.
**Teesra:** Hotel Management kiya toh videsh jaane ke chances zyada hai. Sabse bada sapna yahi tha us samay jeevan ka.

Jaipur shift hona mere liye ek turning point raha.
Maine apne andar ek naya insaan dekha.

Hotel management college ka discipline ekdum strict tha—hamesha clean, crisp aur ironed kiye kapde pehenna, clean collars, sahi socks, chamakte shoes, aur ekdum clean-shaven rehna.
Ulta haath laga kar daily shave check kiya jata tha aur sahi nahi hai toh ghar jaao.
Main hamesha se ek aisa insaan tha jisko subah uthke ready hoke ache kapde pehenna bohot pasand tha. Occasion ho na ho, ready hona zaruri hai. Mujhe lagta tha usse meri energy achi rehti hai.
Ye maine meri daadi **The Great Shanti Devi** se seekha hai.
Woh aaj 80+ saal ki hogai hai, lekin ek bhi din aisa nahi hoga jab aap unhe properly dressed nahi dekhoge.

Toh mujhe yeh college ka process aur discipline pasand aaya. Mujhe laga, mera college ek aisi jagah hai jo mujhe behtar banne me madad karega aur mere goal tak le jaega.

Aur dheere-dheere, teachers ne dusre students ko bolna shuru kar diya ki grooming Jai ki jaisi honi chahiye. Dekho ache se.
Wahi extracurricular activities—jo bachpan me mujhe daant sunwati thi—yahan meri pehchaan ban rahi thi.

*Jaipur aane ke sirf do mahine ke andar, mujhe college me.*
**Mr. Fresher award** *mila, main class representative bana jo school me kabhi nahi hota tha.*
*Aur uske baad, meri academics me bhi tareef hone lagi.*

*Ek cheez samajh aa gayi thi—Jab tum apne strengths ko samajh kar agey badhne lagte ho, toh duniya tumhe pehchaan ne lagti hai.*
*Aur apne upar kaam karne ka sabse accha tarika hai ki uss jagah rehne lago jaha tumhe koi nahi janta. Tum kuch bhi naya try kar sakte ho Tum baal colour kara sakte ho. Tum new trends ke kapde pehen sakte ho, jo tumne kabhi nahi pehne. Tum alag accent me baat kar sakte ho. Tum English bolne ki koshish kar sakte ho. Kisi ko nahi pata tum kaun ho toh, pehle kaise baat karte the. Tum woh banne ki koshish kar sakte ho jo tum banna chahte ho.*
*Aur tum jo chahte ho log tumhe uss nazar se dekhne lagte hai.*

*Maine is process me seekha— Tumhare muh kholne se pehle hi log tumhari ek image bana lete hai.*
*Tum kaisi family se ho, kitni kamai hogi tumhari, tum kaise rehte ho?*
*Woh sach ho ya nahi.. par log image create kar lete hai.*
*Personal grooming sirf accha dikhne ke liye nahi hoti, yeh darshati hai ki aapne apne aap ko kitna respect karte ho aur kitne confident ho.*
*Jab tum chhoti-chhoti cheezon ka dhyaan rakhte ho—jaise saaf kapde, polished shoes, posture, hygiene, aur presentation—tab tum bina kuch kahe yeh bata dete ho ki tum apne aap ko aur apni zindagi ko kitna seriously lete ho.*

*Mujhe bohot ache se guitar bajana nahi aata tha*
*Main beginner level par tha*
*But mujhe ye acche se aata tha ki guitar lekar confidently baithna kaise hai.*
*Surr bohot ache nahi the, par gaane ka shokh bohot tha.*
*Sabko lagta tha ki ye toh performer hai.*

*Log isko kehte hai*
*Fake it till you make it*
*Mein bolta hu '**Faith it, till you make it**'.*

*Kaam hath me lo, efforts daalne ke liye ready hojao aur baaki sab upar wale par chhod do.*

## The Power of Appearance

Tum apne aap ko duniya ke saamne kaise pesh karte ho—tumhari grooming, dressing aur body language—yeh sab decide karta hai ki duniya tumhe kaise treat karegi.
Acchi appearance tumhari life me naye mauke leke aane ka kaam karti hai.
Mere college me yeh sab details matter karti thi— Pehle toh yeh sab overwhelming laga, phir saath wale dost college par gussa hone lage ki itna bhi kyu strict hona
Magar phir ek baat hum sab ko samajh aayi:
Jab tum accha dikhte ho, toh tum accha mehsoos karte ho. Aur jab tum accha mehsoos karte ho, toh tum behtareen perform karte ho. Jab teachers ne meri grooming aur professionalism ko ek example ki tarah dikhana shuru kiya, tab sirf mere looks nahi, mera overall confidence bhi badhne laga. Aapka bhi confidence boost up hota hai jab aapki koi tareef karta hai.

**Moral of the story is..**

✔ **First Impression Pal Bhar Me Banta Hai** – Log tumhe sirf kuch seconds me judge kar lete hain ki tum kitne door jane wale ho.

✔ **Confidence Badhta Hai** – Jab tum acche se groomed hote ho, toh tum andar se bhi zyada capable feel karte ho.

✔ **Discipline Dikhta Hai** – Chhoti-chhoti aadatein jaise kapde press karna ya sahi footwear pehnna yeh dikhata hai ki tum apne aap ko seriously lete ho.

✔ **Naye Mauke Milte Hain** – Bahut baar tumhara presentation hi decide karta hai ki tumhe opportunity milegi ya nahi.

Duniya tumse waise hi behave karti hai jaise tum apni image create karte ho. Isliye, jo tum dikhate ho, wahi tum paate ho.

## The Science behind it

**Log Sabse Pehle Kya Notice Karte Hain?**
Jab koi tumse pehli baar milta hai, uska dimaag kuch key areas ko turant scan karta hai

✓ **Face & Expression** – Kya tum approachable, confident aur well-groomed dikh rahe ho?

✓ **Posture & Body Language** – Kya tum seedhe khade hote ho aur apne aap ko assurance ke saath carry karte ho?

✓ **Clothing & Cleanliness** – Kya tumhare kapde fit aur well-maintained hain? Kya woh tumhara discipline, self-respect aur effort dikhate hain?

✓ **Shoes & Accessories** – Kya tumhare shoes aur accessories wisely choose kiye gaye hain aur acche se maintained hain?

Log shayad consciously in sab cheezon ka analysis na karein, par unka subconscious mind sirf kuch seconds me tumhare baare me ek opinion bana leta hai.

**Inner-Outer Connection**
Andar Ka Confidence, Bahar Ka Impression

Accha dikhna sirf doosron ko impress karne ke liye nahi, khud ke andar se confident feel karne ke liye hota hai.

✓ **Confidence in Conversations** – Jab tum accha aur presentable feel karte ho, toh tumhari awaaz me authority aati hai aur tum bejhijhak baat kar pate ho. Yaad karo woh time jab tumhe apni favourite dress pehni thi. Kahar dha rahe the tum :)

✓ **Body Language & Energy** – Acchi grooming aur dressing tumhari posture aur poise ko naturally improve karti hai. 3 piece suit pehen ke tum bed par nahi lait te ho na? Tum seedhe baithte ho.

✓ **Opportunities & Perception** – Chahe business ho ya social life, ek well-dressed aur well-groomed insaan ko zyada capable aur trustworthy maana jata hai.

✓ **Efforts Ka Asar Hamesha Dikhta Hai**
Grooming aur dressing ka matlab show-off karna nahi, balki self discipline aur self-respect dikhana hai.
Yeh tumhe control deta hai ki duniya tumhe kaise dekhe.
Soch ke dekho tum bhi logo ko aise hi judge karte ho.

*"Tumhari appearance trust banane ka pehla kadam hai. Tum isse kaise maintain karte ho, yahi decide karega ki log tumhe kaise yaad rakhenge."*

## Grooming & Dressing with Intent

Ek duniya jahan first impression sab kuch hota hai, grooming aur dressing sirf show-off karne ki baat nahi hai—yeh doosron par ek powerful impact daalne ki ability hai.
Tumhari personality bina bole hi logon par asar daalti hai, aur yeh sab tumhare presentation se start hota hai.

**Grooming aur Dressing ko samjho.**

1. **Grooming – Tumhari Pehchaan ka Pehla Kadam**

Grooming ek sabse aasaan par sabse powerful tareeka hai discipline, attention to detail aur self-care ko dikhane ka.
Iska matlab mehenge products ya ghanton tak mirror ke samne rehna nahi, balki ek neat aur polished look maintain karna hai jo tumhari personality aur profession se match kare. Isme aata hai:

✔ **Skincare & Hygiene** – Saaf twacha/skin aur achhi hygiene tumhari cleanliness aur self-care ko dikhati hai. Ek fresh face, trimmed nails aur well-maintained hair tumhe aur zyada organized aur presentable dikhata hai. Zyadatar ladke in cheezon par dhyaan nahi dete, jo ki galat hai. Manicure Pedicure sirf ladkiyo ke kaam nahi hai. Nails tumhare bhi bade hote hai, zarurat tumhe bhi hai.

✔ **Hair & Beard Care** – Tumhara hairstyle aur beard tumhare face aur personality ke hisaab se hona chahiye. Bikhra hua look aksar careless attitude ka impression deta hai (not for artists), jabki ek well-groomed appearance discipline dikhata hai.
Ek aur cheez samjho, **good beard or no beard**. Agar acchi beard nahi aarahi toh mat rakho. It's okay**. Mooch nahi toh mard nahi** ek stupid concept hai jo kuch mooch wale insecure aadmiyon ne nikala hai. Mooch toh billi ke bhi aati hai?

✔ **Fragrance & Freshness** – Accha smell karna ek underrated game-changer hai. Ek mild par noticeable fragrance tumhari presence ko enhance karta hai bina doosron ko overpower kiye.
Grooming ka matlab ameer dikhna nahi hota—iska matlab hota hai zimmedar dikhna aur har waqt opportunity ke liye ready rehna.

## 2. Dressing - Tumhara Personal Brand Statement

Tumhare kapde sirf tumhe dikhane ke liye nahi hote—yeh tumhari kahani batate hain, tumse pehle tumhare baare me baat karte hai. Chahe tum boardroom me ho, kisi networking event me ya ek casual outing pe, tumhara dressing naye mauke dilata bhi hai aur tumse mauke cheen bhi leta hai.

### Kaise Dress Karein Jo Impact Daale?

✓ **Mauke Ko Samjho** – Setting ke hisaab se dress karo. Ek well tailored suit corporate event ke liye perfect hai, jabki smart casuals informal networking me best lagte hain.

✓ **Fit, Fashion Se Zyada Zaroori Hai** – Kapde kitne bhi mehenge ho, agar fit accha nahi hai toh impact nahi dalenge. Ek well-fitted, clean aur ironed outfit, ek sloppy designer piece se behtar dikhta hai.

✓ **Color Psychology Samjho** – Rang emotions aur perceptions par asar daalte hain:

- **Dark colours** (black, navy, grey) – Power aur authority dikhate hain.
- **Light colours** (white, beige, pastels) – Approachable aur calm vibe dete hain.
- **Bright colours** (red, yellow, royal blue) – Confidence aur energy ka impression dete hain, par inhe wisely use karna chahiye.

✓ **Accessories Matter** – Sahi accessories (watch, belt, shoes, tie, jewellery) tumhare outfit ko enhance karte hain, overpower nahi. Choose minimal and elegant.

✓ **Shoes Speak Louder Than Words** – Bahut log tumhare attention to detail ka andaza tumhare jooton se lagate hain. Clean, polished footwear professionalism aur self-respect ka symbol hota hai.

Kapde us jagah ke liye mat pehno jahan tum ho, balki us jagah ke liye jahan tum pahunchna chahte ho.

Dekho hum sab ka **The Ultimate Goal** hai successful banna. Right?

Ab uske liye aapko ye samajhna hoga ki successful banne ke liye aapko 2 cheezein chahiye..

1. Aapko ek chance milna chahiye kuch karne ka (job, business, etc)
2. Chance milne par aapko accha perform karna hoga

Ye dono steps sath hone chahiye
Inme se sirf ek hua toh kaam nahi chalega
Jaise agar chance nahi mila toh perform kaise karoge?
Aur agar chance mil gaya par perform nahi kar paaye toh bhi kya fayda?
Samjho.. Aap jaise dikhte ho woh aapka first impression banata hai aur aapko help karta hai chance dilane me. aur,
Soft Skills jo hai woh aapko help karti hai uss chance par acha perform karne me. (hum aagey seekhenge)

**Activity:**
Right occasion ke liye ek right outfit kaise choose karein?
**First up, dress for the ROLE, GOAL and OCCASION**
Then, Ask yourself these question.

- **Aap kaun ho, aapki designation kya hai jaha aap jaa rahe ho?**
  Aap ek company ke boss ho, kisi ghar ke daamaad ho, kaun ho?
- **Aap kaha jaa rahe ho?**
  Aap meeting me jaa rahe ho, festival, family function?
- **Kaun log honge waha?**
  Aapke rishteydaar, ladki wale, colleagues.
- **Waha aapka goal kya hai? Kya pana chahte ho waha jaakar?**
  Ladki ke parivar ko impress karna, rishteydaaro ko shock karna, team ko motivate karna, etc.
- **Woh goal paane ke liye aap kya message dena chahte ho?**
  Yeh toh bada aadmi hai. Classy. Sophisticated. Traditional.

Kya kapde pehne jaaye jo aapko woh message dene me help karega jo aap dena chahte ho?
3 piece suit authority dikhata hai, saari traditional feel deti hai, saafa lagane se aapka culture dikhega, etc.

## Chapter 3

# THE HABIT OF KNOCKING DOORS

College ka first year end hone se pehle hi mujhe ek 5 Star hotel se job offer mil gaya tha, par mere ek teacher ne mujhe suggest kiya ki abhi accept na karun. Second year aate-aate, mujhe need feel hui aur maine padhai ke saath kaam bhi shuru kar diya.

### Mera Jobs Ki Duniya Me Pehla Kadam (2012)

Mujhe hamesha se communication ki power ne attract kiya tha. Mujhe samajh agaya tha ki 'baat karne se baat banti hai', aur maine agar acche se baat karne ka hunar seekh liya, toh zindagi me koi bhi bada goal achieve kar sakta hoon.

Jaise log radio shows sunke sochte hain, "Yaar, RJ banna kitna cool hoga!"—meri bhi wahi feeling thi. Mujhe ek Radio Jockey banne ka shokh chadha aur mera ek naya dream bana. Is dream ko pura karne ke liye, maine socha ki sabse pehle mujhe speaking skills improve karni hongi.

Main YouTube videos dekhkar roz practice karne laga. Phir maine mentors dhoondhna start kiya jo mujhe Speaking Skills sikha sakein.

**Ek cheez yaad rakhein..** jab bhi kuch naya kaam karna chaho. Ek accha mentor/trainer dekho aur unse seekhna chalu karo. Aisa nahi hai ki aap unke bina nahi seekh paoge. Par aap bohot time aur energy save karoge. Ab aap bol sakte ho paise nahi hai.

**Solution** - 10 trainers ko message karo aur unko bolo ki main ye kaam aapke liye free me karunga, mujhe aapse ye sikhna hai.

Ex. Social Media Handling, video editing (ye sab aap youtube se free me seekh sakho).

Ek na ek aapko saath rakh lega aur kaam sikha dega. Kya aap 10 doors knock karoge?

Kuch din dhoondhne ke baad mujhe ek lady mili—jo ek professional RJ thi aur radio station me kaam karti thi. Maine bina soch-vichar kiye unhe call kiya aur seedha bola, "Kya aap mujhe train kar sakti hain?" Unhone haan keh diya aur apne course me join karne ke liye kaha. Meri shuruaat hochuki thi. Har ek cheez jo unhone sikhai, main roz ghanton tak usse practice karta. Yeh sirf seekhne ke liye nahi, balki kyunki mujhe yeh process sacch me pasand tha. Kuch hi din ki training ke baad, unhone kaha, "Jaake 94.3 MY FM pe audition do." Main ekdum shock ho gaya. "Main? Abhi audition? Itni jaldi?" Meri hesitation dekh ke, unhone muskurakar kaha.

*"Wahan full-time RJ nahi, sirf interns chahiye. aur tu accha karlega I know. Ab agar woh bol rahi hai toh maan lete hai.*

*Yaar dekho yeh ek badi baat thi. Main bohot dara hua tha. Par maine hamesha yeh maana hai ki mauke chaiye toh darwaza khud khatkhataana padta hai. Isliye, maine apne darr ko godi me liya aur audition dene nikal gaya.* ***Mera Pehla RJ wala Audition*** *dene.*

Audition ke din, interviewer ne ek newspaper haath me diya aur kaha, "Aaj ki headlines padho aur 5 links banao (Links woh chhoti chhoti lines hoti hai jo RJ's songs ke beech me bolte hai).
Maine turant likhna shuru kiya. Ek gehri saans li, confidence gather kiya, aur phir unke kehne par poore RJ style me deliver kiya.
Interview khatam hote hi interviewer ne dekha aur sirf bola—
"Kuch toh hai tujhme, par pata nahi kya hai?"
**Kab se join kar sakta hai. Maine kaha 'AAJ SE'"**

Aur bas, ussi moment me jo ladka radio stations ko door se admire karta tha, jo RJs ko larger-than-life personality maanta tha,
wo aaj Jaipur ke top RJs ke saath ek studio me baitha tha, unke liye links likh raha tha, 94.3 MyFm ke liye outdoor broadcasting kar raha tha.
Uss din mujhe ek badi seekh mili— "Har baar tum ready feel nahi karoge. Par agar tum acchi niyat aur karm se aage badhte raho, toh naye naye darwaze khulte rahenge."

## Seekhna Tha, Rukna Nahi Tha

Mera 94.3 MY FM ka safar sirf do mahine ka hi tha, jaha door se sochta tha 'ki kaisa hoga Radio Station?' waha main kaam karke nikal chuka tha.
Radio station me kaam karna ek alag excitement tha, par mujhe pata tha ki mujhe sirf ek jagah rukna nahi hai, bass aagey badhte rehna hai,

Mere andar ek aisi energy thi jo hamesha naye raste dhoondhne, nayi cheezein seekhne, aur kabhi bhi na rukne ke liye majboor karti thi. Aur mujhe aisa feel hota tha kuch bhi impossible nahi hai.
Main sab kuch seekhna chahta tha, naye experiences lena chahta the. Mujhe is duniya mein sab kuch experience karna tha. Aur main jaanta tha ki yeh sirf ek shuruat hai.
Isliye, maine comfortable hone ke bajaye, apne liye agla challenge dhoondhna shuru kiya. Sabse pehle, maine call centres me apply kiya aur back to back 2 BPOs me kaam kiya. Ek teleperformance jo mere accommodation ke paas open hi hua tha (7-8 floors ki badi si building bani thi, usme kaam karne ka mann hua) aur phir ek BPO international calling ke liye tha jaha main Australia mein 'Duct Cleaning Services' sell karta tha outbound calls par. Night shift, ek raat me 250 se 300 foreigners se baat karni hoti thi. Usme log irritate bhi hojate the 'ek bhai ne toh mujhe suna diya ki life me kuch accha karlo :D.'
Teleperformance me maza araha tha, waha shayad kuch time aur kaam karta lekin un dino maine eyebrow piercing karwai thi, unhone usse remove karne ko boldiya tha. Toh woh job chhodna pada.

Goal tha communication skills ko improve karna aur behtar banna.
Phir, maine Jaipur ke do best hotels me ek ke baad ek kaam kiya.
2 months each. (Agey bataunga is bare me)
Waha jaakar samajh aaya ki aise bhi log hote hai ek din hotel me rehne ke liye 2 lac Rs. kharch kar dete hai. Matlab din me aaye, khaya peeya, ghume hotel me aur agle din chale gaye 2 lac Rs. dekar. Meri salary 10,000 Rs. kuch thi.
Yeh sirf jobs nahi thi, yeh mere naye safar ki tayyari thi.

Mujhe samajh aa gaya tha ki real world me safal hone ke liye sirf talent kaafi nahi hota—discipline, professionalism, growth mindset, networking aur adaptability jaisi skills bhi utni hi zaroori hoti hai. Aur yeh seekhne ke safar me, main ek behtar version me badal raha tha.

Ye baat abhi toh bohot interesting lag rahi hai ki college ke sath jobs chal rahi hai par kaafi baar me college nahi jaa pa raha tha aur ye ek bohot bada struggle tha. Kyuki...

Harr kuch din me mere pita ji ko college se phone jata tha. Aur phir samajh jaao. Kuch samay toh pitaji ne khoob samjhaya, phir papa ko calls jaane band hogaye college se aur life me shaanti aai.

Ab mere pita ji thehre the court wale aadmi, pure din criminals se deal karte the. Unko hua ek din doubt ki ye mera chhora itna toh sudhar nahi sakta ekdum se, case kya hai college jakar hi samajte hai.

Fortunately, uss din main college me hi tha aur class me ek teacher bolne aaye ki director sir office me bula rahe hai.

Dekho school me Principal ma'am se maar aur college me hamare super handsome Director sir se daant khane ki mujhe aadat si hogai thi.

Main office me jaise hi gaya.. samne mere pitaji bethe the.

I was like, yeh kya hogaya ekdum. Don aaj yaha kaise?

Waqt badal gaya, jazbaat badal gaye.

Ek hi pal me behad khauf wala maahaul bann chuka tha.

Pape ne pucha, 'college aata hai ye regular ab?'
Sir ne bola 'BILKUL NAHI. Bohot chutti leraha hai.'
Papa bole 'toh phir mujhe aap phone kyu nahi karte.'
Sir bole 'sir khoob karte hai.. aapko lagta nahi hai'
Papa bole 'aise kaise, abhi karo'.
Sir ne try kiya 2-3 baar aur phone nahi laga.
Kisi ko samajh nahi aaya kya horaha hai.
Phir unhone bola 'hoga kuch network issue' aur baat ko taal diya.

Maine un chand seconds me 33 koti devi deta ko yaad karliya tha ki bass koi papa ke phone ki block list check na karle.
Woh maine ek din slam book bharwane ke bahane sab teachers ke numbers leliye the.

Again, isme koi samajhdari nahi thi, I was silly, Please yeh galtiyan aap na hi karein toh acha hoga. Apna hi nuksaan hai.

*Dost log movie dekhte dekhte bata rahe the ki unhe college me bola tha 'agar Jai ke sath rahe toh final exam me nahi bethne denge'. Aur phir humne popcorns order karliye.*

***Aakash - Jai - Vikas - Dhawan***
*(ek aur Vikas missing hai)*

**Secret Talk – Maine Uss Waqt Hotel Jobs Kyun Apply Ki**

Meri class ka ek student Hotel Oberoi, Jaipur me job par laga tha.
Pura college uske baare me baat kar raha tha—teachers bhi, students bhi. 'Yaar pata hai uska oberoi me selection hogaya'.
Mujhe yeh sunke curiosity hui.
Maine poocha, "Isme badi baat kya hai?"
Ab college me kisiko meri jobs ke baare me idea nahi tha.
Toh ek bhai ne haste huve jawab diya, "Agar koi badi baat nahi hai, toh tu bhi wahan kaam kar ke dikha na?"

Uske bass yeh kehne ki der thi, main gaya Oberoi Rajvilas, black suit daal kar walk-in interview dene apni fatfati par.
Usse yaad aaya, papa ne apni purani bike (Hero Honda CD 100) mujhe dene ke liye haa kardiya tha. Bass problem ek hi thi.. uske brakes tab hi lagte the jab aap uske brakes par khade hojao. still, bike toh hai hi.

Hotel gaya, interviews diye aur main select hogaya.
Unhone kaha kab join kar sakte ho, maine kaha aaj.
Bohot acha experience tha, kaafi kuch seekha, telephone operator kaam kiya initially toh reservation ko samjha.
Overall do mahine kaam kiya, aur phir chhod diya.

Mujhe na kisi se compare hona pasand nahi tha.

Phir maine usse bhi bade hotel, Taj Rambagh Palace, Jaipur (world's best) me apply kiya, wahan koi jaan ne wala bhi mil gaye, aur main udhar bhi select hogaya, do mahine kaam kiya, aur chhod diya.

Ab mujhe lagta hai ki itni jaldi nahi chhodna chahiye par shayad woh ek bachpana tha jisme mujhe koi darr nahi tha aur me sab kuch thode hi time me experience karna chahta tha.
Is chakkar me maine 2012 se 2016 tak me:
Do 5-star resorts - ek 5-star business class hotel
Ek 5-star heritage/palace property aur Ek 7-star hotel
me kaam karliya tha.

## Comparison – Sabse gandi cheez hoti hai

Yeh ek dangerous game hai, jo hume bachpan se sikhaya jata hai. Mujhe school me compare kiya gaya. Mujhe ghar me compare kiya gaya (jo ki unintentionally harr ghar me hota hai), Society me compare kiya gaya. Rishteydaaro ke baccho se compare kiya tha. Woh ek uncle ka ladka hota haina jo zyada hi padhai karta hai aur hamari zindagi difficult banata hai. Usse mujhe nafrat thi.

Mujhe aur mere chhote bhai (Chinu) ko bhi kuch logon ne ek silent competition me daal diya—jo hume kabhi chahiye hi nahi tha. Mujhe aaj bhi woh words yaad hai 'tu nikal yaha se, humare toh Chinu hi theek hai'. Mera bhai hamesha yeh sochne laga ki usey mujhse better karna hai life me, career me. Behtar dikhna hai, kamana hai, kyuki sabne uske dimag me ye drill kardiya ki woh chhota hai par mujhse zyada samajhdaar hai. Aur mujhe is race me padna hi nahi tha. Main kamm samajhdaar hi khush tha apni life me. Kuch time baad jab main life me acha perform karne laga toh Chinu mere liye bohot khush hone laga, mujhse seekhne laga par surrounding me kuch wahi baatein hone lagi jisse usko pressure aaya, aur usey lag gaya ki kahi ye behtar na dikhne lag jaye mujhse. Pareshan rehne laga, perception management me phass gaya aur apni problems apne andar hi rakhne laga.

Humein ek sacch samajhna zaroori hai—asli competition sirf humare dimaag me hota hai. Jis din maine apne chhote bhai se kaha, Tu apni jagah best hai, aur main apni jagah. Tera mera koi competition nahi hai kyunki hum bhai hai aur hamara goal ek hi hai 'apne ghar ko behtar banana, aur saath me khush rehna'. Unnecessary pareshan mat ho. Jis stupid competition me humein daal diya gaya tha, woh sirf humein pareshan hi karega. Is chakkar me tu hamesha 'good boy' banne ki race me reh jaega aur khush nahi reh paega. Ussi din hum dono ne woh bekaar ka pressure chhodna chalu kiya. Par kyuki ye ek bohot purani programming hai toh sahi hone me time lagta hai.

## PLEASE... GHAR KE BADO SE MERI EK REQUEST HAI

Band karo comparison. Bhai behen ke beech. Parivar ke beech. Dusro ke baccho ke saath. Yeh sirf aapke baccho ko weak banaega. Aapka ego toh uss samay ke liye satisfy hojaega lekin baccho ko long term issues ho sakte hai. Unka self esteem down ho sakta hai for long.

Agar aapko koi pasand nahi hai toh usse door raho aur apne kaam se kaam karo.
Usko baar baar mat batao uski kamiyaan jis tarike se aap bata rahe ho aur usko apne hi logon se compare mat karo. Woh unki poori zindagi ke liye ek self doubt paida kar sakta hai.

Logon ko apni speed se grow karne do, apne tareeke se aur apne time se.
Kyuki success kisi se better hone me nahi, balki apni best version banne me hai.

Agar aap kisi ki life me kuch add karna hi chahte ho toh usse milkar bolo 'tu jo kar raha hai best kar raha hai, aur support karna ho toh bolo 'main tere sath hu'. I wish you a lot of happiness and luck'.

Zaruri nahi hai aapki zindagi jaisi rahi hai uski bhi waisi hi rehne wali hai.

**Aapse ek aur baat karna chahta hu**

Mostly maine dekha hai ki aap log college join karte ho aur phir wait karte ho ki college aapko job dila dega. Mil rahi hai toh theek hai par uspar dependent nahi raho.

Main shock hoajata hu jab graduates se sunta hu ki abhi placements nahi horahe hai college se. Bhai zarurat hi nahi hai. Apne upar kaam karo itna ki aapko kabhi zarurat hi na ho college ke paas jakar help lene ki. Main phir kahunga ki agar me kar sakta hu toh aap bhi kar sakte ho. Kabhi nahi li maine college se help, na hotel jobs ki aur na kisi aur industry ki.

Log puchte hai mujhse ki kis field me scope hai.. aapko bhi hoga yeh sawal. Bhai..
**Scope field me nahi.. aap ke andar hai**
Aapne soch liya aur decide karliya na ki mujhe is field me fodna hai. Aapko koi nahi rok paega.
Apna bag pack karo aur akele nikal jao mehnat karne.
Yaad rakhna.. fast jana hai toh akele jao. Aur dur jana hai toh saath me company rakho.
Career ke start me sirf speed pakdo.
Jo experience kar sakte ho karo...

Main galat bhi ho sakta hu par mera maan na hai ki 'choosing career is like eating mithai... 4 mithai khaoge tab hi toh pata lagega ki aapko pasand kaunsi hai?'
Aur 17-18 saal ke bacche ko hamesha thodi pata hota hai ki usko kya chahiye. Hojati hai galti nahi samajh araha ek do saal me toh aagey badho. Pareshan mat raho!
Aapki mental health se zyada important kuch nahi hai. Aur harr chhoti cheez ka mental health par effect mat hone do. Strong bhi toh banna padega.
Ye phase me mujhe kuch badi skills sikhai.. jaise!

## Communication Skills – Sabse Badi Taaqat

Communication ka matlab sirf baat karna nahi, yeh ek process hai jisme hum apne vichar, emotions aur information exchange karte hain. Yeh verbal, non-verbal ya written ho sakti hai, aur personal aur professional success ke liye ek crucial skill hai.

Acchi communication sirf ek skill nahi hai—yeh samajhne aur samjhane ki kala hai.
Isme actively yani ki ache se sunna, apne ideas ko clearly express karna aur body language ka sahi use karna aata hai.

## Communication Itna Zaroori Kyun Hai?

Socho kisi bhi successful leader, business person ya influencer ke baare me—sabme ek common cheez hoti hai: unke communication skills.

✓ Jab tum acchi tarah apni baat rakhna seekh jaate ho, toh tumhara self-belief aur confidence bhi badhne lagta hai.
✓ Accha communication tumhe jobs, opportunities, promotions aur naye connections dilane me madad karta hai.
✓ Business ho, leadership ho ya personal life—effective communication tumhe aur zyada prabhavshali banata hai.
✓ Jab tum apni baat clearly express karte ho, toh misunderstandings kamm hoti hain aur clarity badhti hai.

Agar tumhe safal banna hai, toh communication seekhna zaroori hai—kyunki duniya sirf unhi ki sunti hai jo apni baat sahi tareeke se rakhna aur samjhana jaante hain.

Main bohot zyada politics na samajhta hu na uss baare me baat karta hu par.. hamare **Prime Minister Modi ji** ki body language bahut hi confident aur powerful hai. Unki personality se hum ye important cheezein seekh sakte hain jaise ki:

- **Confidence** (Aatmavishwas): Modi ji ki chaal, posture aur speech mein confidence saaf dikhta hai.

**Seekh**: Hamesha straight khade raho, shoulders peeche aur sir upar rakho.

- **Eye Contact:** Modi ji logon ki aankhon mein dekhkar baat karte hain, jo unki sincerity aur honesty ko dikhata hai.

**Seekh**: Direct eye contact rakho, ye tumhari baaton mein weight aur sacchai dikhayega.

- **Positive Gestures**: Modi ji haath ke gestures effectively use karte hain, jo unke words ko aur powerful banate hain.

**Seekh**: Apni baaton ko gestures ke saath support karo, log tumhe dhyaan se sunenge. Woh hamesha apne speeches me open arms rakhte hai. Notice karna.

- **Control and Calmness**: Difficult situations mein bhi Modi ji ki body language calm aur controlled rehti hai.

**Seekh**: Mushkil waqt mein shant aur composed raho, taaki dusre tumhe trust karein aur tum par rely kar sakein.

- **Smile aur Warmth**: Modi ji jab bhi kisi se milte hain toh warm aur welcoming smile dete hain.

**Seekh**: Logo se muskurate hue milo, ye tumhari personality ko approachable aur friendly banayega.

## Types of Communication

**1. Verbal Communication** (Boli Jane Wali Baatcheet)
Isme clear bolna, sahi shabdon ka chunav karna aur tone ka sahi use aata hai. Kaise bola jaa raha hai, yeh kabhi-kabhi shabdon se zyada important hota hai.
**Tip**: Filler words, jaise "um," "like," "you know", avoid karo. Yeh tumhari confidence aur clarity ko kamm kar dete hain.

**2. Non-Verbal Communication** (Sharirik Bhaasha)
Isme body language, facial expressions, haath ke ishare, posture aur eye contact aate hain. Kabhi-kabhi tumhari actions shabdon se zyada powerful hoti hain.
**Tip**: Achha eye contact maintain karo. Yeh dikhata hai ki tum confident aur baat ache se sunn rahe ho.

**3. Written Communication** (Likhi Hui Baatcheet)
Emails, messages, ya social media posts — tum kis tareeke se likhte ho, yeh logon ko tumhare prati vichar banane me help karta hai. Ek galat likha hua message confusion paida kar sakta hai, jabki ek accha likha message trust build karta hai.
**Tip**: Koi bhi important message bhejne se pehle usse zor se padho. Isse galtiyan aur ajeeb lagne wale sentences pakad me aayenge.

**4. Listening Skills (Sunne Ki Kala)**
Samajhne ke liye suno, jawab dene ke liye nahi.
Bahut log sunte toh hain, par asal me kisi ki baat ko samajhne ki koshish nahi karte. Active listening ka matlab sirf sunna nahi, balki samajhna aur ache se response karna hai.
**Tip**: Paraphrasing practice karo. Jaise agar koi kuch kahe, toh confirm karne ke liye bolo “Toh tumhara matlab yeh hai ki......”
Yeh tumhari listening skills ko aur better karega.

## Verbal Communication
### Sirf Bolna Nahi, Asar Chhodna Zaroori Hai

Verbal communication ka matlab sirf bolna nahi hai, balki apni baat is tareeke se kehna hai jo logon par asar chhode. Yeh humari daily life me har jagah important hota hai—chahe restaurant me order dena ho, pasandida ladki ya ladke se baat karna ho ya kisi company me salary negotiate karni ho.

Bharat jaisa desh jahan har kuch kilometers me bhasha aur lehja badal jata hai, wahan yeh skill personal aur professional dono growth me madad karti hai.

**Shabdon Ki Taqat**
Shabd rishton ko bana bhi sakte hain aur bigaad bhi sakte hain.
Socho, jab tumne last time kisi family member se jhagda kiya tha—zyadatar samasya shabdon se nahi, balki usse kehne ke tareeke se hui thi. Tumhari tone, pitch, aur bolne ki speed yeh decide karti hai ki doosre log tumhe kaise perceive karenge.

**Verbal Communication Me Common Galtiyan**

- **Sunne ke bina bolna** – Bahut log yeh sochte hain ki aage kya bolna hai, lekin samne wale ki baat dhyan se nahi sunte.
- **Zyada mushkil shabdon ka istemal** – Sirf fancy words ka use karne se communication accha nahi hota, clarity se hota hai.
- **Bina sune interrupt karna** – Beech me baat kaatne se baatcheet frustrating ho jaati hai. Samne wala interest kho deta hai.
- **Lack of confidence** – Bahut dheere bolna ya hesitate karna tumhari baat ka impact kam kar deta hai.

Agar tum verbal communication me maahir banna chahte ho, toh sirf bolna nahi, sunna bhi seekho. Saaf, self-confident aur respectfully baat karna hi tumhe ek accha communicator banayega.

**Aapko ek bohot important law ke baare me batata hu...**

Mehrabian's Law ko log aksar 7-38-55 Rule ke naam se bhi jaante hai, aur yeh communication mein non-verbal signals ke importance ko explain karta hai.

**Mehrabian's Law kya hai?**

Albert Mehrabian, ek psychologist, ne yeh law diya jisme unhone bataya ki jab koi humse baat karta hai, toh humari understanding teen cheezon par depend karti hai:

**7% Words**
Sirf 7% communication words se hoti hai.

**38% Tone of Voice**
38% communication aapke tone of voice, yahi ki aap kaise bol rahe ho—voice ka pitch, speed, enthusiasm se hoti hai.

**55% Body Language**
Sabse zyada, 55% communication aapki body language, jaise facial expressions, gestures, posture se hoti hai.

Mehrabian's Law har situation par apply nahi hota.
Yeh sirf tab relevant hai jab emotions ya feelings express ki jaa rahi ho—

**Example:** Agar koi bol raha hai, "Main tumse naraz nahi hoon," lekin uski aankhon mein gussa dikh raha hai aur tone rude hai, toh aap uski body language aur tone ko zyada importance doge, na ki words ko.

Communication sirf bolne ka khel nahi hai—kaise bolte ho aur uss samay aap kaise dikhte ho, woh zyada matter karta hai, especially jab aap feelings express kar rahe ho.

## Non-Verbal Communication – Bina Bole Bhi Baat Hoti Hai

Non-verbal communication ka matlab hai bina shabdon ke apni baat kehna. Isme facial expressions, body language, gestures, posture, eye contact, tone of voice, aur logon ke beech ka physical distance sab kuch shamil hota hai. Socho, tum ek interview ke liye enter karte ho, par seedha baithne ki jagah slouch ho jaate ho, jhuk jaate ho, interviewer se aankh nahi milate, fidget karte ho, aur apne haath me haath fasa kar beth jate ho.

Chahe tumhare answers perfect ho, tumhari body language yeh signal degi ki tum ya toh interested nahi ho, ya nervous ho, ya phir overconfident. Lekin agar tum confidently baitho, accha posture maintain karo aur natural eye contact rakho, toh bina kuch kahe hi tum ek credible aur engaged personality lagoge.

Challenges Log Face Karte Hain

- **Apni Body Language Ka Pata Na Hona** – Bahut log yehi nahi samajh paate ki unka body language unki baat se alag signal de raha hai.
- **Cultural Differences** – Kuch cultures me direct eye contact confidence dikhata hai, jabki kuch jagah ise aggression maana jata hai.
- **Galat Interpretation** – Kabhi-kabhi log gestures ya facial expressions ko galat samajh lete hain, jo misunderstandings create karta hai.
- **Nervous Energy Control Na Kar Pana** – Fidgeting ya eye contact avoid karna galat message bhej sakta hai.

**Yaad rakho-**
Shabdon se pehle log tumhari energy mehsoos kar lete hain.

## Written Communication: Shabdon Ki Taqat

Written communication ek bohot powerful tool hai jo ideas express karne, information share karne aur logon se connect hone me madad karta hai.

Verbal communication me tone aur body language message clear karne me madad karte hain, par written communication sirf shabdon par depend karta hai.

Isliye, clarity, structure aur tone sahi hona zaroori hai, taaki tumhari baat doosre insaan tak sahi tareeke se pahunch sake.

### Written Communication Itna Zaroori Kyun Hai?

Aaj ke time me emails, reports, WhatsApp, text messages aur social media posts har jagah use hote hai.

Ek accha likha gaya message naye rishton ko banata hai, logon ko influence karta hai, aur conflicts tak solve kar sakta hai.

Wahin, galat tareeke se likha gaya communication misunderstandings, confusion aur reputation damage tak la sakta hai. **Example** - Kapil Sharma ka likha hua tweet. Yaad hai?

### Effective Written Communication Ke Key Elements

#### 1. Clarity aur Simplicity

Accha likhne ka matlab mushkil shabdon ka istemal nahi, balki baat ko aasaan aur clear banana hai.

Hamesha socho: Kya ek 15 saal ka baccha aur 70 saal ki daadi isse samajh sakte hai? Agar nahi, toh simplify karo.

#### 2. Proper Structure

Ek well-structured message hamesha zyada impact dalta hai. Iska ek clear format hota hai:

- **Introduction** – Tumhara message kis baare me hai, yeh short aur clear batao.
- **Body** – Details, explanations ya arguments rakho.
- **Conclusion** – Important points summarise karo ya koi action dene ke liye likho.

Agar tum apne likhne ka tareeka sudhar loge, toh tumhare words sirf padhe nahi, mehsoos kiye jayenge.

**Tone Aur Professionalism**

Tumhara tone tumhare message ka mood set karta hai.

- **Formal tone** – Business emails, reports, aur professional settings ke liye.
- **Friendly tone** – Personal messages ya casual office conversations ke liye.
- **Persuasive tone** – Marketing, sales aur proposals likhne ke liye.

**Grammar Aur Punctuation**

Galat grammar aur punctuation tumhare message ka meaning change kar sakta hai.
Kuch bhejne se pehle proof read zaroor karo.
Tools jaise Grammarly tumhari writing ko refine karne me madad kar sakte hain.

**Brevity Aur Impact**

Aaj kal logon ka attention span chhota hai.
Zyada lafzon me baat ghumaane ki jagah, seedha mudde pe aao.
Kam shabdon me zyada kehna seekho.

**Written Communication Improve Karne Ke Tips**

✓ **Apna message zor se padho** – Isse awkward wording samajh aayegi.
✓ **Bullet points aur headings use karo** – Yeh content ko scan karna easy banata hai.
✓ **Pehle likho, fir edit karo** – Pehli draft perfect hone ki zaroorat nahi, pehle freely likho, baad me refine karo.
✓ **Apne audience ko samjho** – Ek formal report aur WhatsApp message ek jaise nahi lagne chahiye.

Agar tumhe apni baat likhne ka sahi tareeka aa gaya, toh tum bina bole bhi logon par asar daal sakte ho.

**Listening Skills – Samajhne Ki Kala**

Jaisa ki humne pehle discuss kiya. Listening skills ka matlab sirf sunna nahi, balki actively kisi ki baat ko sunna, samajhna, process karna aur uspar dhyaan dena hai.
Hearing ek passive act hai, par listening focus, patience aur engagement maangta hai.
Yeh effective communication ka ek sabse zaroori hissa hai, jo rishton ko majboot banata hai, misunderstandings door karta hai aur learning enhance karta hai.

**Types of Listening – Kaunse Tareeke Se Sunna Zaroori Hai?**

1. **Active Listening (Poori Tarah Dhyaan Dena)**

Iska matlab hai speaker ki baat ko dhyaan se sunna aur usme actively participate karna.

- Sar hilana (nodding) ya ek chhota verbal responses dena ("I see," "That makes sense")
- Sahi sawal poochna jo conversation ko aage badhaye
- Jo suna hai uska summary ya paraphrase karna taaki samne wale ko lage ki tumne sacch me dhyaan diya
- Empathetic Listening (Emotions Ko Samajhna)

Yeh sunne ka tareeka sirf shabdon tak seemit nahi hai, balki bolne wale ke emotions ko samajhna zaroori hota hai.

- Conflict resolution ya emotional situations me yeh sabse effective hota hai
- Speaker ki feelings ko samajhne ki koshish karna
- Sirf jawab dene ke liye sunne ki jagah, unke emotions ko genuinely feel karna

Agar tum sacch me ek acche listener ban gaye, toh sirf conversations nahi, balki rishton ko bhi ek naye level par le ja sakte ho.

**2. Critical Listening (Soch Samajh Kar Sunna)**

Iska use tab hota hai jab tum kisi information ko analyse kar rahe ho—jaise important conversations, debates, negotiations, ya business decisions me.

Isme message ki authenticity ko question karna aur soch samajh kar respond karna zaroori hota hai.

**3. Reflective Listening (Samajhne Aur Confirm Karne Ka Tareeka)**

Iska matlab hai jo speaker ne kaha, usko summarise ya repeat karna taaki clarity rahe.

Isse miscommunication avoid hota hai aur dono parties ek hi page par rehti hain.

**Listening Me Sabse Badi Mushkilein**

- **Distractions** – Phone notifications, external noise, ya apne personal thoughts tumhe distract kar sakte hain.
- **Jaldi response dene ki aadat** – Bahut log poori baat sunne se pehle hi sochne lagte hain ki ab kya bolna hai.
- **Bias aur assumptions** – Pehle se banayi gayi soch kabhi-kabhi message ko galat samajhne par majboor kar deti hai.
- **Emotional reactions** – Jab emotions control me nahi hote, toh objectively sunna mushkil ho jata hai.

**Apne Listening Skills Ka Self-Check Karo**

- Kya main bina phone dekhe poori tarah speaker par dhyaan deta/deti hoon?
- Kya main interrupt kiye bina doosre ki poori baat sunta/sunti hoon aur end me follow up question puchta hu?
- Kya main kisi ki baat ko accurately summarize kar sakta/sakti hoon?
- Kya log mujhse apni baatein share karne me comfortable feel karte hain?

Listening ek skill nahi, ek art hai. Jo isme maahir ho gaya, uska communication game doosron se kayi kadam aage hojaega aur rishtey behtar hojaenge.

## Common Communication Challenges Ko Kaise Overcome Karein?

Bahut log nervousness, clarity ki kammi, ya log kya sochenge iske dar ki wajah se acchi communication nahi kar paate.

### 1. Public Speaking Ka Dar

- **Practice mirror ke samne karo** – Apne aap ko bolte hue dekho, gestures aur expressions par dhyaan do.
- **Apni speech record karo** – Suno aur dekho ki kaha behtar ho sakta hai.

### 2. Soch Ko Accurately Express Karna Mushkil Lagna

- Baat karne se pehle apne ideas organise karo.
- Mushkil shabdon ke chakkar me mat pado—seedhe aur simple tareeke se baat rakho.

### 3. Conflicts Ko Handle Karna

- **Shaant raho aur ache se suno** – Samne wale ko pehle pura bolne do. Listen to understand, not to reply.
- **Blame karne ke bajaye "I" statements use karo** – Jaise, "Mujhe aisa mehsoos hota hai...", na ki "Tum hamesha aisa karte ho..."

Main usually CEO, Senior Manager ya Businessmen ko train karta hu. Maine ek common pattern jo almost sabhi senior profiles me notice kiya hai woh hai,

- **Conversation ke beech phone use karna**
  Chahe aap bahut busy ho, phone nikaal ke message dekhna ya scroll karna yeh signal deta hai ki saamne wala unimportant hai. Chahe aap CEO ho ya minister, yeh rude behaviour lagta hai aur aapki image par asar daalta hai. Log shayad aapko bolenge nahi par ye aapki authority ko impact karta hai.
- **Closed-off posture (baazu band karke ya peeche jhuka rehna)**
  Arms crossed ya chair pe peeche jhukna defensive aur uninterested lagta hai. Isse saamne wale ke saath ek invisible barrier ban jaata hai.
- **Eye contact avoid karna ya baar-baar ghadi dekhna**
  Nazar na milaana ya baar baar time dekhte rehna impatient aur distracted lagta hai. Logon ko feel hona chahiye ki aap unki baat sun rahe ho aur unko value de rahe ho. Bhale hi aapke dimag me 1000 cheezein chal rahi ho.
- **Team member ko dusro ko saamne rudely bolna**
  Agar aap kisi ko public mein, WhatsApp group ya email mein point-out karte ho—chahe galti ho ya feedback ho—woh shayad seedha na bole, par unka self-respect hurt hota hai. Yeh unki aapke prati loyalty aur team morale dono pe negative impact daalta hai. Koshish karo feedback sahi tarike se ya phir akele me do.
- **Baar-baar “mere paas time nahi hai” kehna**
  Jab aap us position par ho jahan aapke upar logon ke career ki responsibility hai, toh aapko time management jaisi skills ko seekh lena chahiye.
  Team ko baar-baar yeh bolte rehna ki “time nahi hai” ya “bohot kaam hai” kehna na sirf rude lagta hai, balki aapki professionalism aur credibility ko bhi nuksan pahunchata hai.

Kuch agar nahi aata toh accept karo aur sawal pucho. Team ko samajh aata hai ki aapko jawab nahi pata.
Agar aapne seekhna band kardiya toh aapki growth ruk jaegi.

## Practical Communication Techniques

Behtar Baat Karne Ke Tareeke

### 1. 3-Second Rule

Jawaab dene se pehle 3 second ruko. Count 1 2 3, aur phir jawab do. Yeh impulsive replies rokta hai aur tumhe sochne ka waqt deta hai, taaki tum zyada clear aur impactful baat kar sako. Aur kahi kuch galat na boldo.

### 2. The Power of Storytelling

Log facts bhool sakte hain, par kahaniyan yaad rakhte hain.
Agar tumhe kisi rok ke rakhna hai, toh apni baat ek chhoti kahani ke format me batao. (Agey baat karenge is topic par)

### 3. The Mirroring Technique

Agar tum kisi ke body language, tone, ya pace ko subtly mirror karte ho, toh rapport aur connection jaldi build hota hai.

### 4. Confident Sound Kaise Karein?

Steady pace me bolo – Na bahut tez, na bahut dheere.

- **Pitch thodi lower rakho** – Bahut high-pitched voice nervous lag sakti hai.
- **Pauses ka sahi use karo** – Kabhi-kabhi silence bhi powerful hota hai.

Acchi communication ek skill nahi, ek superpower hai.
Agar tum isse master kar loge, toh life me har jagah ek edge milega.

## Communication in Different Situations

### Alag-Alag Logon Se Kaise Baat Karein?

- **Bosses/Seniors Se Baat Karna** – Respectful, concise aur solution-oriented raho.
- **Doston Se Baat Karna** – Natural raho, par conversation interrupt ya dominate mat karo. And stop assuming.
- **Strangers Se Baat Karna** – Open-ended questions se start karo aur genuine interest dikhao unki journey me.

### Mushkil Conversations Kaise Handle Karein?

- **Shaant aur composed raho** – Apne emotions par control rakho.
- **Positive language use karo** – "Main aapki baat samajhne ki koshish kar raha hoon" bolo, "Aap galat hain", nahi.
- **Interrupt mat karo** – Puri baat suno aur fir calmly jawab do.

### Networking Tips

- **Apne aap ko confidently introduce karo** – "Hi, main [Name] hoon, aur [Field] me kaam karta hoon." Practice it 1000 times.
- **Apni value clear rakho** – Dusre bande ko samajh aaye ki tum kya karte ho aur kaise helpful ho sakte ho.

### Fun Challenges for Readers

1. **One Minute Storytelling Challenge –**

Ek random topic uthao aur 1 minute me simple aur engaging tareeke se explain karo. Isko regular practice karo.

**2. Silent Conversation Exercise –**
Bina bole sirf gestures aur expressions se communicate karne ki koshish karo. Isse body language aur non-verbal skills improve hoti hain.

**3. No-Filler-Word Challenge –**
Do minutes tak bina "um," "like," "you know" kahe bolo.
Isse tum clear aur confident bolna seekhoge.
Jitni acchi tumhari communication hogi, utni hi behtar tumhari personality lagegi—aur naye naye doors khulenge.

## Activity:

**Apni communication skills ko test aur improve karo**

**Step 1 - Apna ek video record karo**

Ek chhota topic select karo aur apni video record karo (1-2 minute). Ensure karo ki lighting, framing sahi ho aur aap clear dikh rahe ho.

**Step 2 - Mute karke video dekho**

Ab video ko bina awaaz ke dekho aur observe karo:

- Kya main confident lag raha hoon?
- Meri body language aur facial expressions engaging hain ya stiff?
- Gestures natural hain ya zyada distracting?

**Step 2 - Ab sirf audio ko suno**

Ab phone ko ulta rakhdo aur sirf apni awaaz suno:

- Kya clarity aur aapka pronunciation theek hai?
- Tone aur energy engaging hai ya dull lag rahi hai?
- Kya koi aapko sunna chahega?
- Kya main "um," "uh," "like" jaise filler words zyada use kar raha hoon?

**Ye video sirf aapke liye hai so judge karo apne aap ko jitna kar sakte ho..**

Jo improvement areas tumhe samajh aaye, unhe note karo.

Phir adjustments ke saath dobara record karo.

Yeh activity tumhari verbal aur non-verbal communication ko refine karne me help karegi aur tumhe ek aur zyada impactful speaker banayegi.

## Street Smartness

Hamesha book smartness ki baat hoti hai—kitabon se seekhna, exams pass karna, degrees lena, top karna.
Par asal duniya me jo log survive, adapt aur succeed karte hain, unme ek aur cheez hoti hai—Street Smartness.
Yeh ek practical skill hai jo tumhe tezi se sochne, logon ko samajhne, tricky situations handle karne aur challenges ko opportunities me badalne me madad karti hai.

**Street Smart Logon Me Yeh Qualities Hoti Hain:**

- **Quick Thinking** – Pressure me bhi tezi se aur sahi decision lena.
- **Situational Awareness** – Apne aaspaas kya ho raha hai, yeh samajhna aur uske according adjust hona.
- **People Skills** – Logon ki nature samajhna, emotions read karna aur alag-alag personalities ke saath deal karna.
- **Problem-Solving Ability** – Jab resources kam ho tab bhi smart solutions dhoondhna. Judgaad samajhte ho?
- **Survival Instincts** – Naye aur unfamiliar situations me bhi safe rehna.

**Street Smart Kaise Banein?**

- **Apni Instincts Par Bharosa Rakho** – Tumhara gut feeling aksar sahi hota hai. Agar kuch galat lag raha hai, toh usse ignore mat karo.
- **Observe & Learn** – Dhyaan do ki log kaise behave karte hain, deals kaise banti hain, conflicts kaise solve hote hain.
- **Baat Karne Ka Art Seekho** – Negotiation, tough situations handle karna aur samne wale ko convince karna—sab tumhari communication skills par depend karta hai.
- **Resourceful Bano** – Agar sab kuch available nahi hai, tab bhi kaam kaise chalega, yeh dhoondhna street smartness hai.
- **Risk & Safety Samjho** – Kahan risk lena chahiye aur kahan step back karna chahiye, yeh samajhna sabse zaroori hai.

## Jugaad

**India's National Superpower!**

India mein sab kuch mile ya na mile, ek cheez guaranteed milegi: **Jugaad**!
Simple shabdon mein kahu toh— "kamm resources mein, dimag ka full use karke, impossible ko possible bana dena!"

**Jugaad ki asli power kya hai?**
Ye sirf comedy nahi hai, boss! Jugaad ki mentality tumhe sikhati hai:

- **Problem solving**: Har mushkil ka solution hota hai, agar tum dimaag lagao.
- **Creativity**: Normal cheezon mein naye ideas dekhne ki kala.
- **Adaptability**: Har condition mein survive karne ki skill.

**Lekin Jugaad mein ek dikkat bhi hai:**
Temporary solution accha hai, par hamesha "*theek hai yaar chalta hai*" attitude mat rakho. Lambi race mein permanent aur strong solution dhoondhna zaruri hai. Jugaad temporary fix hai, permanent solution nahi.

**Toh kya seekh mili?**

- Life mein creative bano, Jugaad apnao, par permanent solutions bhi zarur dhundho.
- Problems se daro mat, unhe solve karne ka unique aur innovative tareeka socho.
- Jugaad sirf ek word nahi, hum Indians ka inbuilt talent hai. Be proud of your Jugaad instinct, but never stop learning and improving!

## Street Smarts vs. Book Smarts

✓ **Book Smart** – Rules jaanta hai, instructions follow karta hai aur structured environments me excel karta hai.
✓ **Street Smart** – Jaanta hai kab rules bend karne hain, jaldi adapt karta hai aur unpredictable situations me excel karta hai.

**Street Smartness Ka Matlab Careless Hona Nahi Hai**
Na reckless hone hai, balki sharp, aware aur adaptable hone hai.
Chahe business ho, relationships ho ya daily life—street smart logon ke paas hamesha ek edge hota hai.
Baat sirf yeh nahi ki tum kya jaante ho, baat yeh hai ki tum apni knowledge ka istemal kaise karte ho!"

SCAN HERE

Scan this code to watch a detailed video on 'Being Street Smart'.
**Agar tumhe aur aise hi videos dekhne hain, toh visit karo:**
**www.YouTube.com/@JaiPareek**
**www.Instagram.com/JaiPareek**
Seekho kaise real duniya me street smart ban ke apni jagah banayi jaati hai.

## Chapter 4

# 2013 CHANGED ME AS A PERSON

### Woh Sapna – Jo mere liye sab kuch tha!

Jo sapna maine pehle aapse share kiya tha—"Videsh me rehne ka"—wo meri life ka sabse bada sapna tha.

Bade hote hue maine dekha tha ki mere papa un rishtedaron ko ek alag respect se dekhte the jo India ke bahar rehte the. Aur vacations ya festivals me ghar aate the.
Mujhe un relatives se problem nahi thi, woh toh hamare liye goals the par mere papa ka unke around behavior mujhe kuch sikha raha tha. Mujhe chahiye tha ki mere papa ko log meri wajah se waise hi izzat dein aur waise hi treat karein.

Mujhe Kishangarh se pyaar hai par uss samay mujhe lagta tha ki abhi yaha rehna mere liye right decision nahi hoga. Pyar mujhe bohot tha meri jagah se par woh comfort aur mere around mindset mujhe aagey badhne nahi de raha tha. Bahar ki duniya badi lagti thi, zyada accepting log, aur mujhe vishwas tha ki waha mujhe mere jaise log milenge jo alag sochte hai.
College ke dino me, mujhe ek aadmi mila jo students ko training ke liye videsh bhejta tha. Mujhe laga, yeh hai mera chance apne sapne ko sacch karne ka. Isko bolenge yeh bhej dega. Easy.

Maine apply kiya, papa se lekar paise diye, aur poori tayyari shuru kar di. Life suddenly bohot exciting hogai, harr ek din excitement se bhara hota tha. Sab acha lagne lag gaya kyunki dimag me sirf ek cheez chalti thi ki kuch din me mein desh chhod ke bahar jaane wala hu. Interviews diye aur selection hogaya. Phone wallpaper, desktop screen par harr jagah hotel ki photo lagi hoti thi.

Phir agent ne ekdin inform kiya ke selection hogaya hai mera, approvals agaye hai aap ready hojao kuch din me hi aapko Malaysia jana hoga internship ke liye Hotel Equatorial me.
Holi Diwali sab festivals ek hi din me agaye mere liye. I felt like the luckiest person on this planet.
Mumbai se flights thi toh Mumbai tak ke train tickets book kiye aur finally Mumbai jaane wala din aaya. Mujhe lagbhag 25 log station par chhodne aaye the. Friends, family, relatives.
Aise hi main Mumbai ke liye train me chadha, mere bhai Lucky ki awaaz aayi— "We are proud of you, tu hamare parivaar ka pehla insaan hai jo videsh jaa raha hai. khoob agey badh bhai"
Main aur mera ek dusra bhai Abhishek Mumbai ke liye nikal gaye, Mumbai pahunche, ek relative ke ghar ruke aur khoob shopping kari. Gate way of India ghuma, vada pao khaya, local train me safar kiya, Shah Rukh Khan ke ghar ko 1 ghante tak nihara aur 2-3 din me jo jo Mumbai ke bare me suna tha woh sab experience karliya.

Phir ek din visa lene gaya. Main usually shirts pehenta tha skinny hone ke kaaran. Usdin mere haath me ek t-shirt aaya aur maine usey pehen liya bina soche samjhe kyuki jaldi se visa lena tha.
Agent ke office gaye. Uski team ne kuch formalities ki aur phir finally Visa handover karne MAIN agent aaya. Jaise hi woh aaya usne mujhse kuch sawaal kiya aur ekdum se uski nazar mere haath par padi. Mere haath me ek tattoo hai.
Suddenly, uske chehra ke expressions badal gaye.
Usne pucha, ye permanent tattoo hai? 'I said haa'.
Woh bohot rude voice me bola
Tumne mujhe bataya kyu nahi?, hotel me tattoo allowed nahi hai
**"Tumhara visa cancel karna padega"**

Main shocked tha. Meri aawaz kanp rahi thi, "Sir, meri kal flight hai. Yeh mera bapchpan ka sapna hai. Please mat kijiye aisa mere sath. Aap kahoge toh mein isse roz hide kar lunga. Full sleeves pehen lunga,, make up laga lunga"
Usne meri taraf dekha bhi nahi. Seedha kaha,
**"Visa cancel kar raha hoon,"** aur ek dusre room me chala gaya.

Us pal, main blank ho gaya. Agle 10 minute tak kuch sunayi nahi diya aur na kuch samajh aaya. Mujhe sirf meri saanse sunai de rahi thi. Maine unn sab rich aur powerful rishtedaron ko call kiya jo kehte the, "Kuch chahiye ho toh bolna, Mumbai me sab kuch ho jata hai apne bolne par."

Kisi ne help nahi ki. Kuch samay baad unhone calls uthana bhi band kar diya. Mujhe lag raha tha meri life end hochuki hai.
Us din samajh aane laga ki aise toh sab log aapke saath honge, lekin jab aapke sapno par baat ajaegi na, aapko akele hi agey jana hoga, akele sab handle karna hoga.
Iss samay main bohot weak tha, mera dimag chalna band hogaya tha aur main sachh me bohot dukhi hogaya tha.
Do din baad meri kishangarh ke liye train thi toh aagle do din main sirf akela beth kar ye search karta hota tha ki is tattoo ko remove ya hide kaise kar sakta hu.

Mujhe lag raha tha ki jiss baare me maine 3 saal padhai ki, woh sab waste hogaya hai. Mujhe tattoo ki wajah se hotels me koi job nahi dega.

Mumbai me mere relative koi badi position par kaam kar rahe the. Unhone mujhe pareshan dekha aur bola 'life thodi khatam hogai hai teri'.
Baat toh sahi thi lekin us samay mujhe woh bohot kadvi lagi.
Waha sirf ek chhoti bacchi thi 'Mili' jo mujhe dekh kar samajh pa rahi thi ki main pareshan hu. Aur jitna ho sakta tha koshish kar rahi thi mujhse baat karne ki. Bina mujhe kuch solution diye.

Main us samay bass samajhna chahta tha is pain se bahar kaise nikla jaaye. Main **resilience** seekhna chahta tha.

Samjho ek rubber band hai—jitna bhi stretch kar lo, woh phir se apni original shape mein aa jaata hai.
Ussi tarah, resilient log bhi life ki problems aur challenges se jaldi ubhar ke normal ho jaate hain, bounce back karlete hai.

Mujhe samajhna tha ki Rejection end nahi hai—yeh sirf ek naya raasta dikhane wala mod hota hai.

**Rejection means redirection.**

## Obstacles Are Opportunities in Disguise

Jab zindagi hamare saamne achanak se koi challenge phenkti hai, toh aksar lagta hai ki sab chhod do, give up kar do.
Lekin har setback/challenge ke andar chhupa hota hai ek lesson, ek naya perspective, ek nayi raah dhoondhne ka moka.
Mera visa cancel hona ek heartbreaking experience tha, lekin usne mujhe ek badi baat sikhayi—apne upar bharosa karna, soch ko naya mod dena, aur wo strength dhoondhna jo shayad mujhe khud nahi pata tha ki mere andar hai.

Aapko ye feeling ekdum se bhi aa sakti hai aur hosakta hai kuch time baad aaye. Sabka apna pace hota hai.

Uss experience ne mujhe **Resilience** ka matlab sikhaya
**Resilience** ka matlab hota hai musibat ke baad bhi khud ko sambhal lena, stress aur problems ke saamne bhi apna balance na khona aur buri se buri situation se nikalkar ek stronger version baahar aana.
Yeh stress se bachne ka nahi, stress ko effectively handle karne ki skill hai.
Jo log resilient hote hain, wo pressure me shaant rehte hain, badlav ke saath jaldi adapt kar lete hain, aur har difficulty se jaldi recover karte hain.

Zindagi me stress unavoidable hai—kabhi kaam ka pressure, kabhi personal struggles, kabhi sudden/unexpected crisis.
Lekin jo log resilience build karte hain, ye skill ko seekh lete hai, wo stress ko control karte hain, stress unhe control nahi karta.

**Resilience se:**

- Burnout, anxiety, emotional thakan se bachav hota hai.
- Mental well-being better hoti hai.
- Decision-making aur life satisfaction dono improve hote hain.

## Resilience Zaroori Kyun Hai?

✓ **Ye Failures Ko Handle Karna Seekhata Hai** – Zindagi kabhi na kabhi tumhe gira degi. Resilience tumhe wapas khade hone ki taqat deta hai.
✓ **Emotional Strength Badhata Hai** – Tum mentally zyada strong bante ho aur aane wale challenges ke liye tayyar rehte ho.
✓ **Adapt Karna Sikhata Hai** – Setbacks sirf raaste ke mod hote hain. Resilience tumhe adjust karna aur aage badhna sikhaata hai.
✓ **Winners Aur Quitters Me Farq Karta Hai** – Jo log girke bhi chalte rehte hain, wahi asli winner hote hain. Aisa koi successful insaan nahi hai jo bohot baar gira na ho. Farq sirf itna hai ki woh girne ke baad waha beth ke ye nahi soch rahe the 'yaar main phir gir gaya'. Woh utha aur aagey badh gaye.

## Resilience Kaise Build Karein?

✓ **Failures Ko Zindagi Ka Hissa Maano** – Failure se daro mat, usse seekho. Har setback kuch na kuch sikhaata hai.
✓ **Jis Par Control Hai, Us Par Dhyaan Do** – Kya galat hua, usme atke mat raho—solution dhoondo.
✓ **Buri Haalat Me Bhi Positive Raho –** Dimaag ko train karo ki tight situations me bhi learnings leta rahe. Easy nahi hai par possible hai.
✓ **Strong Logon Ke Saath Raho** – Jo log tumhe sambhal sake jab tum thak jao, ya phir jinhe dekh kar tum tough situations handle karna seekho. Nahi mil rahe toh khud ke liye woh insaan bann jao.
✓ **Ruko Mat, Chalte Raho** – Chahe dheere hi sahi, progress toh progress hoti hai.

Bunny ki baat yaad hai?
Main daudna chahta hu, girna chahta hu, udna chahta hu bass.. rukna nahi chahta.
Usse seekh lo aur chalte raho.

Mere saath jo tattoo incident hua tha, wo mere sapne ko khatam kar sakta tha, par aisa nahi hua. God's grace.

Usne mujhe aur strong, samajhdar, aur zyada determined banaya. Yahi hota hai resilience ka asar—jo rokta nahi, naya raasta dikhata hai.

Jab zindagi tumhe giraaye, khud se sirf ek sawaal poochhna:
"Kya main apne aap ko khatam hone dunga, ya isse aur strong hokar bahar niklunga?"
Issi sawaal ka jawab tumhari kismat likhega.

Aapki life mein problem kabhi khatam nahi hogi
Agar aapko aise lagne lage ki problems aani band hogai hai toh samajh jana aap apna ek stronger version bann chuke ho aur problems aapko zyada bother nahi kar rahi hai.
Woh aati hai aur aapka dhyaan usko fix karne me chala jata hai balki usse pareshan hone me.

Pehle aap ek problem oriented person the.. jo sirf problems ke barae me sochte the.
Ab aap ek solution-oriented person hein, Jo problem ke aate hi solution par focus karta hai. Time waste nahi karta.

**Resilience Builder Activity: "The Setback Tracker"**

**Objective**: Tumne zindagi me jitne setbacks face kiye hain, unko ek nayi nazar se dekhna, aur apni andar ki taqat pehchanna.

**Step 1: Ek Tough Moment Yaad Karo**

Ek aisi situation socho jahan zindagi ne tumhe zor se maara tha—shayad koi exam fail hua, job chali gayi, rejection mila, ya koi sapna toot gaya.

**Write it down:**

"Jo setback maine face kiya woh tha..."

✍ ____________________________________________

**Step 2: Tumne Kya Seekha?**

Apne aap se poochho: "Is experience ne mujhe kya sikhaya?"

(Example: Main mentally zyada strong bana / Mujhe pata chala kaun mere saath hai / Maine ek naya raasta dhoonda)

✍ ____________________________________________

**Step 3: Tum Kaise Bounce Back Hue?**

Koi bhi 3 chhoti ya bade actions likho jo tumne liye jisse tumne thoda bhi recover kiya ho

1. ____________________________________________
2. ____________________________________________
3. ____________________________________________

**Step 4: Tumhara Resilience Score (Self-Check)**

1 se 10 ke scale par rate karo ki aaj tum kitne strong feel karte ho us setback ke comparison me.

(1 = Abhi bhi uska asar hai, 10 = Maine usse bahut kuch seekha aur grow kiya)

Mera Resilience Score: ___ /10

**Apna Resilience Mantra Banao**

Apne liye ek line ka personal mantra likho jo tumhe hamesha yaad dilaye ki tum kitne strong ho.

(Example: "Main jhukta hoon, par tootta nahi." ya "Main har baar aur zyada strong hokar wapas aata hoon.")

✍ ____________________________________________

# Stress Management

## Samajhna Aur Sambhalna Seekho

Stress zindagi ka ek natural hissa hai. Chahe kaam ka pressure ho, personal struggles ho, ya achanak challenges, stress sabhi ko hota hai. Lekin farq sirf is baat se padta hai ki tum us stress ko kaise manage karte ho—kyunki ya toh stress tumhe tod dega, ya tumhe aur strong banayega.

### Stress Kya Hai?

Stress tumhare sharir ka response hai kisi challenge ya demand ke saamne.

- **Positive Stress (Eustress)**: Jab stress tumhe energize karta hai —jaise kisi presentation ya competition ke liye tayyari karte waqt.
- **Negative Stress (Distress)**: Jab pressure itna zyada ho jaye ki tum anxious ya thake hue feel karo.

### Stress Ke Common Signs

Stress tumhare body, mind aur behavior ko affect karta hai.

- **Physical Symptoms** – Sar dard, thakan, body pain, tez heartbeat.
- **Emotional Symptoms** – Chidchidaapan, ghabrahat, overwhelmed feel karna.
- **Behavioral Symptoms** – Neend me dikkat, zyada ya kamm khana, zimmedari se bacchna.

Agar stress chronic ban jaye, toh burnout, depression aur health issues hone lagte hain. Isliye, stress manage karna seekhna bohot zaroori hai.

Stress ko samajh lo, sambhal lo, aur jeevan ka control apne haath me le lo.

Stress se dosti kar lo, dushmani nahi.

## How to Manage Stress Effectively

**Stress Ko Dost Kaise Banayein?**

**1. Apne Stress Triggers Ko Pehchano**

Stress manage karne ka pehla step hai samajhna ki stress ho kyun raha hai?

- Work pressure?
- Paise ki dikkat?
- Relationships?
- Future ka uncertainty? Ya aur kuch.

➡ **Likho ki kya cheez tumhe stress deti hai aur tum uss waqt kaise react karte ho.**

Isse tumhe clarity milegi aur tum apne stress ko control kar paoge.

**2. Mindfulness Aur Deep Breathing Practice Karo**

Mindfulness ka matlab hai present moment me rehna, bina kisi judgment ke. BEING IN NOW!

Yeh anxiety kamm karta hai aur tumhe apne emotions ko samajhne me help karta hai.

➡ **Deep Breathing Technique (4-7-8 Rule):**

- 4 seconds tak gehri saans lo
- 7 seconds tak saans roko
- 8 seconds me dheere-dheere saans chhodo

Yeh tumhare dimaag ko shaant karta hai aur control wapas deta hai. Sara breathing ka game hai. Ispar achi research karo.

**3. Physically Active Raho**

Exercise se endorphins (feel-good hormones) release hote hain, jo stress kam karte hain aur mood lift karte hain.

➡ **Yoga** – Relax hone ke liye

➡ **Strength Training** – Body ka tension release karne ke liye

➡ **Dance ya Sports** – Mood ko instantly boost karne ke liye

**4. Time Management Aur Prioritization Seekho**
Overwhelm hone ka reason hota hai poor time management.
➡ **Eisenhower Matrix: (on next page)**

- Urgent
- Important
- Not Urgent
- Not Important

Focus karo jo sacch me matter karta hai uspar.

➡ **2-Minute Rule**: Jo kaam 2 minute me ho sakta hai, turant karo.

➡ **Realistic Goals Set Karo**: Apne upar zyada pressure mat daalo, sab kuch ek din me mat karo.

**5. Support System Build Karo**
➡ **Apna ek go-to person dhundho** – Friend, family ya mentor. Kabhi-kabhi sirf emotions share karna hi mann halka kar deta hai aur aapko problem ka solution dedeta hai.
**Pro Tip:** Aise logon ke saath raho jo positive aur uplifting ho. Jo sirf stress badhate hain, unse dur raho.

**6. Healthy Lifestyle Maintain Karo**
➡ **Sahi Khaana Khao** – Junk food temporary comfort deta hai, par balanced diet tumhe strong banati hai aur active rakhti hai.
➡ **Achhi Neend Lo** – Neend ki kami se stress badhta hai. 7–9 ghante ki quality sleep lo. Don't oversleep.
➡ **Caffeine & Alcohol Limit Karo ya band karo** – Zyada caffeine se anxiety badh sakti hai aur shaam 4 baje baad coffee avoide karo. Alcohol se mood, sleep aur rishtey kharab ho sakte hai.

**7. Growth Mindset Develop Karo**
Stress ko bojh nahi, ek challenge samjho jise tum jeet sakte ho.
Apne aap se poochho:
➡ "Main is situation se kya seekh sakta hoon?"
➡ "Yeh challenge mujhe kaise grow karne me madad karega?"
Growth mindset tumhe har halat me strong aur flexible banata hai.

## The Eisenhower decision matrix

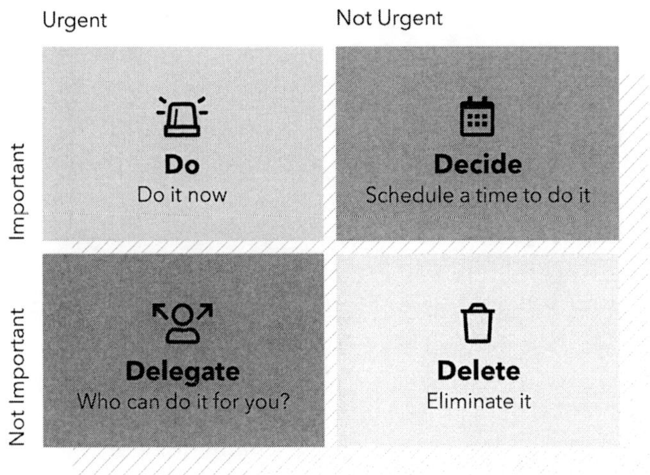


Eisenhower Matrix ek simple time management tool hai jo aapko decide karne me madad karta hai ki kaunsa kaam pehle karna hai, kaunsa baad me, aur kaunsa karna hi nahi hai.

**Iska motto hai:**

"What is important is seldom urgent, and what is urgent is seldom important."

### Eisenhower Matrix ke 4 Box:

**Box 1: Urgent + Important → Do it now**

Ye woh kaam hote hain jo turant karne zaroori hain, jaise:

- Client ko phone call
- Aaj ki deadline wala kaam
- Health emergency

Yeh kaam aapko khud turant karne chahiye.

**Box 2: Not Urgent + Important → Plan karo**
Ye kaam abhi urgent nahi hain, lekin future me bohot important honge:

- Koi course/skill seekhna
- Fitness & health routine
- Networking event me jana

Yeh kaam aap calendar me mention karke rakho.

**Box 3: Urgent + Not Important → Delegate karo**
Ye kaam jaldi karne wale lagte hain, lekin zaroori nahi hote aapke liye.

- Kisi aur ki email ka reply
- Routine admin work
- Bahut saare chhote phone calls

Yeh kaam kisi aur ko karne ko de do (delegate).

**Box 4: Not Urgent + Not Important → Avoid karo**
Ye woh kaam hain jo na to zaroori hain, na hi urgent, sirf time waste karte hain:

- Excessive social media scrolling
- Gossip
- Repeated Netflix binge without purpose

Yeh kaam avoid karne chahiye.

"Urgent ka matlab hai jaldi karna.
Important ka matlab hai aapke goals se judna."

## Stress Toh Aayega

Par Tumhara Reaction Tumhare Control Me Hai?

Stress ko samjho, relax karo, active raho aur positive soch rakho—tum stress ko apni taqat aur growth ka source bana sakte ho.
Jab bhi overwhelmed feel ho, ek gehri saans lo, pause karo, aur stress par control le lo. You've got this!

**Ek baat share karta hu, aapke kaam aegi.**
Main 5 saal hotel industry ka hissa raha hu. Most of the times mere paas bar ke access hota tha, jo alcohol chahiye woh available thi, jitni chahiye thi consume kar sakta tha.. par maine aaj tak alcohol ko taste nahi kiya. Aur na main cigarette leta hu.

Aur main apni life me bohot difference feel kar pata tha jab un log ke sath hota hu jinka alcohol or smoking par control nahi hai.
Unke paas paisa ho ya na ho, unka addiction unko paise kharch karne par majboor karta tha. Unke rishtey kharab horahe the, health affect horahi thi, par woh aadat nahi chhoot rahi thi.
Mere bohot sare classmates jab hotel management karne aaye the tab unhe koi addiction nahi tha par kuch hi saalo mein woh addicts bann gaye aur regret karte the ki kyu woh 'ek baar try karna hai' wale trap me phas gaye.
Hotel me shift ke baad kuch colleagues ek room me bethe hote the, mera mazak banate the 'tu mard nahi hai - hai toh ekbar peeke bata' 'kya hi zindagi jee rahe hai tu'. Subah sab zameen par soye milte the, kisi ka pair kiske muh par hai, kisi ke kapde kaha.
Kuch nahi pata hota tha unhe.

Apni boundries set karna seekhna hoga aapko. Ye nashe wali life bohot fancy aur cool lagti hai bahar se par ye ek ganda trap hai. Aapko apne aap ko lekar bohot strict hona padega. Ghar chhodte hi aksar logo ko maine freedom ke naam par apni life kharab karte dekha hai. Hope aap woh galti nahi karenge.

## Stress Buster Activity: "My Stress Toolkit"

**Objective:** Apne stress triggers ko pehchano aur apna personal stress buster toolkit banao—taaki jab bhi stress aaye, tum usse pro ki tarah handle kar sako.

**Step 1: Tumhe Sabse Zyada Stress Kis Cheez Se Hota Hai?**

Thoda socho—kya hai jo tumhe stress deta hai:

- Studies?
- Job?
- Family expectations?
- Paise ki tension?
- Future ka uncertainty? Etc.

✍ **Write - Top 3-4 cheezein jo mujhe stress deti hain:**

1. ______________________________
2. ______________________________
3. ______________________________
4. ______________________________

**Step 2: Stress Ka Tum Par Kya Impact Hai?**

Har kisi ka stress alag dikhayi deta hai, kisi ko gussa aata hai, kisi ko anxiety, sar dard, koi rone lagta hai, koi cigarette peeta hai. Agar tum apne stress ke signs pehle pehchaan loge, toh usse sambhalna aasan ho jaayega.

✍ **Jab main stressed hota hoon, tab mein** ______________

______________________________

______________________________

______________________________

______________________________

**Step 3: Apna Stress Buster Toolkit Banao**

Ab likho 5 cheezein jo tumhe stress kam karne me help karti hain.

**Example**

- 2 minute deep breathing
- Walk or nature time
- Music sunna, gaana ya instrument bajana
- Journal likhna
- Kisi trusted insaan se baat karna
- Exercise / Dance / Body movement
- Kuch creative karna (drawing, cooking, etc.)
- Pray ya meditate karna
- 10-minute ka screen break
- Etc.

✍ **Mere Top 5 Stress Busters:**

- ____________________________________________________
- ____________________________________________________
- ____________________________________________________
- ____________________________________________________
- ____________________________________________________

**Step 4: Quick Reset – Abhi Try Karo!**

- 4 second tak gehri saans lo
- 4 second tak saans roko
- 4 second tak dheere se saans chhodo

Ab Yeh 5 baar repeat karo—aapko halkapan aur shaanti mehsoos hogi.

## Daily Check-Ins

**Din ke end me apne aap se poochho:**

- Aaj aapko kya achha feel hua?
- Aaj aapko kya stress hua?
- Kal aap kya alag kar sakte ho jisse woh stress phirse na ho?

Yeh likhne me sirf 3 minute lagenge, par aapko emotions par control milega.

**Yeh Activity Kaam Kyun Karti Hai?**
Stress kabhi khatam nahi hota, par tum smart aur strong ban sakte ho usse sambhalne me.
Tumhara dimaag ek bohot important tool hai, agar tum issy sahi se use karna seekh gaye, toh koi bhi stress tumhe weak nahi bana paega. Tum apni life ko jaisa chahoge waisa chala paoge.

Ab baat karte hai us sabse badi learning ki jo meri zindagi ka game-changer bani. Jisne meri soch hi badal di.
Aur woh learning hai... **SRR FORMULA**

## S + R = R (Situation + Reaction = Results)

**Matlab**: Jo tumhare saath hota hai (Situation) + Tum kaise react karte ho (Reaction) = Uska outcome (Results)

Har event tumhare control me nahi hota, lekin tumhara reaction hamesha tumhare haath me hota hai.
Aur wahi reaction, tumhara result/outcome decide karta hai.

**Example:**
**Event**: Traffic me phas gaye ho, meeting ke liye late ho rahe ho.
**Reaction 1**: Gussa ho jaate ho, horn bajate ho, stress lete ho.
**Reaction 2**: Shaant rehte ho, podcast sunte ho, clear mind ke saath pahunchte ho. Apne aap se bolte ho, main kuch nahi kar sakta is traffic ka. Ab jab open hoga tab hi ja paunga.

**Result**: Tumhara reaction hi decide karega ki tum har challenge me stress me rahoge ya uss situation me aane ke baad bhi khush rahoge.

Zindagi ke challenges tum control nahi kar sakte,
par apna reaction ya response control kar sakte ho.
Aur wahi tumhara result shape karta hai.
Jab bhi zindagi tumhe challenge de, ruk jao, socho, aur reaction wisely choose karo—yeh sab kuch badal deta hai.

Mumbai se aane ke baad teen din tak main isolation me raha.
Tab mere paas do choices thi—
**Pehli -** Apne failure me dooba rahun ya control le loon.
**Dusri -** Agar abhi abroad nahi ja sakta, toh yaha rehkar aisa kya kar sakta hu jisse mujhe waisi hi khushi mile.

Chapter 5

# GOA CALLED ME

Room me akela aur pareshan betha betha main sochta raha ki ye mere sath kyu hua?
Station par mujhe bina mann se bye bolne aaye kuch rishtedaron ke chehre par mujhe ek chhoti si hasi dikh rahi thi jo kehna chahti thi, 'Ja aaya videsh'. 'Fail ho gaya na yaha bhi.'
Us waqt laga jaise log mere fail hone par khush hain.

Infact ghar walo ko laga kisi pandit ko dikhana chahiye
Ek pandit ke paas gaye toh unhone kaha 'beta ab 7.5 years ghar par betho, tumhare sade sati lagi hai. Kitna bhi haath peir maroge, kuch nahi hopaega.'
Yaha pehle hi dukh khatam nahi horahe aur ye bhai sahab aur masaley laga gaye.

Lekin un teen dino me maine ek cheez ki jo maine kabhi nahi ki thi — **Maine pehli baar apni zindagi main ek bada plan banaya.**
Maine apne aap se poocha,
"Agar abhi videsh nahi ja raha, toh India me sabse achhi jagah rehne ke liye kaunsi hai jo mujhe waisi hi feel de jaise main videsh me reh raha hu?"
Ek aisi jagah jahan freedom, energy aur opportunity teeno milein.
Jaha mujhe koi nahi jaanta ho aur main apne aap ko jitna badalna chahu, badal sakoon.

Dimag me jawab aaya – **Goa**.

Maine turant Google pe Goa ke top hotels search kiye. Maybe 30-40. Ek calling script banayi aur sabko ek ek karke call kiya internship vacancy ka pata karne ke liye.
Kuch ne mana kiya aur kuch ne mujhe CV send karne ko kaha.

Agli subah mujhe ek strange number se call aaya,
Maine call uthaya toh pata chala ki woh call **Taj Exotica, Goa** se tha— One of the best resort properties in the world.
Unhone bola, "Aapka CV mila humein, we have a vacancy aur aap industrial training ke liye aa sakte ho."
Maine turant bags pack kiye aur family ko bola,
"Iss baar mere saath mat aana. Main khud se karunga jo karna hai."
Aur mein nikal gaya akela train se Goa....

25 ghante ki train journey karne ke baad main pohocha Goa.
Actually South Goa, jo ki luxury aur peace ke liye jana jata tha.
North Goa jao party ke liye aur South shaanti ke liye.

Main ek vegetarian hoon jo kabhi akela apne state se bahar nahi gaya tha, aur Goa ki streets me fish aur pork bik raha tha woh bhi aise jaise paani puri ka thela laga ho.
Jo ladka is umar mein bhi apni maa ke haath se khana khata tha, wo ab ek nayi duniya me jagah jagah ghoom kar khana dhoondh raha tha.
Ab main unplanned pohoch toh gaya, rehne ka kya karna hai ye toh socha hi nahi. Main 5-6 ghante tak idhar udhar ghumta raha, logo ke ghar ki bells baja kar poocha 'ek room available hai kya 6 months ke liye?', almost har darwaza knock kiya Benaulim area ka. Phir finally ek Goan family ne mujhe $1^{st}$ floor par ek room diya.

Is process ne mujhe ek cheez ka confidence dediya tha ki main ab is duniya ke kisi bhi kone me jaakar rehne ki jagah dhoondh sakta hu.
Main ye Jaipur me college time me bhi karta tha. Jaha mere saath wale pareshan hote rehte thi ki accommodation nahi mil raha, sirf girls ke liye PGs available hai. Wahi main, ache ache bungalows me rooms lekar rehta tha. Funda simple tha.. knock 100 doors for whatever you need, ek toh door open ho hi jaega aapke liye.

Agar nahi hua toh 100 aur kardo, isbar pakka hoga. Bas ruko mat. Agle din mujhe hotel jana tha. Taj me internship start karne ka excitement ke saath andar se ek darr bhi tha—
Mujhe pata hai sab final hai magar phir bhi darr sa lag raha tha ki yaha bhi unhone mujhe tattoo ke wajah se reject kar diya toh?"

Malaysia ka visa cancel hone wala zakham abhi bhi taza tha.
Main hotel full sleeves shirt pahan kar gaya.

Kuch din Taj Exotica me maine **Garde Manger department** me bhi kaam kiya aur bohot achi food carving karne lag gaya tha main.

# Adaptability

Har Situation Me Khud Ko Dhalne Ki Kala

Adaptability ka matlab hota hai naye conditions, challenges aur changes me khud ko adjust karna— woh bhi positive aur flexible mindset ke saath.

Naye ideas ke liye open rehna, uncertainty ko accept karna, aur jab sab kuch plan ke hisaab se na ho, tab bhi success ka rasta dhoondhna.

Aaj ke fast-paced world me, adaptability ek priceless skill hai— workplace, personal life, ya relationships me jo log badlav se darte hain, woh ruk jaate hain.

Jo log badlav ko gale lagate hain, wo aage badhte hain.

## Adaptability Zaroori Kyun Hai?

✓ **Change Ko Handle Karne Me Help Karti Hai** – Zindagi unpredictable hai. Adaptable log hamesha aage badhte hain.

✓ **Naye Opportunities Ka Darwaza Kholti Hai** – Jaldi adapt karo, jaldi naye chances milenge.

✓ **Confidence Build Karti Hai** – Tum kisi bhi situation me khud par bharosa karna seekhte ho.

✓ **Problem-Solving Strong Karti Hai** – Jab sab kuch asaan na ho, toh adaptable log hi creative solutions nikalte hain.

## Adaptability Me Aane Wale Challenges

✗ **Fear of Change** – Change uncomfortable lagta hai, isliye log use avoid karte hain.

✗ **Rigid Thinking** – Purani aadaton se chipke rehna, naye tareeke try na karna.

✗ **Lack of Confidence** – Apne aap par doubt karna. Kya main nayi cheezein seekh paunga?

✗ **Emotional Resistance** – Jab sab plan ke hisaab se na ho, toh ghabrahat, frustration me ulajh jaana.

✗ **Fixed Mindset** – Sochna ki “main aisa hi hoon, main badal nahi sakta.”

**Adaptability Kaise Develop Karein?**

✓ **Naye Experiences Try Karo** – Jitna zyada alag situations ka exposure hoga, utna hi tum adapt karna seekhoge.
✓ **Discomfort Ko Accept Karo** – Growth comfort zone ke bahar hoti hai.
✓ **Curious Raho, Seekhte Raho** – Duniya tezi se badal rahi hai. Seekhna kabhi bandh mat karo.
✓ **Perspective Change Karo** – Challenges ko problem nahi, growth ka moka samjho. Angle change karke dekho.
✓ **Khud Pe Bharosa Rakho** – Tumhare paas saare answers nahi honge, lekin pehla kadam lena zaroori hai.

Adaptability Skill hi mujhe Malaysia Visa rejection se Goa me opportunity tak lekar gayi.
Is skill ne hi mujhe naye shahar me dar ke bawajood aage badhne ki taqat di. Mujhe sikhaya ki setbacks tumhe define nahi karte—tumhara response karta hai.

**Apne aap se poochho:**
"Jab zindagi mujhe achanak badlav deti hai, kya main resist karta hoon... ya adapt karke grow karta hoon?"
Tumhara jawab hi decide karega ki zindagi me tum kitni door jaoge.

## Activity: My Adaptability Score

**Objective:** Tum kitne adaptable ho, is par reflection karna aur badlav, uncertainty, aur challenges ko kaise behtar handle kar sakte ho, yeh samajhna.

**Step 1: Quick Self-Check – Apne Aap Ko Rate Karo**
Neeche diye gaye statements ko 1 se 5 ke beech rate karo
1 = Kabhi nahi, 5 = Hamesha

**Statement 1**: Jab kuch unexpected hota hai, tab bhi main shaant rehta hoon.
Rating (1-5): _______

**Statement 2:** Jab sab kuch plan ke hisaab se na ho, tab bhi main jaldi adjust kar leta hoon
Rating (1-5): _______

**Statement 3**: Main naye tareekon se kaam seekhne ke liye hamesha open hoon
Rating (1-5): _______

**Statement 4:** Jab situation tough ho jaaye, tab bhi main give up nahi karta
Rating (1-5): _______

**Statement 5**: Mujhe lagta hai challenges mujhe grow karne ka moka dete hain
Rating (1-5): _______

Total Score: _______ /25

**Reflection:**
**Score 5–10:** Tum seekh rahe ho – thoda aur flexible banne ki koshish karo
**Score 11–20:** Tum raaste par ho – apne comfort zone se bahar nikalte raho
**Score 21–25:** Tum adaptability expert ho – kisi bhi challenge ke liye ready ho

### Step 2: Apna Adaptive Moment Yaad Karo

Ek aisa moment yaad karo jab tumne koi bada change ya challenge face kiya aur uske saath adjust kiya. Shayad tumne sheher badla ho, job change ki ho, failure face kiya ho, breakup hua, ya kuch naya jaldi seekhna pada ho.

**Situation kya thi?**
Answer: ___________________________________________
**Tumne adapt karne ke liye kya kiya?**
Answer: ___________________________________________
**Tumne us experience se kya seekha?**
Answer: ___________________________________________

**Adaptability ek skill hai** – jitni zyada baar tum badlav ko accept karoge, utni hi zyada tum life me grow karoge.

### Step 3: Challenge Yourself – Small Adaptability Dares

Agle 3 din me inme se koi ek try karo:

- Kuch aisa khana jo tumne kabhi nahi khaya ho
- Apne regular jagah jaane ke liye naya raasta choose karo
- Kisi naye insaan se baat shuru karo
- 2 ghante bina phone ke kaam karo
- Koi nayi skill seekho (chahe sirf 15 minute ke liye hi sahi)
- Kisi aisi cheez ke liye "ha" kaho jisse tum usually avoid karte ho

Tum kaunsa karoge? ________________________________________
Jab kar loge, likho kaisa feel hua: _____________________________

**Why This Works:**
Jitne zyada chhote badlav tum face karte ho, utne hi zyada strong aur confident ban jaate ho jab bade badlav aate hain.
Adaptability tumhari superpower hai — ye tumhe har situation me grow karne, survive karne aur jeetne me madad karti hai.

**Jab bhi kuch plan ke hisaab se na ho, apne aap se poochho:**

- Main isse kya seekh sakta hoon?
- Main kaise adapt karke aage badh sakta hoon?

Yahi soch ek winner ki hoti hai.

# Discipline: The Key to Success

Discipline ka matlab hai wahi kaam karna jo zaroori hai, chahe tumhara mann kare ya nahi.
Yahi wo bridge hai jo tumhare goals ko achievements me badal deta hai.
Log sochte hain motivation success ki key hai, lekin motivation kabhi na kabhi khatam ho jata hai. Discipline hi wo force hai jo tumhe tab bhi chalaye rakhta hai jab motivation zero ho.

## Discipline Kya Hai?

Discipline ka simple bhasha me matlab hai acchi aadaton ko follow karna, routine banana, aur apne goals ke liye committed rehna.

**Yeh tumhe madad karta hai:**

- Focused rehne me
- Time manage karne me
- Strong habits banane me
- Long-term success achieve karne me
- Aur mood ko side me rakhkar jo karna hai woh karne me :)

## Discipline Kaise Develop Karein

### 1. Clear Goals Set Karo

- Kya chahiye life me, yeh clear karo
- Bada goal, chhote aur manageable tasks me break karo

### 2. Routine Banao

- Daily schedule fix karo aur usse follow karo
- Tasks ko apni lifestyle ka hissa banao, jaise brushing your teeth

### 3. Distractions Hatao

- Apne aas-paas ka environment clean aur organized rakho
- Focus banaye rakhne ke liye **Pomodoro** jaise techniques use karo

**4. Self-Control Practice Karo**

- Jo cheezein tumhe goals se door le jaati hain unhe “No” kaho
- Procrastination se bacho—chhota start karo, momentum build hoga

**5. Consistent Raho**

- Discipline ek muscle jaisa hai—jitna use karoge, utna strong banega
- Bure din par bhi kuch na kuch zaroor karo, thoda kuch karna, kuch bhi na karne se behtar hai

**6. Progress Track Karo**

- Journal ya checklist banao
- Chhoti chhoti wins ko celebrate karo taaki motivation bana rahe

## Discipline vs. Motivation

**Motivation temporary hai** – kabhi hai, kabhi nahi
**Discipline permanent hai** – Ye moods par depend nahi karta

**Example:**

- **Motivated** insaan tab gym jaata hai jab uska mann ho
- **Disciplined** insaan gym jata hai kyuki usko jana hoga, mann ho ya nahi

**Discipline Ke Rewards**
✓ Tum zyada productive ban jaate ho
✓ Log tumhari respect karte hain
✓ Tum goals jaldi achieve karte ho
✓ Strong habits develop hoti hai jo lifetime chalti hain

Success sirf smart ya lucky hone se nahi milti—
Success regular aur disciplined rehne se milti hai.

Aaj se start karo, bhale hi chhota start ho bass disciplined raho, aur dekho zindagi kaise badalti hai.

## Activity – Discipline Tracker: Win Your Day!

**Objective:** Discipline ek din me nahi banta—yeh daily chhoti habits se banta hai. Discipline ka matlab perfection nahi, roz ka show-up hai, especially jab mann na ho.

### Step 1: Apne Power Habits Choose Karo

3 chhoti habits choose karo jo tumhari life better banayengi—personal, professional ya health related.

**Examples:**

- Subah 6 baje uthna
- 30 min reading
- Daily exercise/walk
- 10 baje tak social media avoid karna
- 3 litre paani peena
- Roz 3 goals likhna
- Junk food avoid karna
- Etc.

**Tumhari 3 Daily Power Habits:**

1. ______________________________________________
2. ______________________________________________
3. ______________________________________________

## Step 2: 7-Day Discipline Tracker

**Day 1**
Habit 1: __________ Habit 2: ____________ Habit 3: _____________
Notes/Feelings: _____________________________________________

**Day 2**
Habit 1: __________ Habit 2: ____________ Habit 3: _____________
Notes/Feelings: _____________________________________________

**Day 3**
Habit 1: __________ Habit 2: ____________ Habit 3: _____________
Notes/Feelings: _____________________________________________

**Day 4**
Habit 1: __________ Habit 2: ____________ Habit 3: _____________
Notes/Feelings: _____________________________________________

**Day 5**
Habit 1: __________ Habit 2: ____________ Habit 3: _____________
Notes/Feelings: _____________________________________________

**Day 6**
Habit 1: __________ Habit 2: ____________ Habit 3: _____________
Notes/Feelings: _____________________________________________

**Day 7**
Habit 1: __________ Habit 2: ____________ Habit 3: _____________
Notes/Feelings: _____________________________________________

**Goal**: Is week kamm se kamm 80% habits complete karo.
Roz chhoti jeet jeeto, discipline banega!

## Step 3: Reflect and Reward

**Week ke end mein apne aap se poochho:**

- What was the hardest part?
- How did I feel after completing my habits?
- What is that one thing I will improve next week?

## Reward Yourself:

Small treats for big wins – apna favourite khana, movie night ya nayi book le lo. Apne efforts ko celebrate karna zaroori hai.

**Why This Works:**

Discipline motivation se nahi, consistency se banta hai.
Roz chhote actions, tumhe time ke saath unstoppable bana deti hain.
Yeh tracker tumhara din tumhare control mein laata hai aur mental strength build karta hai.

**Remember**
Jab kabhi mann kare skip karne ka, khud se bolo:
"Aaj discipline, kal freedom."

Chhoti jeet se hi bade sapne sach hote hain.

*"Discipline is choosing between what you want now and what you want most."*
*— Abraham Lincoln*

In sab learnings ke beech mujhe mila **'daddy of learning'**

# The Power of Subconsious Mind

Toh ji, The Power of Your Subconscious Mind by Dr. Joseph Murphy ek aisi kitab hai jo zindagi badal sakti hai—agar hum iske concepts ko samjhein aur apply karein.

**The Power of Your Subconscious Mind**

Hamari zindagi mein jo kuch bhi hota hai—success ho ya failure, khushi ho ya dukh—uske peeche sirf ek cheez ka haath hota hai: *Hamari soch.*

Dr. Murphy ne apni book me 2 minds ke baare me baat ki hai.

**1. Conscious Mind (चेतन मन)**

Ye woh mind hai jo tum abhi use kar rahe ho.

Jo tum soch ke karte ho – jaise decisions lena, plan banana, kisi se baat karna, ya sochna ki aaj kya pehna jaaye.

✓ Sirf 5–10% role hota hai iska tumhari life decisions me.

✓ Ye logic, reasoning aur planning karta hai.

✓ Par iska power limited hai.

**Example**: Jab tum kisi naye raste pe gadi chala rahe ho, har signal, turn aur brake consciously lete ho.

**2. Subconscious Mind (अवचेतन मन)**

Ye mind background me chalta hai, bina bataye. Ye Ginnie hai chirag se nikla hua. Jo tum kahoge woh karega, bass isse baat karna seekh jaao.

Ye tumhare beliefs, habits, fears, aur emotional patterns ko control karta hai.

✓ 90–95% decisions subconscious mind se chalte hain.

✓ Jo baar-baar tum sochte ho, wahi subconscious me store ho jata hai. Ye mind tumhe universe se connect karta hai.

✓ Iska power unlimited hai — yahi tumhari reality banata hai.

**Example**: Jab ek baar tum driving seekh jaate ho, tum bina soche gadi chala lete ho – ye subconscious ka kamaal hai.

## Subconscious Mind Ka Power Kya Hai?

**1. Jo tum isme daaloge, wahi tum paoge.**
Agar tum baar-baar sochoge, “Mujhse nahi hoga,” toh tumhara subconscious maan lega ki tum weak ho – aur tum waisa hi behave karoge.
Lekin agar tum sochoge, “Main kar sakta hoon,” toh tumhara subconscious tumhare body, actions, aur emotions ko success ke liye tayyar karega.

**2. Yeh har baat ko sach maan leta hai.**
Subconscious ko farak nahi padta ki tum sach bol rahe ho ya jhooth — woh jo baar-baar sunta hai, usey hi reality bana deta hai.
**Example**:
Agar tum har roz socho, “Main successful hoon,” aur usi tarah se kaam karo toh tumhara subconscious uss thought ke hisaab se kaam karega.
Wahi cheezein tumhari life me attract hongi jo tumhe success ki taraf le jaengi.

### Kaise Kaam Karta Hai Yeh Power?

**Example 1: Health**
Agar tum har din socho, “Main healthy hoon, meri body strong hai,” toh subconscious tumhari body ko uss thought ke hisaab se heal karne lagega. Bohot saari studies hai ispar, please padhna.

**Example 2: Money**
Agar tum socho, “Main paisa kama raha hoon, naye mauke aa rahe hain,” toh subconscious tumhare liye waise log aur situations attract karega jisse tum financially grow karo.

**Example 3: Fear vs. Faith**
Agar tum darr mein jeeyoge, subconscious uss darr ko hi reality banayega.
Lekin agar tum faith aur trust ke saath jeeyoge, toh wahi faith tumhari nayi reality banega.

## Subconscious Mind Ko Program Kaise Karein?

**1. Positive Affirmations**
**Har din, positive lines repeat karo:**

- "Main successful hoon."
- "Main fearless hoon."
- "Main paisa attract karta hoon."

Subconscious inhe maan ne legega.

**2. Visualization (Dimage me tasveer Banao)**
Roz 5 minutes aankhein band karke apne goals ka scene imagine karo—jaise tum already achieve kar chuke ho.
Yeh seedha subconscious tak jaata hai.

**3. Gratitude (Shukr Guzari)**
Jitna tum thankful rahoge, utna tumhara subconscious positivity store karega.
Gratitude = magnet for more blessings.

"Subconscious mind ek garden hai. Jo beej tum daaloge (soch), wahi phal banega (result)."
— Dr. Joseph Murphy

**Yaad rakhna...**
Zindagi mein jo tum baar-baar sochte ho, wahi tum ban jaate ho. Subconscious mind sirf ek power nahi hai—yeh tumhara silent partner hai jo har waqt tumhare sapno ko pura karne mein laga hua hai... bas tum usse sahi direction dena seekh jao.

Chapter 6

# I UNDERSTOOD HARD WORK

**Taj Exotica, Goa**

*Ab Main Mehnat Ka Asli Matlab Samjha*

Taj Exotica ek 56 acres main faili hui resort property hai, aur trainee ke role me maine jaldi samajh liya ki trainee ka matlab hota hai cheap labour. Mujhe month ka 1200 Rs. stipend milta tha.

Main roz 15 ghante kaam karta, jisme se 6–7 ghante sirf villas ke beech chalte hue guests request poori karte karte nikal jaate the. Mujhe yaad hai waha itni garmi aur humidity hoti thi ki mere socks sookhte hi nahi the. Ghar aake kuch ghante rest karta utni der me phirse shift par nikalna hota tha toh geele socks hi pehen kar chala jata tha. Iss kaaran mere peir me chaaley (Blisters) hojate the jo ki training end hone ke kaafi time baad theek huve.

Vegetarian hone ke kaaran maine 6 me se 4 mahine sirf salads aur pizzas par hi guzare.

Bohot pareshan ho jaata tha, lekin wahi meri mehnat ki samajh ka base ban gaya. Main hotel ke har department ko samajhna chahta tha, kal ko apna hotel kholna pade toh pata hona chaiye na.

Toh maine Front Office, Food & Beverage Services, F&B Production aur Housekeeping, chaaro departments me kaam kiya. Par mera favorite hamesha se Front Office hi tha.

Ek mahina maine South Indian kitchen me bhi kaam seekha, 3 AM se shift start hoti thi—wahaan pata chala agar aap 3-4 baje uthne ki aadat daal lo toh aapki productivity ka level alag hoga.

**Moral of the story ye hai ki**

Training woh phase hota hai jaha 50% students kaam chhod dete hai. Lekin ye phase sabse zyada important hai, ye aapko aapke career se introduce karta hai. Agar aapne ye phase ko ache se seekh kar nikal liya toh aapki aagey ki life easy hojaegi. Aur yaha agar kaam chhori kardi, toh aapka kaam aapko bojh lagne lagega.

Main hamesha **Burj Al Arab, Dubai** hotel se fascinated tha—duniya ka sirf ek 7-star hotel (kehte hai 7 Star catagory abhi tak bani nahi hai par jis din banegi Burj Al Arab ko us category me daal diya jaega). Main usi hotel me kaam karna chahta tha.
Woh ek sapno ki jagah thi, luxury aur perfection ka symbol. Lekin main kabhi kisi se nahi mila tha jo wahaan kaam kar chuka ho.

Phir Goa me mujhe pata chala ki Mr. Kompella, hamare L&D Manager, us hotel me kaam kar chuke hain.
Woh strict the—aise koi bhi insaan jinke paas jaane se pehle do baar sochna padta tha.
Lekin ek din maine decide kiya, "Mujhe unse baat karni hi hai."

Staff cafeteria main koi bhi kisi ke saath beth kar lunch kar sakta tha. Maine dekha tha kabhi kabhi kuch log seniors ke paas bhi beth jaate the aur discussion karte the.

Lunch ke time, main jaan-bujh kar, guts collect karke Mr. Kompella ke paas jaakar baith gaya. Dil zor se dhadak raha tha, lekin maine himmat karke poochha:
"Sir, Burj Al Arab me kaam karne ke liye kya chahiye hota hai?"
Unhone mujhe dekha, 3 second pause liya, aur phir bole:
"Good hotel brands on your CV, powerful interpersonal skills, and years of experience."
Unki baat seedha dil me lagi aur maine kaha 'apne chances kamm hai bhai, chalo yaha se'.
Mere paas sirf 4 mahine ka experience tha, woh bhi 2 hotels me—aur dono job maine bina bataye chhod di thi.
Tab samajh aaya – Main ready nahi tha. Burj Al Arab bohot door hai aur woh shayad ek sapna hi reh jaega.

## Jaipur Wapsi – Ek Nayi Taqat Ke Saath

Internship complete karke main Jaipur wapas aaya—ek naye determination ke saath.
Agle 6 mahine tak maine agents se baat ki kyunki mere abroad jaane ka sapna aur zyada bada ho chuka tha. Abhi me confident feel karta tha aur mere paas Taj Exotica, Goa ka training certificate bhi tha. Pehli job jo maine complete ki hai.

Lekin us dauraan main kuch agents se mila jo frauds kar rahe the—students ko jhoothe sapne dikha kar paise le kar bhaag rahe the.
Agar tum bhi abroad jaana chahte ho, toh dhyan rakho.
Log dhokha dene ke liye kisi bhi hadd tak ja sakte hain.

Ek agent ne mujhse 10 din tak regular baat ki, 2 companies me interviews bhi karwaye, offer letter bhej diya aur toh aur Singapore ke tickets bheje aur bola,
"Flight book ho gayi hai aapki, aap Singapore ja rahe ho next month , paise bhejdo."
Maine bola, "Thoda ruk jao, adhe ghante me bhejta hu"

Maine turant airline ko call kiya, PNR number bataya aur pucha ki is name se koi booking hai kya?
—unhone bola, "Koi booking nahi hai is name se."
Maine agent ko call kiya aur bataya toh usne mujhe block kar diya.
Darr sa lagne laga tha ki mere life me videsh jana likha bhi hai kya?
Kahin woh pandit sahi toh nahi bol raha tha.

Mere experiences ne mujhe sikha diya tha – cautious hona zaroori hai aur kisi par 100% trust nahi karo. Log kitna neeche gir chuke hai paise kamane ke liye aapko koi idea bhi nahi hai. Toh aapko apne aap ko prepare karke chalna chahiye...

Which leads us to a skill called **COGNITIVE THINKING.**

## Cognitive Thinking

Cognitive thinking ka matlab hai situation ko analyse karna, soch samajh ke decision lena, aur problems ko effectively solve karna. Isme aata hai critical thinking, logical reasoning, aur situational awareness—jo kisi bhi field me success ke liye essential hai.

## Frauds Se Bach Gaya

Jab agent ne mujhe kaha ye raha aapka ticket ab paise bhejo
Main excited aur khush toh tha, par maine socha ekbar phir bhi check karte hai ki ye real hai ya nahi aur maine airline ko call kiya. Cognitive thinking skill ne mujhe help kiya fraud ko pakdne me.

**Kuch red flags samjho -**

🏴 **Red Flag 1**: Bahut saare agents bina kisi proof ke bada paisa demand kar rahe the. Kyuki log itne zyada pagal hogaye hai bahar jaane ke liye, woh bina kuch soche samjhe paisa de rahe hai.
Aapne stories suni hogi ki skilled logo ko bahar bula kar labors ka kaam karwaya ja raha hai. (agey ek aur story bataunga)

🏴 **Red Flag 2**: Pressure tactics use kar rahe the – "Abhi paise do, warna chance chala jayega!" Is kaaran insaan me FOMO (fear of missing out) develop hota hai aur woh paisa dedeta hai.

🏴 **Red Flag 3**: Ye agents bohot professional hote hai. Language, documents, processes bohot ache tarike se use karte hai, aapko lagega ye toh genuine insaan hai.
So, please jo aap apni society ko ye feel karana chahte ho ki aap videsh rehte ho, woh idea toh theek hai lekin decision jald baazi main mat lena, aap phas jaoge.

## Cognitive Thinking Zaroori Kyun Hai?

✔ **Decision-Making Me Help Karta Hai** – Jab pressure me ho, tab bhi sahi choice lene me madad milti hai.

✔ **Frauds Se Bachata Hai** – Tez dimaag fraud ko detect kar leta hai aur nuksan hone se bachata hai.

✔ **Problem-Solving Improve Karta Hai** – Jab challenge ho, logic se solution nikalta hai, emotion se nahi.

✔ **Learning & Growth Me Madad Karta Hai** – Jitna zyada analyse karoge, utne zyada mature aur aware banoge.

## Cognitive Thinking Kaise Develop Karein?

✓ **Question and analyze Everything** – Har cheez ko face value pe mat lo. Poore doubt ke saath poochho, "Yeh sach haina? Verify kar sakta hoon?"
Aisa bhi ho sakta hai ki aap pressure ke kaaran ye sochne lag jao ki agent ko bura na lag jaye, ye mujhe reject na karde par trust me reject hona behtar hai fraud me fasne se.

✓ **Curious Raho** – Nayi cheezein seekhte raho, knowledge tumhara thinking sharp karega. Jitni zyada knowledge tumhare paas hogi, utna behtar tumhara thought process hoga.

✓ **Mind Games Khelo** – Puzzles, brain teasers, problem-solving exercises khelte raho.

✓ **Observe & Listen** – Chhoti cheeze dhyaan se dekho, wahi badi sacchai dikhati hain.

**Cognitive Thinking Ne Mujhe Kaise Help Kiya?**
Mujhe zyada aware, strategic aur ready banaya.
Hard work akela kaafi nahi hai—smart thinking bhi chahiye.
Agli baar jab koi bada decision aaye, apne aap se poochho:
"Kya main critically soch raha hoon, ya sirf emotionally react kar raha hoon?"

Sahi mindset tumhara pura future badal sakta hai.

## Activity – Brain Gym: Train Your Thinking

**Objective:** Life jab aapko problems degi tab cognitive thinking aapko clarity, logic, aur smart strategy se solve karna sikhayegi.

**Step 1: What–Why–How Framework**

Koi bhi challenge lo (chhota ya bada) aur is tareeke se tod do:

- **What is the real problem?**

**Example**: "Mujhe interview calls nahi aa rahe."

Tumhara Answer: ______________________________

- **Why is this happening? (Possible reasons)**

**Example**: "CV weak hai / skills missing hai."

Tumhara Answer: ______________________________

- **How can I solve it? (2–3 solutions)**

**Example**: "Knowledge upgrade karun?, short course karun?, feedback lu?."

Tumhara Answer: ______________________________

**Step 2: Think in Outcomes**

Agar main Action A leta hoon → kya hoga?

Agar main Action B leta hoon → kya hoga?

Action A & Possible Outcome: ______________________

Action B & Possible Outcome: ______________________

**Step 3: Rapid Problem Solving (5-Minute Drill)**

Koi real-life problem lo aur 5 minute me "What–Why–How" method se solve karo.

**Timer lagao. Goal hai:** Pressure me bhi clearly sochna seekhna.

**"React mat karo. Socho!."**

**Tough situation me 30 seconds pause lo,**

Is process ko use karke, actions loge toh better results milenge.

Cognitive Thinking tumhare decision-making muscles ko strong banata hai, stress me calm rakhta hai, aur time + energy dono bachaata hai. Samajh nahi aa raha toh case studies padho online.

Chapter 7

# DREAMS DO COME TRUE

Ek din mujhe ek agent mila, jo mujhe genuine lag raha tha, usne kuch brands ke sath mere interviews bhi karwaye aur ek Interview me main select hogaya.
Jaise hi agent ne mujhe bataya toh maine confirm karne ke liye brand ko call kiya and unhone positive response diya.

Process chalu hua aur kuch din baad mere paas flight tickets aur visa aaya, maine flight ticket verify kiya aur woh bhi sahi nikla :)

Basss... main SINGAPORE ke liye, apna bachpan ka sapna poora karne, ghar se AKELA nikal gaya.

Ye picture us moment ki hai jab mera sapna poora hone ja raha tha. Main dara hua toh tha par bohot khush tha.

Woh jo NRI tag mere relatives par laga hota tha, ab mere upar bhi lagne wala tha. Darr ye tha ki abhi phir se koi mujhe rok na le jaise tattoo ke kaaran roka tha.
Par isbaar aisa nahi hua.
Main life me pehli baar flight me betha tha aur itna khush tha ki mujhe kuch samajh hi nahi araha tha.
Ye ek connecting flight thi, pehle hum Chennai ja rahe the aur phir Singapore. Main flight ko enjoy karne ki jagah soch raha tha jaldi se singapore land kardo taaki koi naya panga na aa jaaye.

## AUR FINALLY MAINE SINGAPORE LAND KIYA

Main sirf apne around dekh raha tha ki duniya itni khoobsurat bhi ho sakti hai. Kuch der main sirf beth gaya kyuki mujhe koi lene nahi aane wala tha.
Maine socha pehle vibe ko feel karte hai phir load lenge ki hostel kaise jana hai. Subah ki 3 baj rahi thi aur nai jagah thi toh raat me bahar jaane ki himmat nahi horahi thi. Toh main ek chhote bacche jaisi excitement lekar airport par idhar udhar ghumne laga.

Phir maine ek SIM card kharida aur ghar phone laga kar bataya ki Pareek sahab pohoch chuke hai bidesss (Videsh).
Subah 6 baje jo agent ne hostel bataya tha waha ke liye cab li.
Aur finally main Raju bhai se mila. Jo harr baat me bolte the **'koi poblem nahi hai'** Unke POBLEM me PROBLEM thi, but he was very cute and helpful.
Main hostel ke room me gaya toh waha 15 ladke aur the—aur sab life me struggle kar rahe the.

Jaise hi main room me gaya, sabne mujhe gher liya aur gaali dene lage, *'zindagi barbaad kar di Singapore aake tumne. Tumhare liye yahaan kuch nahi hai, wapas chale jao. Hum pareshan horahe hai yaha jobs nahi hai aur, tum aur agaye ho.'*
Woh hote haina kuch log jo kisi dusre desh me bethe hote hai haalaat ke kaaran, mera khyaal se ye woh sab the... Inki harr baat demotivate karne wali thi. Aisa lag raha tha ye mujhe abhi wapas India bhej denge.

Bas mujhe 10 baje ka intezaar tha— mera first day at work start hone wala tha aur main is excitement ko kill nahi karna chahta tha par ye log ne toh bilkul hi mera morale down kar diya tha.
Socho jis din ka aap 10 saal se intezaar kar rahe the.. aur jab woh din aaya aur aapko bola ja raha hai ki ye kya kardiya, pagal ho kya.

Main ready hua.. Metro pehli baar dekhi thi life me.. 10 jagah pucch kar station gaya, card banwaya aur metro me chadha.

Yaar kya mazedaar hota hai Videsh.. Itna saaf, khoobsurat, baahar sports cars dikh rahi hai jo TV aur internet par dikhti thi. Unreal tha.

Phir main apne workplace par pohocha aur waha jaate hi ek naya challenge samne aaya.
Hum teen Indian ladke induction ka wait kar rahe the, jaha company ka introduction hota hai, welcome kiya jata hai aur kaam samjhaya jata hai.
Ek Chinese lady aayi, kuch bhi baat nahi ki, humko uniforms diye aur bola jaao kaam karo.

Jis department ke liye mujhe hire kiya tha, uski uniform brown color ki thi. Maine enter karte hi dekh liya tha.
Aur jo uniform humko di gai thi woh yellow color ki thi, jo ki kitchen cleaner ne pehen rakhi thi.

Mere saath wale dono Indians ne uniform li aur kaam karne chale gaye. Main wahin khada raha—andar se gussa ubal raha tha.
Mann kar raha tha ki unhe bolu, "Baat kar behen kuch toh main itni door cleaner banne nahi aaya hoon." Par woh kuch nahi bol rahi.

Tab maine khud se ek sawaal poocha – **ya toh jo bola jaa raha hai woh karo, jaise baaki ke 2 ladko ne kiya, ya isko bolo ki mujhe is department me kaam nahi karna hai. Risk ye hoga ki aapko wapas ghar bhej denge.**

Main us lady ke paas gaya aur bola,
"Excuse me ma'am, kya main aapse ek minute baat kar sakta hoon?" (english me bola). Unhone kaha bolo.
Maine gehri saans li aur unse bola:
"Maine 3 saal hotel management padha hai, aur India ke best brand Taj ke saath training li hai. Main aapke business ke liye ek asset ban sakta hoon. Kitchen me safai toh koi bhi kar dega par main aapke yaha ek guest experience create kar sakta hu jo aapki brand value badhaega. Mujhe ek aise role me hona chahiye jahan main apni eudcation, skills and experience ka use kar sakoon.'
Paanch minute tak main sirf bolta raha aur woh sunti rahi.

Phir ek pause aaya..
Unhone mujhe dekha, **aur brown wali uniform nikaal kar dedi.**

**Lesson** – Jab tum khud ko value karte ho, duniya bhi tumhari value samajhne lagti hai. Plus tumhe **negotiate** karna aana zaroori hai.

Ye sort hua lekin us hostel me jaane ka mera mann nahi kar raha tha. Mujhe finally Singapore me acha feel hone laga tha.
Chharo taraf angrez dikh rahe hai.. english sunai de rahi hai.. videshi khana dikh raha hai. Par hostel toh jana tha shift ke baad.
Shift khatam hone se pehle meri mulaqat ek Philippines se aayi colleague se hui.
Baat karte karte usne mujhse casually poocha,
"Tum Singapore me kahaan rehte ho?" Maine apni saari frustrations aur rehne ki dikkat usse share kardi. Usne turant bola, "Humare ghar me ek bed khali hai, 4 BHK hai—2 rooms boys ke, 2 girls ke. Ek room me ek bed available hai, dekhna chaho toh aa sakte ho."

Main khush.. Maine kaha chalo...
Shaam ko kaam ke baad main turant us jagah gaya. Wahaan pahunchte hi mujhe us ghar se pyaar ho gaya.
Itna zyada sundar. haaye!! Duplex. Wooden floors. Mehek raha tha. Bhaag ke gaya, purane hostel se saman uthaya, negativity ko bye bola, aur Singapore me nayi journey start ki ek khubsurat ghar se—jahan ek cute dog bhi tha, 'Charlie'.

Main purane accommodation se itna pareshan tha ki maine Kaide se zyada details hi nahi li. New accommodation ka rent meri around 60% salary tha - haha!

Lekin har ek dollar worth tha. Main finally ek ghar me Philippines aur Russia ke logon ke saath reh raha tha. Jisme ek gay tha aur ek lesbian. Waha main sexual preference jaisi cheez ko samjha aur ye bhi samjha ki unhe judge nahi karna chahiye, because ye log galat nahi hai.. jaise straight log naturally dusre gender ki taraf attract hote hai waise woh naturally same gender ya agar bisexual hai toh dono gender ki taraf attract hote hai. Unko kudrat ne aisa hi banaya hai. Aur ye hamesha se ho raha hai, shayad aapke around bohot log honge but darr ke kaaran bata nahi rahe.
Woh shayad aap bhi ho sakte ho.
Aap jab foreigners ke sath rehte ho na toh aap bhul jate ho ki unke liye aap bhi toh foreigner ho. Agar aap apne aap ko ache se carry karte ho toh woh bhi aapko us nazar se hi dekhte hai jis izzat wali nazar se aap unko dekhte ho. Kuch dino me hum log friends bann gaye, sath ghumne lage. Main unke taur tarike seekhne laga, aur apne sikhane. Life skills, understanding of food, culture, behavior, — Is process me maine seekha ki jab tum open mind rakhte ho, toh zindagi tumhe unexpected jagah par le jati hai.
Challenge zaroor aata hai par uske sath-sath solution bhi aata hai. Jitna zyada seekhne ke liye khud ko open rakhoge, utna hi life tumhe grow karne ka moka degi

**Ek baar ki baat hai..**
Main aur mera Filipino room mate bohot close friends bann gaye the. Woh mujhse sab kuch share karta tha.. family, personal life everything.

Ek din me ready hone ja raha tha, maine cupboard me se ek fresh towel nikala aur side me uska bed the us par rakh diya. Hum dono ke beds ke beech ek almirah thi jisme mera samaan hota tha.
Woh aaya aur ekdum se mujhe gusse me bola **'what is this'?**
Mujhe samajh nahi aaya kya hua. Woh bola **'this'**
Maine bola 'towel hai mera', nahane ja raha hu
Woh upset hogaya aur bolne laga ki tumne bohot unhygienic harkat ki hai. It's not fair. Aise thodi kisi ke bed par apna towel rakhte hai aur woh upset hokar room se bahar chala gaya.

Us point par mujhe bohot bura laga, kyuki woh mera friend tha.
Phir ek thought aaya ki ya toh main usse ladai karloon ki isme kya hua ek towel hi toh hai. Ya phir, main learning loon ki inke culture me ya routine me mera towel unke bed par hona hygienic nahi hai.
Maine woh galti accept ki, usey sorry bola and things got normal.

Aise meri Singapore me learnings ke shuruwaat hui aur sabse pehle maine seekha **'Negotation Skill** kitni important hai and **Cultural Awareness** ki samajh aapko alag culture ke logo ke saath acche se rehne me madad karegi'.

## Negotiation

Negotiation ka matlab hai do ya zyada logon ke beech aapas me baat karke aisi agreement par pahuchna jahan dono ya saari parties khush ho aur unko apna fayda nazar aa raha ho.

Alag-alag goals, perspectives aur needs ke beech communication, problem-solving aur decision-making se ek behtar solution dhoondhna—yahi negotiation hai.
Yeh sirf jeet ya haar ka game nahi hai—yeh value create karne aur collaboration build karne ka process hai.

Kisi ko lagta hai maine achi deal karli bhale hi samne wale ko bohot nuksaan ho raha ho toh woh accha negotiator nahi hai.

### Negotiation Ke Key Elements

✔ **Preparation** – Apne goals aur saamne wale ki needs ko samajhna.
✔ **Active Listening** – Dhyaan se sunna, unki problems aur expectations samajhna.
✔ **Persuasion** – Apna point effectively aur respect ke saath rakhna.
✔ **Compromise** – Beech ka raasta dhoondhna, thoda adjust karna.
✔ **Emotional Intelligence** – Emotions ko control me rakhna, shant aur composed rehkar decision lena.
✔ **Clarity** – Terms aur expectations clearly communicate karna.

### Negotiation Zaroori Kyun Hai?

✔ **Behtar Opportunities Milti Hain** – Job, salary, ya accommodation—jo deserve karte ho, woh paane ka raasta hai ye.
✔ **Confidence Build Hota Hai** – Apne liye stand lena life-changing hota hai. Agar main yellow uniform le leta toh life kuch aur hoti.
✔ **Problem-Solving Improve Hoti Hai** – Jo mile usme adjust nahi, balki better solution dhundhna.
✔ **Influence Badhata Hai** – Jab apni value present karte ho, log sunte hain aur aapki respect karte hai.

## 'Master Of Negotiation' Kaise Banein?

Uniform wali story mind me rakhkar niche wale points ko padho

✓ **Apni Worth Jaano** – Tum kya value dete ho, yeh clear rakho
✓ **Clear Communication** – Seedhe, confident aur respectful tareeke se apni baat ko rakho
✓ **Solution-Oriented Raho** – Shikayat nahi, solutions offer karo jo dono ke liye fayde ka ho
✓ **Sunna Aur Adjust Karna Seekho** – Samne wale ki needs ko samajh ke approach change karo
✓ **Persistent Raho** – Pehla "No" hamesha final nahi hota, phirse try karo

Singapore ka struggle ek bada test tha, lekin us test ne meri life ko uss direction me turn kardiya jidhar main jana chahata tha. Ya sacch kahu toh itna accha toh maine socha bhi nahi tha.

**Lesson?**
Agar jahan ho wahan khush nahi ho—usse apni kismat mat samjho. Awaaz uthao, negotiate karo, aur apni zindagi khud badlo.

Change karne ki power tumhare haath me hai—
**ASK, BELIEVE, WORK FOR IT AND RECIEVE.**

## Activity: The Deal Maker Challenge

**Objective:** Real life me negotiation practice karo, confidence build karo, aur seekho kaise apni baat manwaani hai—relationship kharab kiye bina.

**Step 1: Tumhe Kya Chahiye?**

Aaj kuch chhota negotiate karne ka plan banao—

**Example**:

– Shopkeeper se better rates me saamaan lena
– Boss ya teacher se time extension lena
– Parents se kisi workshop ya event me jaane ki permission

Mera negotiation ka goal: ________________________________

**Step 2: Apna Pitch Prepare Karo – 3P Formula**

- **Purpose** – Tumhe yeh kyu chahiye?

**Mera reason:** ________________________________

- **Position** – Tum kya value dete ho? (loyalty, effort, value)

**Mera value point**: ________________________________

- **Plan B** – Agar "No" mila, to alternate kya hai?

**Mera Plan B:** ________________________________

**3 Idiots movie yaad hai?**

Farhan ne apne papa se jo negotiation kiya tha?

Jab usne engineering chhod ke photography pursue karne ka decision liya, usse hum 3P model mein divide kar sakte hain:

**1. Purpose (Maksad):**
**Kya tha Farhan ka asli maksad?**
Farhan ka sapna tha wildlife photographer banna. Usne realize kiya ki engineering uska passion nahi hai. Uska purpose sirf degree lena nahi, balki zindagi mein woh karna tha jo usse sach mein khushi de.
*"Papa, main khush nahi hoon. Main kisi aur ke liye jee raha hoon."*

**2. Position (Ravayya / Jazbaat ka taur-tarika):**
**Usne apne papa ke samne kaise baat rakhi?**
Farhan ne shant, emotional aur heartfelt tone mein apne jazbaat express kiye.
Usne blame game nahi khela, balki apne dil ki baat seedhe aur imaandari se rakhi.
Usne sirf apni feelings share ki, jisme guilt, pressure aur sapno ka sach tha.
Yeh position powerful thi kyunki usme sacchai thi, ego nahi.

**3. Plan B (Vikalp):**
**Agar papa nahi maante toh?**
Farhan ke paas koi solid Plan B nahi tha, lekin uski emotional appeal itni genuine thi ki uske papa pighal gaye.
Lekin practical duniya mein, Plan B ho toh aur achha hota.

**Real life mein, tum negotiation ke time yeh bol sakte ho:**
"Agar yeh kaam nahi bhi chala, toh jo maine padha usse related job toh mujhe 2 saal baad bhi mil jayegi, Atleast mujhe regret toh nahi hoga ki jo karna chahta tha uske liye maine koshish bhi nahi ki."

Ye wala maine apne papa ke samne use kiya tha jab mujhe job world chhod kar business me jana tha and it worked.

### Step 3: Real Life Challenge – Negotiation Karo

Aaj hi try karo. Calm raho, demand ya blame nahi—baat cheet karo. Baat karne se baat banti hai.
**Agar nervous feel ho to use this line:**
“Main aapse kuch discuss karna chahta hoon. Kya hum dono baat karke kuch behtar solutions nikaal sakte hain?”

**Step 4: Reflect Karo**
✔ Maine jo chaha tha, kya woh mujhe mila?
✔ Negotiation ke dauraan mujhe kaisa feel hua?
✔ Next time main kya better kar sakta hu?

Negotiation aggressive hone ka nahi, smart aur mindful hone ka game hai.
Chhoti chhoti negotiations tumhe badi deals ke liye ready karti hain—salary, business, partnerships, etc.

**Pause Power**
Jab samne wala reply de, 2-3 seconds ruk ke jawab do.
Ye confidence dikhata hai aur tumhe clarity deta hai.

Kabhi kisi local sabzi wale ko observe karo, woh negotiation ki masterclass hai. Woh us art me behtar isiliye hai kyuki woh din me kaafi logo se interact karta hai aur zyadatar log us price me nahi lena chahte jo woh pehli baar me batata hai.

Ab Negotiation ke sath ek aur skill hai jo aapko seekhni zaruri hai
Ye aapko baaki negotiators se alag banayegi. Woh hai..

## Positive Diplomacy

Baat Karne Ka Art Jo Rishte Bachaye Aur Results De

Positive diplomacy ek aisi skill hai jo tumhe conversations, disagreements, aur negotiations ko gracefully handle karna sikhati hai. Yeh ek aisi communication style hai jisme tact, respect, aur emotional intelligence ka use hota hai.
**Iska goal hai** – apni baat kehna, bina kisi ko hurt kiye, aur aisa solution dhoondhna jo sabke liye beneficial ho.

**Yeh tumhe madad karta hai:**
✓ Apne views honestly express karne me, bina kisi ko offend kiye
✓ Conflicts ko shanti se handle karne me
✓ Trust aur strong relationships banane me
✓ Negotiations me win-win solution dhoondhne me

**Example**:
✗ **Aggressive**: "Yeh idea bakwaas hai. Kabhi kaam nahi karega."
☑ **Diplomatic**: "Main samajh raha hoon aapka point, par kya hum kuch aur options explore kar sakte hai?"

**Positive Diplomacy Zaroori Kyun Hai?**
✓ **Bekaar ke conflicts se bachaata hai** – Baat cheet productive hoti hai aur unnecessary conflicts nahi hote
✓ **Achhe rishte banata hai** – Log respect aur fairness ko value karte hain
✓ **Teamwork improve karta hai** – Personal aur professional dono settings me useful
✓ **Leadership skill enhance karta hai** – Tumhe ek respected aur trusted leader banata hai

Positive diplomacy ka matlab ye nahi ki tum apni baat chhupa rahe ho, iska matlab hai tum apni baat ko is tareeke se rakh rahe ho jisse saamne wale ko respect mile, aur tumhe result bhi mil jaye. Aise log hi duniya me logon ka trust jeet te hain aur aage badhte hain.

## Positive Diplomacy Kaise Practice Karein

**1. Apne Shabdon Ko Samajhkar Chuno**

❌ "Tum galat ho"
✅ "Mera nazariya thoda alag hai. Chalo baat karte hain."
❌ "Yeh kaam nahi karega"
✅ "Kya hum kuch aur possibilities explore kar sakte hain?"

**2. Emotions Ko Control Karo**

Conversation chahe heated ho, tumhara calm rehna zaroori hai.
React mat karo—soch samajh ke respond karo.

**3. Active Listening Karo**

Sirf reply dene ke liye mat suno—samajhne ke liye suno.
Pehle saamne wale ki baat ko acknowledge karo, phir apna point rakho.

**4. Common Ground Dhoondo**

Jahan difference hai uspar focus karne ke bajaye, jahan agree karte ho usse highlight karo.
**Example**: "Hum dono hi best outcome chahte hain. Chalo dekhte hain waha tak kaise pahuch sakte hain."

✅ "I" Statements Use Karo, "You" Nahi
❌ "Tum kabhi meri nahi sunte!" → Yeh blame lagta hai
✅ "Mujhe kabhi-kabhi lagta hai ki meri baat nahi suni jaati. Kya hum baat kar sakte hain?" → Discussion open karta hai

**5. Solution Pe Focus Karo**

Problems ginate rehne ke bajaye, solution pe kaam karo.
**Example**: "Kaise ek aisa raasta nikalein jo dono ke liye kaam kare?"
***Diplomacy ka matlab compromise nahi—***
Yeh smart communication ka tareeka hai, jo respect bhi dilata hai aur result bhi.

## Positive Diplomacy in Action

### Real Life Mein Kaise Kaam Aati Hai

**Scenario 1: Workplace Disagreement**
❌ **Negative**: “Tumhara idea bekaar hai. Ye kaam mere tareeke se karna chahiye.”
✅ **Diplomatic**: “Tumhare idea mein kuch achhe points hain. Shayad hum ise kisi aur approach ke saath combine kar sakte hain?”

**Scenario 2: Family Conflict**
❌ **Negative**: “Tum hamesha bina pooche decision le lete ho!”
✅ **Diplomatic**: “Main bhi decision-making ka hissa banna chahta hoon. Kya agli baar hum milkar baat kar sakte hain?”

**Scenario 3: Business Negotiation**
❌ **Negative**: “Tumhara price bahut zyada hai. Hum deal nahi kar sakte.”
✅ **Diplomatic**: “Aapka offer hum appreciate karte hain. Kya hum kuch aise options explore kar sakte hain jo humare budget mein fit ho?”

**Positive Diplomacy Ek Powerful Skill Hai**
Jo tumhe difficult situations mein bhi confidence ke saath conversation navigate karne deti hai.
Agar tum respectful, solution-focused aur emotionally intelligent raho, toh tum apna point bhi rakh sakte ho aur rishte bhi bana ke rakh sakte ho.

Is skill ko master karo, aur log tumhe ek leader, problem-solver, aur trustworthy insaan ke roop main dekhenge.
Nahi toh tum ek baar toh deal jeet jaoge, par shayad woh rishta kho doge toh tumhe hamesha profit de sakta tha.

## Cultural Awareness

### Har Culture Ko Samajhna, Respect Karna, Aur Usse Seekhna

Cultural Awareness ka matlab hai alag-alag cultures ke beliefs, values, behavior, aur customs ko samajhna, respect karna, aur appreciate karna.

Yeh skill tumhe sikhati hai ki kaise har insaan ke cultural background ka asar unke perspective, behavior aur decisions par hota hai—aur kaise tum diverse environments me mil jul kar kaam kar sakte ho.

**Yeh Zaroori Kyun Hai?**

✓ Ye samajhne se strong relationships bante hain
✓ Global environments me tum better adapt kar paate ho
✓ Communication aur teamwork improve hota hai
✓ Misunderstandings aur conflicts se bachaav hota hai

**Cultural Awareness ke Key Elements**

✓ **Recognition** – Differences ko samajhna aur acknowledge karna
✓ **Respect** – Har culture ke traditions aur views ko value dena
✓ **Sensitivity** – Stereotypes, bias ya judgment se bachna
✓ **Adaptability** – Apne communication aur behaviour ko logon, situation ya culture ke according adjust karna
✓ **Empathy** – Sochna ki doosre logon ke experiences unki duniya dekhne ka nazariya banate hain. Aur tumhari soch aur unki soch me farq aa sakta hai, isme kuch galat nahi hai.

## Mera Pehla Cultural Challenge

Singapore me kaam Ka Environment

Mere colleagues the China, Philippines, Malaysia aur India ke.
Har culture ki communication style alag thi:
✓ **Chinese** – Direct aur efficiency ko importance dete.
✓ **Filipinos** – Warm, friendly aur team-oriented. Little sensitive.
✓ **Malaysians** – Respectful lekin assertive.
✓ **Indians** – Hardworking lekin mostly apne group me hi rehna.

Mujhe observe karna, sunna aur apni approach ko adjust karna padta tha har insaan ke saath interaction karne ke liye.

**Lesson**:
Global workplace me safal hone ke liye, tumhe apna communication style culture ke hisaab se badalna aana chahiye.

**Mera Dusra Cultural Challenge – Ghar Ka Environment**
Nayi jagah shift hone ke baad, main Filipinos aur Russians ke saath reh raha tha.
✓ **Filipinos** – Friendly, family-oriented, aur khana share karne wale
✓ **Russians** – Pehle reserved, lekin trust banne ke baad caring and involved.

**Har cheez alag thi:**
✓ **Food habits** – Aise dishes jo maine kabhi dekhe bhi nahi the
✓ **Communication** – Kuch bohot bolne wale, kuch bilkul shant
✓ **Lifestyle** – Celebrations, social life, aur stress handle karne ka tareeka bhi alag

**Lesson:**
Cultural awareness sirf logo ke baare me nahi hoti,
Yeh tumhare lifestyle aur habits accept karne ki ability bhi hoti hai.
Jo duniya tumse alag hai, usse samajhne ka jazba hi tumhe zyada grow karne me help karega.

## Cultural Awareness Ke Kuch Real-Life Examples

✓ **Non-verbal communication samajhna** – Jaise eye contact, gestures, aur personal space (proxemics) ka meaning har culture me alag alag hota hai.
**Proxemics** - Kis insaan/rishtey se kitna door khade hokar baat karna
✓ Workplace me religious ya cultural holidays ka respect karna.
✓ International clients ya partners ke saath business adjust karna.

## Cultural Awareness Develop Kaise Karein?

✓ **Observe & Listen** – Jaldi assumption mat banao. Dekho, suno, aur samajhne ki koshish karo ki log kaise behave karte hain aur communicate karte hain.
✓ **Sawalon Se Seekho, Naa Ki Judge Karo** – "Tum aisa kyun karte ho?" ke bajaye poochho, "Mujhe is tradition ke baare me aur batao?"
✓ **Naye Experiences Try Karo** – Alag-alag khane, festivals, aur living styles ko explore karo. Nayi cheezon ke liye open raho.
✓ **Differences Ka Respect Karo** – Har baat se agree karna zaroori nahi, lekin apne words ya actions se disrespect bhi mat karo.
✓ **Adapt & Integrate** – Global environment me tumhara success tabhi aayega jab tum apni approach ko cultural context ke hisaab se adjust kar paoge.

Singapore jana mere liye sirf ek career move nahi tha—woh ek cultural awakening thi.

**Maine seekha:**
Duniya tumhare hometown, tumhare desh, ya tumhare beliefs se kai zyada badi hai.
Jitna tum apne dimaag ko alag cultures ke liye open karte ho, utni zyada opportunities tumhari life me aati hain.
Global Success ka raaz sirf skills ya hard work nahi hai—wo hai tumhari **ability** har tarah ke logon se connect karne ki.
Jo log duniya ko samajhne lagte hain, duniya unhe samajhne lagti hai. Jo log dusro ko judge karte hai, woh agey nahi badh paate.

## International Business Etiquette

Global Success Ka Dusra Step

International business Skills aapko sikhati hai ki ek global professional environment mein kaise behave karna chahiye—kaunse customs, norms aur manners follow karne chahiye jab tum alag-alag cultures ke logon ke saath kaam karte ho.

**Isme aata hai**: communication style, greeting ka tareeka, meeting ka protocol, negotiation ka approach aur workplace ka behaviour—jo country to country badal jaata hai.

## Yeh Zaroori Kyun Hai?

✓ **Strong Business Relationships Bante Hain** – Jab tum cultural differences ka respect karte ho, trust aur cooperation badhta hai.

✓ **Misunderstandings Se Bachav Hota Hai** – Cultural do's and don'ts jaan na awkward ya offensive moments se bachata hai.

✓ **Professional Image Strong Hoti Hai** – follow karne se lasting positive impression padta hai.

✓ **Negotiation Success Badhta Hai** – Local customs samajhne se deals close karna easy hota hai.

✓ **Global Career Opportunities Milti Hain** – Jo professionals adapt kar lete hain alag business cultures mein, unki demand har multinational company mein hoti hai. And trust me word of mouth bohot powerful tool hai.

## Key Aspects of International Business Etiquette

**1. Greetings aur Pehla Impression**

- **USA & Europe**: Firm handshake aur eye contact.
- **Japan**: Bow karna zyada suitable.
- **Middle East:** Light handshake and yaha male-female handshake preferable nahi hota hai specially when you are meeting locals.
- **France**: Close business associates ke beech cheek kiss common hai.

Pehle locals ka greet karne ka tareeka observe karo, fir mirror karo.

**2. Communication Styles**

- **Germany, Netherlands**: Direct aur clear.
- **Japan** and **India**: Indirect, polite, subtle—harmony maintain hoti hai.
- **Latin America, Middle East**: Expressive body language, energetic tone.

High-context (indirect) vs Low-context (direct) samajhna zaroori hai.

**3. Business Card Etiquette**

- **Japan and China**: Dono haathon se card dena aur receive karna, respect ke saath.
- **US, Europe**: Ek haath se casually exchange hota hai.

**Note**: Kisi ke card par uske samne pen se kuch likhna disrespectful mana jaata hai (specially Asia mein).

**4. Meetings & Punctuality**

- **Germany, Switzerland**: Time ka bohot strict discipline.
- **Spain, Brazil**: Meetings 15–30 mins late ho sakti hain.
- **Middle East, India**: Agenda flexible, discussions open-ended hote hain.

**Note:** Meeting ke pehle se hi formality aur timing ka expectation samajh lo.

**5. Dining & Social Etiquette**

- **China, Japan**: Thoda food plate pe chhodna = tum full ho.
- **Middle East, India**: Right hand se khana khana sahi maante hai.
- **France**: Meal ke time business ki baat nahi hoti—coffee/dessert ke time shuru karo.

**Tipping Culture**: Kahin tipping expected hai, aur kahin offensive.

**6. Negotiation Styles**

- **US, Germany**: Fast-paced, fact-based.
- **China, Japan**: Time lagta hai—trust build karna zaroori.
- **Latin America, Middle East**: Personal connection pe focus.

**Note**: Patience + cultural sensitivity = successful deal.

**7. Dress Code & Personal Presentation**

- **Europe, Japan**: Formal, conservative attire.
- **Silicon Valley, Creative Fields**: Business-casual ya casual accepted hai.
- **Middle East**: Cultural/religious norms follow karo—modesty zaroori.

**Note**: Jab bhi doubt ho toh thoda formal pehna better hota hai.

**8. Gift-Giving Etiquette**

- **China and Japan**: Gift ache se wrap karo, dono haathon se do. Clock mat dena—wahan yeh death ka symbol maana jaata hai.
- **Russia and Latin America**: Gift dena common hai, lekin woh thoughtful hona chahiye, extravagant nahi.
- **US and UK**: Business gifts rare hote hain. Expensive gift dena inappropriate lag sakta hai.

**Note**: Gift dene se pehle hamesha local customs check karo.

**Remember,**
"When in doubt, observe first."
Jo log alag cultures ko samajh kar, respect ke saath adapt karte hain, unki value har jagah hoti hai—aur wahi global success ka raasta banate hain.

## Common Challenges

Jab International Business Etiquette Samajhna Mushkil Ho Jaaye

✓ **Unintentional Offense** – Chhoti gestures jaise thumbs-up ya pair cross karna kuch cultures mein rude hota hai.

✓ **Language Barrier** – Bhasha aane ke bawajood misunderstanding ho sakti hai culture ke difference ki wajah se.

✓ **Professionalism ke Alag Standards** – Ek desh mein jo "professional" hai, dusre mein rigid ya informal lag sakta hai.

✓ **Handling Hierarchies** –

- **Japan, China, India**: Hierarchy ko bohot respect diya jaata hai.
- **Netherlands, Scandinavia:** Flat structure ko value dete hai.

### Kaise Improve Karein Apna International Business Etiquette?

✓ **Research Karo** – Travel se pehle country ke cultural norms, greetings, aur business practices ko samjho.

✓ **Observe aur Adapt Karo** – Locals ka tareeka dekho aur meetings, greetings mein unke jaisa behavior adopt karo.

✓ **Open Minded aur Respectful Raho** – Alag cultures ke baare me seekhne ke liye real interest dikhana shuru karo.

✓ **Guidance Maango** – Confused ho toh local colleague ya business partner se politely pucho.

✓ **Patient aur Flexible Bano** – Har culture ka business ka tareeka alag hota hai. Adaptable raho.

Global world mein sirf product ya service kaam nahi karta, tumhara behaviour bhi business ka part hota hai.
Jo jitna samjhta hai doosre culture ko, woh utna hi global opportunities mein aage badhta hai.

Chapter 8

# MUMBAI MERI JAAN

## Singapore Se Mumbai

Singapore mein kaam bohot acha chal raha tha. Mera contract khatam hone laga tha toh main dusri job dhundhne ka ya contract renew karwane ki baat karne ka soch raha tha,
Ek raat main, YouTube par ek video dekh raha tha—Ranveer Singh apni journey ke baare mein baat kar raha tha. 2014 ki baat hai.
Pura ek ghanta main screen se chipaka raha.
Uss waqt mere andar kuch hua. Bollywood ka main bada deewana tha—aur actor banna mera bachpan ka sapna tha.

Jab main 12th class me tha, maine apne pitaji ko kaha tha ki mujhe acting school join karni hai. Unhone kaha ki 'tu mujhe ek degree lekar dede, phir tujhe jo karna hai tu karlena'
Dusri taraf, meri maa is baat ke bilkul khilaaf thi. Woh bilkul nahi chahti thi ki main us industry ke paas bhi jaau kyuki unko lagta tha ki agar me actor bann gaya toh main kabhi ghar wapas nahi aaunga.
Toh woh sapna mera waha daba reh gaya aur maine apne aap ko kaha ki kabhi future me sochenge.

Uss raat Ranveer ki kahani sun kar laga—ab nahi ruk sakta. Shayad ye right time hai bollywood me kismat aazmaane ka.
Jobs dhundhna band kiya, agle din kaam par gaya, unko bola ye contract khatam hote hi mujhe India jana hai, ticket book kiya—aur contract over hote hi nikal gaya Mumbai ke liye.

Ek relative cum friend Roopal ki engagement thi Gujarat main, toh pehle main waha gaya aur celebration ka part bana.

Log genuinely khush the mujhe dekh kar. Samajh rahe ho na?
Us waqt mere paas 800-900 Singapore dollars the. Main papa ke paas gaya, unke haath mein diye aur bola, "Papa, yeh meri pehli international kamaai hai. Aap rakho!"

Papa muskuraaye, aur bole 'waah yaar, kitne hote hai ye India me?' aur apne saath walo ko dikhane lage plastic ke notes.

8 saal baad mujhe pata chala—woh paisa unhone touch bhi nahi kiye the. Locker mein sambhal ke rakhe the, aur kabhi kabhi apne friends ko dikhate the— "Mera beta bahar se kama kar laya hai."

Woh paisa unki aankhon main ek symbol tha—mere poore ho rahe sapno ka, meri mehnat ka, meri ek chhoti jeet ka.

Maine phir papa ko bataya ki mujhe Mumbai jana hai aur wahi kisi acche hotel me kaam dhundh lunga.
Ek aisi city, jahan sapne bante hain ya bikhar jaate hain—aur mujhe apne sapne bananey the.

Mumbai jaakar acting class dhundhne laga
Kuch din nikle toh samajh aaya ki ye itna easy bhi nahi hai jitna me soch raha tha. Life here is tough. Door bethkar sochna aur kisi jagah par aakar kaam karne me bohot farq hota hai.
Mujhe mere budget me ek acting class mili, aur woh bilkul achi nahi thi. Mera dil kar raha tha ki us trainer ko main kuch classes de du.
Travel, food, living me paisa itna kharch hogaya ki kuch din baad paisa aur motivation dono khatam hone lage.
Phir decide kiya—job start karta hu. 9 ghante kaam karunga, aur 4-5 ghante apne sapne ke peeche lagunga.
Hospitality mera comfort zone tha—aur Taj mera favourite brand. Target set kiya—Taj Lands End. Shah Rukh Khan ke ghar ke paas.

Wahi wala Black Suit pehna aur ready hokar Taj Lands End ke liye nikal gaya. Na wahan koi contact tha, na vacancy ke idea.
Main gate pe gaya aur security se bola—"Mr. Sharma ne interview ke liye bulaya hai."

Mr. Sharma exist karte hai? Pata nahi.
Confidence? Asmaan pe.
**Par puchne me kya jata hai? Mana hi toh karenge.**
**What is there to loose?**

Security ne andar bhej diya. Puch puch kar HR ke office tak gaya, candidates baithe the interview ke liye. Sab mujhe dekh ke khade ho gaye. Main akela waha suit mein tha, aur wo sab white shirt, black pants mein. Bola tha na grooming se bohot farq padta hai.

Main bola—"Main bhi interview dene aaya hoon yaar, betho." toh sab hasne lage.
HR se baat ki toh unhone kaha, "Hiring nahi ho rahi abhi."
Maine kaha—"Interview le lo, future mein vacancy ho toh bata dena. Main Mumbai me hi rehta hu"
Back to back teen rounds hue mere aur phir unhone pucha
**"Kab join kar sakte ho?"**
**Maine bola, "Abhi."**
Kyuki roz rehne khane ke paise lag rahe the. Job lag gai toh ye dono ka toh jugaad hojaega.

Us din se tumhara bhai Taj Lands End, Mumbai ka employee ban gaya. Rehna, khana, uniform, sab set hogaya. Bass salary bohot kamm thi. Singapore me jitna kama raha tha uski 20%. Parr yeh meri life ka best decision nikla.

Subah peak hours me mumbai local padak kar hotel aata tha jo ki jaan par khelne se kamm nahi tha. 13-14 ghante kaam, 493 rooms ki property—hamesha sold out. Mujhe shaukh tha guests se baatein karne ka aur woh mere liye faaydemand nikla. Taj ke portal aur TripAdvisor par guests ke ache reviews ne mujhe hotel aur department me highlight kiya.

Ab jab aap aate hi grow karoge toh purane logo ko thodi toh problem hogi hi na. Toh mere kuch colleagues ne manager ko jaake bolna chalu kardiya ki ye toh sirf khada khada guests se baatein karta hota hai, aur kuch kaam nahi karta.
Manager ne mujhe bulaya aur baat kari. Maine kaha sir hospitality me ye toh bohot kaam ki cheez haina, guests khush rahege toh wapas aenge, wapas aenge toh apna business grow karega. (ek lambi conversation hui).
Manager ko meri baat sahi lagi aur unhone mujhe aise department me daal diya jaha se guests ko acha experience dena hi mera kaam hogaya. Guests relations.

Mujhe kaam main aur maza aane laga. Celebrities se interaction hota tha. Maine us time MS Dhoni, Pulkit Samrat, Miss Universe Lara Datta, jaise kaafi celebrities ko hotel me check in kiya tha.
Infact jab Fawad Khan 'Ae Dil hai Mushkil' ke liye pehli baar India aaye the, toh unke check in aur documentation karne ka chance bhi mujhe mila tha. Aur Mahira Khan jab India aai thi tab bhi hotel me welcome maine hi kiya tha.
Kaafi big shots se regular conversation hone lagi. Woh log mujhe naam se jaan ne lage the toh acha feel hota tha.
Kuch guests toh aise bhi the jo Taj mein pichle 2-3 saal se reh rahe the. Hotel hi unka ghar tha, suit rooms ko apne hisaab se convert kiya hua tha.
Super wealthy and successful guests se acche relationships bane —unhi mein se ek future me meri business partner bani.
Mumbai ne mujhe har angle se push kiya—upar uthaya, neeche giraya, office politics, toxicity, stress, loneliness, growth, relationship building, work load.
Wahin se maine seekha human connection ka art—jo baad mein meri coaching career ka foundation bana.

Sab accha tha par main friends nahi bana pa raha tha hotel me.
Mere zyadatar colleagues ki 2 habits thi..

1. **Harr 2 hours me cigarette break lena** - Managers ke sath smoking ke liye bahar jana so that manager ke sath ek informal bonding hojaye. Woh break main leta nahi tha kyuki I don't smoke. Try kiya tha maine ekbar sath jaane ka, par mujhe sahi nahi laga.

2. **Alcohol after shift** - Work stress ke naam par mostly log daily bar mein jaate the daaru peene. Main woh bhi nahi karta tha toh woh bonding wala chance bhi over.

Sabko lagne laga main rude hu, par asli reason tha ki main distract nahi hona chahta tha. Mujhe pata tha main jaunga toh sab kahenge 'ekbar peeke dekh, kuch nahi hota', toh maine avoid kiya.
Ye isiliye bata raha hu aapko kyuki ye aapke sath bhi ho sakta hai. Aapko bhi lonely, left out, FOMO feel ho sakta hai.
Par aapko apne values aur ethics ko nahi bhulna hai.
Wait karo, aapko aapke hisse ke log mil jaenge. Woh aapko waise hi accept and appreciate karenge jaise aap ho.

Picture from **STAR Celebration** jo harr week hotel me hota tha.
Hotel me mera kaam tha - un guests ko acha experience dena jo din ke 15,000 se 1,50,000 Rs. kharch kar rahe hai sirf hotel me rehne aur khane ke liye. Agar kisi guest ko mera kaam acha lagta tha toh woh mere liye email ya company ke software me 'review' likhte the. Kisi week mere naam se review aaya toh us week me **STAR** bann jata tha aur **STARS** ke liye every saturday ek celebration hota tha. Jaha recognition aur accha khana milta tha.
I was fortunate ki mere paas aise bohot saare reviews the, mera har kabhi **STAR** ke liye naam appoint hota tha jo ki easy nahi tha.

Ye picture me jo last me gentleman dikh rahe hai Blair, ye Taj me mujhe mentor assign kiye gaye the, I respect him alot along with Pranali and Gurmeet ma'am. In log ne mujhe basics sikhaye. Last second, Mr. Himadri jo hamare Front Office manager the, mere favorite, inse maine seekha ki kabhi bias nahi hona, jo sahi hai woh sahi hai aur jo galat woh galat. Last third, Mr. Gaurav Mighlani. Inhone mera final interview liya tha aur ek baat kahi thi jisne mujhe hospitality ki sabse badi learning di. Inhone mujhe hire karte hi kaha **'Tu rajasthan se hai Jai, agar tujhe zameen par girna pade toh gir jana lekin apne hotel se koi guest upset nahi jana chahiye.'** Shayad isiliye mera focus guests ko best services dena hota tha.
Aur ye cheez meri life ke ek bohot important point par kaam aai.
Aagey batata hu :)
Pehle kuch skills discuss karte hai jo yaha maine seekhi.

## Self-Belief

Apne Aap Par Bharosa Rakhna

Self-belief ka matlab hai apni abilities, values, aur decisions pe poora vishwas rakhna. Yeh woh andar ki awaaz hai jo kehti hai, "Main kar sakta hoon, chahe duniya kuch bhi kahe."
Yeh vishwas tumhe har challenge se ladne aur naye risks lene ka hausla aur sapno ke peeche daudne ki taqat deta hai.

## Self-Belief Tumhare Liye Kya Kar Sakta Hai?

✓ **Risk lene ki himmat deta hai** – Jaise Singapore chhod ke Mumbai jaana, bina guarantee ke, sirf ek sapne ke liye.
✓ **Faith It Till You Make It** – Jaise Taj Lands End jaakar khud aur upar wale par bharosa rakh kar boldena ki "Mr. Sharma ne bulaya."
✓ **Comfort Zone se bahar nikalta hai** – Pata hai career settled hai, new beginning me bohot mehnat lagegi.
✓ **Tumhe standout karne me help karta hai** – Jaise unhe bolna ki 'interview lelo, vacancy ho tab bula lena'. Main unki baat ko accept karleta ki abhi hiring nahi chal rahi toh ye life nahi dekh pata.

**Kaise Badhayein Apna Self-Belief?**

- **Chhote Risks Lo** – Har chhoti jeet se confidence banta hai aur haar se character.
- **Aise Dress Karo Jaise Tum Already Successful Ho** – Kapdon ka tumhare mindset par bohot bada asar hota hai.
- **Bina Dare Baat Karo** – Har baar sab answer pata ho zaroori nahi, lekin confidently bolne se log vishwas karte hain.
- **Mauke ka intezaar mat karo**—Mauke banao, darwazo par knock karo. Khulenge ya nahi woh baad me dekhenge.

**Yaad rakho, Puchhne mein kya jaata hai?**
**Mana hi toh karenge. Lekin agar haa kardiya toh? :)**

"Agar khud pe vishwas hai, toh duniya tumhare khilaaf ho kar bhi tumhe rok nahi sakti."
Self-belief tumhara sabse bada weapon hai—usey roz sharp karo!

## Aaj Se Hi Shuru Karo - Self-Belief Ke Liye Actions

Challenge Karo Apne Negative Thoughts Ko. Hamari soch hi self-doubt ki shuruaat hoti hai. Agar tum khud se baar-baar kehte ho, “Main nahi kar sakta” ya “Main kabil nahi hoon,” toh tum apni growth khud rok rahe ho. ***Soch badlo, zindagi badlegi.***

### Growth Mindset Build Karo

Growth mindset ka matlab hai hamesha kuch na kuch seekhte rehna, yeh maan na ki tumhari life, skills aur intelligence mehnat aur lagan se improve ho sakti hai.
“Main seekh sakta hoon, main behtar ho sakta hoon. Bass mujhe hamesha seekhte rehna hai”

### Positive Logo Ke Saath Raho

Tumhara environment tumhari self-belief ko direct affect karta hai. Negative aur unsupportive log tumhara confidence cheen lenge. Positive aur encouraging log tumhe upar uthayenge. Woh log choose karo jo kehte hain— ‘Tum kar sakte ho’

### Action Lo, Chahe Ready Mehsoos Na Karo

Confidence baithne se nahi, actions lene se aata hai. Zyadatar log isliye start nahi karte kyunki wo sochte hain, “Pehle perfect ready ho jaun.” Perfect moment kabhi nahi aata—shuru karo, yahi perfect moment hai, Ye book padhli na, muhurt nikal gaya tumhare liye :)

### Success Visualize Karo

Apne aap ko safal hote hue imagine karo. Jab tum apne aap ko jeet te hue dekhte ho, tumhara dimaag aur actions us direction me kaam karna shuru karte hain. Soch me jeet, toh zindagi me bhi jeet.

### Apni Past Successes Yaad Karo

Hum aksar apni galtiyon aur failures pe focus karte hain, par jo hamari purani jeet  hai, use yaad karna bhi zaroori hai.
Apni achievements yaad karo—tumne kitna kuch already achieve kiya hai. Past ki jeet, future ka fuel hai.

Self-belief ek din me nahi banta, lekin har din ke chhote action se mazboot hota hai. Chalo aaj ek chhote action se shuru karte hai.

## Apne Physical aur Mental Health Ka Dhyan Rakho

Tumhara body aur mind connected hain. Agar health kharab hai, toh energy kam ho jaati hai, emotions negative hone lagte hain, aur self-belief gir jata hai.
**Healthy body = Strong mind = Unshakable self-belief**

### Failure Ko Accept Karo Aur Usse Seekho

Fail hone ka matlab yeh nahi ki tum kabil nahi ho—iska matlab sirf yeh hai ki tum seekh rahe ho.
Har successful insaan ne life me failures face kiye hain.
Har haar ek lesson hai, har setback ek setup hai comeback ke liye.
Agar aap haar nahi rahe matlab aap kaam nahi kar rahe ho.

### Keep Showing Up - Hamesha Dikhte Raho

Safal log aur self-doubt wale logon ke beech ka sabse bada farq kya hai?

## Persistence.

Low feel karne wale dinon me bhi apne upar kaam karte raho.
Consistency se confidence banta hai.

### Self-Belief Ek Skill Hai, Talent Nahi

Yeh waqt aur practice se develop hoti hai.
Jab develop ho jaaye, toh tumhara potential limitless ho jaata hai.
Khud par vishwas rakho, action lo, aur self-doubt ko kabhi apne raste me mat aane do.
Agar tum khud par vishwas karte ho, toh duniya bhi tum par vishwas karegi.

Self-belief ka matlab yeh nahi ki tumhe future ka pata hai—iska matlab hai ki chahe kuch bhi ho, tum handle kar loge.

Aur yaad rakhna...
**Puchhne main kya jaata hai?**

## Activity: "The Proof List – Why You Can!"

**Objective:** Apni achievements ko dekhkar khud par vishwas badhao. Apne journey par garv mehsoos karo aur ek aisa self-belief build karo jo kisi bhi situation me hil na sake—even jab poori duniya tumpar doubt kar rahi ho.

**Step 1: Likho 3 cheezein jinpar tumhe garv hai**

Badi baatein nahi, choti choti jeet bhi count hoti hai.

**Example**:

- Maine dance competition me participate kiya aur jeeta.
- Mushkil waqt me apne parivaar ki madad ki.
- Ek difficult situation ko shaanti se handle kiya.

**Likho:**

1.
2.
3.

**Step 2: Kaunse qualities tumne dikhayi?**

**Example**: Confidence, hard work, patience, courage, etc.

Likho: ________________________________________________

**Step 3: Positive Mirror Talk – 1 Minute Challenge**

Ek mirror ke saamne khade ho jao aur zor se bolo (roz):

"Mujhe khud par vishwas hai. Main capable hoon. Maine pehle bhi bohot kuch achieve kiya hai aur aage aur bhi bada karunga/karoongi."

**Step 4: Socho aur likho**

7 din ke baad, ab apne baare me tum kaisa mehsoos karte ho?

**Likho**: ________________________________________________

________________________________________________________

Self-belief tab grow karta hai jab tum apni jeet par focus karte ho, apni strength ko recognize karte ho, aur khud ko yaad dilate ho ki tumne pehle bhi tough time face kiya hai... aur usse strong ban kar nikle ho. Tumhare paas tumhari power ka proof already hai.

Apna ek **"Victory Folder"** banao. Photos, certificates, messages, ya koi bhi cheez jo tumhari jeet ya success yaad dilaye—sab ek jagah sambhalo. Jab kabhi low feel karo, ise khol kar dekho.

# Public Speaking

Public speaking duniya ke sabse valuable skills me se ek hai. Chahe tum ek speech de rahe ho, kisiko koi idea pitch kar rahe ho, ya bas ek group me apne thoughts share kar rahe ho—tumhari confidently communicate karne ki ability tumhe sabse alag bana sakti hai. Lekin sach ye hai ki bohot logon ko audience ke saamne bolne ka sirf khayal hi dara deta hai.

**Good news?**
Public speaking bhi ek skill hai, talent nahi. Sahi approach aur thodi practice se koi bhi ek acha speaker ban sakta hai.

**Why Public Speaking Matters**

- **Confidence build hota hai** – Jitna zyada practice karoge, utna comfortable feel karoge.
- **Career growth fast hoti hai** – Great speakers influence karte hain, lead karte hain, inspire karte hain.
- **Communication better hoti hai** – Apne ideas clearly express karne ki skill daily life me bhi kaam aati hai.
- **Impact create hota hai** – Team lead karni ho, kisi ko sikhaana ho ya story batani ho—ek powerful message zindagi badal sakta hai.

**Common Fears Kaise Overcome Karein**

- **Fear of Judgment**

Yaad rakho, audience tumhe fail hote nahi dekhna chahti, wo tumhe succeed hote dekhna chahti hai.

- **Fear of Forgetting Words**

Apna speech acche se structure karo, key points yaad rakho. Agar kuch bhool jao, pause lo, breathe karo, aur aage badho. Audience ko nahi pata tumhari script kya hai.

- **Fear of Nervousness**

Top speakers bhi nervous hote hain. Uss energy ko use karo—engaged aur expressive banne ke liye.

Jitni preparation, utna kam fear. Public speaking me jeet ka formula hai: **Prepare → Practice → Perform**
Let's dive into how to master this skill.

## How to Become a Powerful Speaker

- **Know Your Audience**

Samjho unhe kya chahiye, kya expect kar rahe hain, aur kis cheez se unka attention bana rahega.

- **Structure Your Speech**

Ek great speech ke 3 parts hote hain:
**Opening** – Shuruaat karo ek story, question ya fact ke saath.
**Body** – Apne main points simple aur clear rakho.
**Conclusion** – Khatam karo ek strong message ya action point ke saath.

- **Voice & Body Language ka Use**

Tone me variation/modulation rakho—monotone avoid karo.
Pauses lo important points pe—impact badhta hai.
Eye contact banao—connection feel hota hai.
Naturally move karo, bina overacting ke.

- **Practice, Practice, Practice**

Mirror ke saamne bolo ya khud ka video record karo aur dekho.
Pehle chhoti audience ke saamne practice karo, phir bada stage.

- **Tell Stories**

Log facts bhool jaate hain, lekin stories yaad rakhte hain. Speech ko relatable aur emotional banao.

**The Secret to Public Speaking**
"Perfect banne ki zarurat nahi—real bano."

Public speaking lines yaad karne ka game nahi hai—ye game hai apna message clarity, passion aur asli feeling ke saath dene ka.
Jitni baar stage par jaoge, utne better banoge.
Jitna avoid karoge, utni nervousness badhegi.
Next time jab bolne ka moka mile, grab it.
Tumhare words logon ko inspire, influence aur change hone me help kar sakte hain.

## Activity: "Craft Your Elevator Pitch"

**Skill**: Clear & Confident Self-Introduction in 30 Seconds

**What's an Elevator Pitch?**

Elevator pitch ek 30-second ka introduction hota hai jisme aap batate ho ki aap kaun ho, kya karte ho, aur saamne wale ko kyun farak padna chahiye.

Bilkul itne time me jitna ek lift ride me milta hai.

Yeh kaafi useful hai jab aap kisi naye insaan se milte ho, interview dete ho, ya kisi event me network karte ho.

**Step 1: Fill in These Blanks**

Format simple hai:

Hi, I'm [Your Name], I am passionate about [your passion or skill]. Currently, I am [what you do or want to do]. I'm [goal, mission or what you seek], "and I'd love to connect or explore opportunities together (optional)."

**Example for students:**

"Hi, I'm Jai Pareek, I am passionate about helping people become better. I'm an International Soft Skills Coach, on a mission to help 1,00,000 small towners learn Soft Skills.

**Step 2: Write Your Own Pitch**

## My Pitch:

_____________________________________________

_____________________________________________

_____________________________________________

_____________________________________________

_____________________________________________

**Step 3: Practice It Out Loud**

- Timer set karo 30 seconds ka.
- Record yourself pitch bolte hue.
- **Dekho**: Smile kiya? Clearly bola? Confident laga?

**Step 4: Test It in Real Life**

Next time koi puche, "Aap kya karte ho?" — Use your pitch.
**Example**: Job fair, seminar, ya friends ke parents ke saath.

India ke Tier 2–3 cities me professional networking common nahi hai, aur log khud ko professionally kaise introduce karein, iska zyada idea nahi hai.
Ye pitch aapko standout karne me madad karega— aapko prepared aur confident feel hoga, har situation me.

Aapka pitch fix nahi hoga—jaise aap grow karte ho, waise hi ise update karte raho! Aur isko aur interesting banate raho.
**Example** - Jab log mujhse puchte hai aap kya karte ho toh main ye nahi bolta ki main 'Soft Skills Coach hu', main kehta hu 'Main logon ko behtar insaan banne me help karta hu'.
Phir baat start hoti hai agey aur iss introduction ke kaaran insaan mujhe yaad rakhta hai.

## Handling Workplace Politics

Workplace Politics ka matlab hota hai office ke andar hone wale power games, groupism, influence aur personal interests ke conflicts. Jab log apni position strong karne ke liye dusron ko neecha dikhate hain, ya unnecessary networking aur manipulation karte hain—usse workplace politics kehte hain.

**Common Examples:**

- Kisi dusre ke ideas ka credit le lena.
- Boss ke saamne dusre ki burai karna.
- Group banakar kisi ek employee ko ignore ya target karna.
- Information chhupana ya manipulate karna to look better.

**Workplace Politics Kaise Handle Karein?**

- **Stay Neutral & Professional**

Gossip se door raho, kisi ki side mat lo. Focus on work aur results.

- **Build Genuine Relationships**

Har department me rishtey banao, lekin fake mat bano.
Difficult time mein yahi connections kaam aate hain.

- **Understand Power Structure**

Samjho kaun decisions le raha hai, aur unka kaam karne ka tareeka kya hai.

- **Clear Communication**

Baatein samajh ke bolo, misunderstandings se badi problems hoti hai.

- **Focus on Performance**

Apna kaam itna accha karo ki kaam bolta rahe, log nahi.
Results hi tumhare biggest support banenge.

“Office politics se daro mat, samjho aur smartly handle karo.
Jitna kaam strong, utna tumhara position strong.”
Aur yaad rahe.. woh sab tumhare colleagues hai. Friends nahi.

**Activity: "Aag Bujhao Nahi, Lagne Hi Mat Do"**

**Step 1: Pehchaano Jhagda Shuru Hone Ki Wajah**
Har jagah—office, college, ya family—conflicts aam tor par yahan se shuru hote hain:

- Miscommunication ya clarity ka na hona
- Ego clash ("Main sahi hoon!")
- Unclear zimmedaari ("Kaun kya karega?")
- Unequal effort (Kuch log zyada kaam karte hain, kuch kam)
- Assumptions aur gossip

Ab likho 2 situations jahan jhagda ho sakta tha (real ya imagine karke):

**Step 2: Tumhara Prevention Plan**
Ab upar likhi har situation ke liye socho—tum kya kar sakte the taaki baat jhagda na bane?
**Example for #1**: Agar log confused hain ki kaun kya karega – Main ek chhoti meeting bulata, kaam divide karta, aur confirm karta ki sabko samajh aa gaya.
Ab likho tumhare ideas: ______________________________________

____________________________________________________________

**Step 3: "Stop, Think, Clarify" Technique**
Jab lage ki jhagda hone wala hai, turant ye 3 steps follow karo:
**Stop** – Turant react mat karo. Saans lo.
**Think** – Asli problem kya hai? Sirf chillana nahi, reason samjho.
**Clarify** – Shanti aur samajh se baat karo.
Bolo: "Chalo baat clear karte hain, jhagda hone se pehle."

**Practice Line Example:**
"I think thoda confusion hai, kya hum 2 minute me clear kar lein?"

**Tumhari version:**
Normally Tum Jhagde Me Kaise React Karte Ho?
□ Avoid karta hoon, chup rehta hoon
□ Seedha jhagad leta hoon
□ Baith ke baat karke solve karta hoon
□ Overthink karta hoon, par kuch nahi bolta

Chapter 9

# THE DREAM BURJ AL ARAB

Mujhe Taj Lands End me kaam karte 10 mahine ho chuke the.
Ek din meri Singapore wali flatmate Ana ka message aaya—'maine tere dream hotel Burj Al Arab me job apply kiya hai, aur kal mera final interview hai.'

Main khushi se pagal ho gaya, aur maine bola, "Tu toh already super star hai—Burj Al Arab ke interview tak pahunchna hi badi baat hai!" Burj Al Arab—duniya ka sirf ek hi 7-star hotel. Aur hotelier ke life woh sabse bada achievement ho sakta hai.
Agle din maine usse poocha, "Kaisa raha interview?"
Usne bola, "Nahi hui select."
Phir bhi, mujhe uspar proud tha—kyunki itni badi stage tak pahunchna hi kaafi hai.

Ussi din, ek interesting incident hua. Hotel me ek VVIP guest ne check in kiya Mrs. Lubna Moosa, Mauritius se.
Gold member in Taj group, gold member in Emirates Airlines.
Full big shot. Unko dekh ke samajh aajaega ki koi toh araha hai.

Kyuki maine new join kiya tha mujhe hotel mein zyada kaam nahi de rahe the. Mrs. Moosa ne jab check in kiya toh mujhe kaha inko room tak escort kardo. 10 minute ka ek process hota hai jisme guest ko kuch important information deni hoti hai aur ek bonding ke liye time mil jata hai so that unki stay me unko hum acche se serve kar sakein. Bohot ache se baat hui hum dono ki.
Agle din, unki ek meeting thi toh woh reception par aai aur unhone Mr. Himadri ko bola ki unhe ek meeting mein jaana hai aur sath me ek insaan chahiye jo unke liye notes le and she said 'agar Jai hai toh usko bhej do'. Himadri sir ne kaha theek hai.
Meeting se pehle Mrs. Moosa aur mera ek acha sa discussion hua India ke logon ke mindset ke baare me. She was amazing, powerful and such a kind heart.. Kaafi kuch seekha unse uss conversation me.

Unki uss meeting ke dauraan mujhe ek strong feeling aayi ki jiske saath unki baat ho rahi thi, wo banda trustworthy nahi hai. Kuch toh woh galat karne ki soch raha hai.

Meeting khatam hone ke baad pata nahi kyun, aisa laga ki mujhe unhe batana chahiye. Darr lag raha tha. Risk tha, job ja sakti thi. Phir bhi maine himmat ki aur unhe bola, *"Ma'am, mujhe lagta hai aapko is insaan se saath deal karne se pehle thoda sochna chahiye."*
Unhone sirf ek shabd bola—"Okay"—aur chali gayi.

Unke is reaction ne mujhe dara diya. Maine khud se kaha, "Bhai tu control kiya kar, aage se chup rehna aur apni *integrity* apne paas rakh, inhone complaint kardi toh gadbad hojaegi."

Agle din Mrs. Moosa mujhe dikhi aur unhone smile karke greet kiya. 'Good morning, Jai. How are you today?;
Mujhe realize hua sab theek hai aur hamare beech ek positive relationship bann chuka hai.
Par na unhone us incidence ke baare me kuch baat ki aur na maine.

Thodi der baad unhe kuch chahiye tha toh woh reception par aai aur unhone dekha ki main kuch soch raha hu. Toh unhone pucha, "Jai, sab theek hai?"

Maine unhe kaha *'yes ma'am, just thinking about a friend, usne Burj Al Arab me interview diya tha, par selection nahi hua'*.

Unhone dhyaan se suna aur bola, *"Tum bhi apply kardo. Acha hotel hai, main gai hu waha ek baar."*

Maine has ke bola,
"Ma'am, meri friend ke paas Singapore me 5 saal ka experience hai, wo Russian hai, model bhi hai. Mere paas total 1.5 saal ka experience tha hospitality industry mein.
Usko reject kiya, mujhe kyun hire karenge woh log?

Maine unhe ye bhi bataya jo Mr. Kompella ne Taj Exotica,
Goa mein kaha tha.

Par Mrs. Moosa ne mujhe dekha aur bola,
**"Tumhe bhi wahan job ke liye apply karna chahiye Jai. Tumhe nahi pata hai ki tum kaun ho"**

Do din tak me himmat joota raha tha... phir finally maine Ana se Burj ke manager ka email mang liya aur unhe bhejne ke liye apna CV ready kiya.
Mujhe pata tha mera CV akela kaafi nahi hai, toh maine ek **collage** banaya Taj mein mujhe mile guest comments ka aur ek notice board ki picture ka— bass wahi mere paas meri mehnat ke saboot the.

Do din baad me is baat ko bhul chuka tha.
Kyuki mere liye woh waise bhi possible hone wali baat nahi thi.
Life jaisi chal rahi thi waise chalne lagi, main apne routine me busy hogaya. Wahi baatein, wahi duniya, wahi sab.

Aur phir, kuch unbelievable hua—
Randomly mere paas ek interview ke liye call aa gaya.
Unhone kaha 'Jai, this is Maureen from Jumeirah group, hamein aapki profile mili hai aur humne aapko short list kiya hai. Aap kab interview ke liye available ho'?
Mujhe aisa laga ki main bolna bhul gaya hu, mere muh se awaz nahi nikal rahi thi but confident toh dikhna tha na. Maine unse baat ki.

Agle 15 din, maine 6-7 interviews diye. Full emotional rollercoaster, blood pressure kabhi high, kabhi low... Telephonic call, Zoom calls, Email conversations. Meri night shift chal rahi thi toh me subah 2 ghante extra ruk kar check karta tha kaunsa room clean horaha hai. Phir us room me jaakar house keeping se request karta tha thodi der ek call karne do. Hath me apna phone lekar, window jaha se samudra dikhta tha udhar face karke maine Burj Al Arab ke ghanto khade reh kar interviews diye.
Kabhi milenge tab baat karenge ki kya kya hua inteviews me.

Pata nahi tha kya hoga, kaisa rahega, andar toh aisa bhi lagta tha ki fake hai, koi fraud kar raha hai mere saath kyuki unhone ye bhi puch liya tha ki aap kab aa sakte ho Dubai aur documents leliye the.
**Phir ek din..** Mere email par...
Ticket. VISA. .Offer letter.. mere sapno ke hotel se—mere paas aaya.

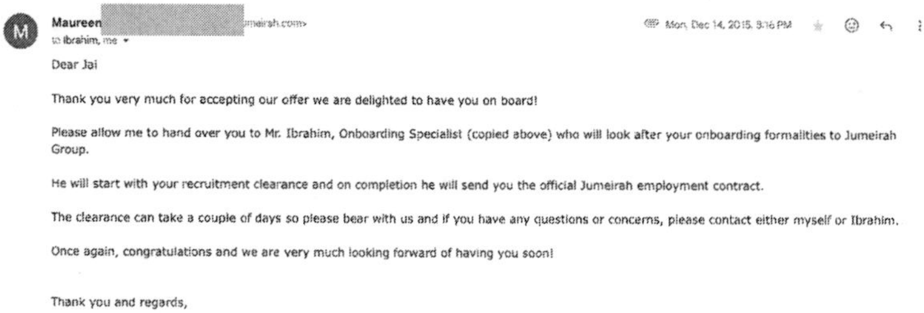
Maureen ...meirah.com> Mon, Dec 14, 2015, 3:16 PM
to Ibrahim, me

Dear Jai

Thank you very much for accepting our offer we are delighted to have you on board!

Please allow me to hand over you to Mr. Ibrahim, Onboarding Specialist (copied above) who will look after your onboarding formalities to Jumeirah Group.

He will start with your recruitment clearance and on completion he will send you the official Jumeirah employment contract.

The clearance can take a couple of days so please bear with us and if you have any questions or concerns, please contact either myself or Ibrahim.

Once again, congratulations and we are very much looking forward of having you soon!

Thank you and regards,

Main clueless tha, kisko batau, kaha jaau.
Mrs. Lubna hotel me hi thi toh maine unko bataya, aur unka response tha: **"Mujhe pata tha, ho hi jaayega."**

Uss moment me main khush toh tha par dara hua bhi tha. Mere sath 2 baar fraud hua tha, aur isbar agar fraud hua toh bohot zyada dukh hoga.

Pata hai,
Akele rehne ka ek nuksaan hai.
Aap apne logo ko sath nahi ho toh khushi share nahi kar sakte. Aur khushi sirf share karne se hi double hoti hai.

Doubt aur khushi ko mann me dabakar main wahi routine wala kaam karne laga. Ek din mere dost Chetan ka call aaya toh maine use bataya aur woh bohot khush hogaya. Usne kaha mujhe bhej me check karta hu genuine hai ya nahi.
Usne check kiya aur bola bhai ye toh genuine hai toh ready hoja Dubai jane ke liye.
Mujhe samajh nahi araha tha kaise react karu. Hotel me express nahi kar sakta. Koi paas me apna nahi hai jiske saath celebrate karlu.
Toh poora excitement apne andar hi rakhna pada.

Ek update aur aai mere paas..
Mere manager aur Mrs. Lubna mere baare me baat kar rahe the toh Himadri sir ne bola tha ki hum Jai ko promote karne wale hai uska 1 year complete hote hi. Idhar main hotel chhodne ka soch raha tha aur udhar ye sab. Sir ke liye meri respect itni zyada thi ki main unka saamna bhi nahi kar pa raha tha.
Kuch hi time pehle maine department me hi ek easy post ke liye trasfer liya tha ye bolke ki mujhe acting classes karni hai job ke saath saath.

Par Burj Al Arab agar mil raha hai toh kaun usey miss karna chahega.
Ye toh once in a life time opportunity thi.
Maine night shift continue ki, resignation letter likha aur raat me unki desk par rakh kar kisi ko bina bataye early morning
Dubai ke liye nikal gaya.

Ab mein aapse discuss karunga woh skills jisne mujhe Burj Al Arab tak.. apne sapne tak pohochane me meri help ki hai.

## 1. Storytelling Skill

Storytelling ek kala hai—jisme hum apni baat ko kisse ke zariye aise pesh karte hain ki sunne wala sirf samjhe nahi, connect kare, inspire ho, aur action le.

Kahani sunana sirf entertainment nahi hai—it's a superpower jo personal aur professional life dono main kaam aati hai.

**Kyun Storytelling ek Superpower hai?**
Log facts se nahi, emotions se connect karte hain.
Jab tum apni struggles share karte ho, log relate karte hain.
Facts bhool jaate hain, kahani yaad rehti hai.
Ek acchi kahani logon ko inspire karti hai—risk lene, apne dreams chase karne, aur khud par believe karne ke liye.
**3 Idiots movie tumhe kyu yaad hai? FRIENDS TV Show? Characters aur unki stories se connected ho tum.**

**Storytelling Skills kaise improve karein?**

- **Hook se shuru karo** – Pehle sentence se attention grab karo. Ye tumhe content creation me bhi kaam aega.
- **Relatable bano** – Apne doubts, struggles aur emotions share karo.
- **Narrative Arc banao** – Kahani mein tension lao, conflict dikhao, phir uska solution.
- **Show, don't just tell** – Facts mat gino, details se scene create karo.
- **Personal touch do** – Jab kahani real hoti hai, tabhi powerful banti hai.

**Remember:**
Logon ko sikhao nahi, unhe mehsoos karwao.
That's the magic of storytelling.

## Activity: "Apni Kahani 1 Minute Mein Sunao"

Log facts bhool jaate hain, kahaniyaan yaad rehti hain.
Ek acchi story inspire karti hai, connect karti hai, aur influence karti hai—chaahe interview ho, business ho, ya roz ki life.

**Step 1: Apni Life ka Ek Moment Choose Karo**
Koi bhi real moment socho jisme tumne kuch seekha ho.

- Koi challenge jo face kiya ho
- Koi success jo tumne earn ki ho
- Koi funny ya emotional experience

**Step 2: S.T.A.R. Method Use Karo**
Kahani sunane ka simple formula:
**S** – **Situation**: Kab aur kaha hua?
**T** – **Task**: Tumhe kya karna tha?
**A** – **Action**: Tumne kya kiya?
**R** – **Result**: Kya outcome aaya? Tumne kya seekha?

**Example:**
"Ek baar mujhe bina tayyari ke ek event mein bolna pada (S). Dar lag raha tha, par bolna zaroori tha (T). Maine haath pe 3 points likhe aur short, honest speech de daali (A). Logon ne taaliyan bajayi, aur mujhe laga main apni soch se zyada capable hoon (R)."

**Step 3: Apni Kahani Likho**
**Title:** ____________________________________________
**S:** ____________________________________________
**T:** ____________________________________________
**A:** ____________________________________________
**R:** ____________________________________________

**Step 4: Record Karo Aur Usko Ache Se Dekho**

**Timer Set Karo: 1 Minute**
Ek achi jagah bethkar, story sunate huve apna ek video record karo

**Ab Dekho aur analyze karo**:
Kya tum clear ho?
Emotions dikh rahe hai?
Connection feel hua?

**Step 5: Share Karo**
Apni story kisi dost ya family member ko sunao.
**Puchho**: "Kya kuch mehsoos hua?"
Unka feedback lo aur improve karo.

Apni 3 personal stories ready rakho—interview, networking ya social media ke liye.

Tumhari kahani tumhari superpower hai
Yaad karo woh log iss duniya me nahi hai, tumhare paas sirf unki kahaniyan hai jisko yaad karke tum khush hote ho aur kuch nahi.

Small towners - Tumhari journey hi tumhari strength hai.
Jab tum usse sahi tarike se share karte ho, log tumhe yaad rakhte hain aur respect karte hain.

## Sample Story Template

**(Create your own story today)**

**1. Background: Main Kaun Hoon, Kahaan Se Aaya Hoon**

"Main ek simple family se aata hoon. Na koi extraordinary talent, na hi koi special background. Par ek cheez thi — sapna. Apni zindagi ko kuch aur banana."

**Tone**: Honest, grounded

**Purpose**: Audience se connection

**2. Challenge: Woh Cheez Jo Aapko Agey Nahi Badhne De Rahi**

"Shuruat mein sab kuch easy nahi tha. Main jahan tha, wahan se sapne sirf sapne lagte the. Confidence nahi tha, resources nahi the, aur sabse bada— guidance nahi thi."

**Problem show karoge** — log relate karenge

**3. Decision: Maine Choose Kya Kiya**

"Ek point aaya jahan do raste the — ya toh system ke flow mein chalte raho, ya khud ka raasta banao. Maine dusra option chuna."

Turning point highlight karo. Inspire without bragging.

**4. Effort & Learning: Kaise Lada Aur Kya Seekha**

"Job kiye, naye sheher gaya, naye log mile. Har jagah se kuch na kuch seekha — kaise baat karte hain, kaise soch badalte hain, kaise haar ke agey badhne ka jazba laate hain."

Process dikhao, not just success

**5. Fall: Jab Sab Girta Hua Mehsoos Hua**

"Ek waqt aaya jab sab kuch ho kar bhi lagta tha — main khud se door ho gaya hoon. Kaam tha, paisa tha, par sukoon nahi tha."

Emotional connect banata hai yeh part

**6. Healing & Growth: Waqt Jo Sab Badal Gaya**
"Tab samjha — success sirf bahar ki cheez nahi hai. Andar ka balance, self-worth, aur clarity — ye sab utna hi zaroori hai. Wahi journey mujhe meri manzil tak le gayi."

**7. Contribution: Ab Kya Kar Raha Hoon**
"Aaj main wahi sab logon ko sikha raha hoon, jahan main kabhi confused tha. Jo cheez mujhe chahiye thi, ab main wohi duniya ko dene ki koshish karta hoon."
Now the hero gives back.

**8. Message to Audience: Tum Bhi Kar Sakte Ho**
"Agar aap kisi confusion, pressure ya self-doubt se guzar rahe ho — toh yeh kahani aapke liye hai. Kyunki agar main badal sakta hoon, toh aap bhi badal sakte ho."

Finish strong, leave them inspired.

Iss skill ne mujhe jobs dilai hai, businesses start karne me help kiya hai, travel karwaya hai, content creator banne me help ki hai aur book likhna sikhaya hai.
Aapko nahi pata ye skill aapko kaha kaha help karegi.

## Interview Skills

Interview dena sirf sawalon ke jawab dena nahi hota—it's about presenting yourself as the best choice.
Burj Al Arab ne mujhe sirf mere resume ki wajah se hire nahi kiya. Unhone mujhe isliye hire kiya kyunki maine:

- Unhe meri stories ke zariye woh feel karwaya jo mere guests feel karte the
- Unhe mera hospitality ke liye passion dikhaya
- Zyada experience na hone par bhi apni value prove ki

### Key Learnings from Burj Al Arab Interview

- **Multiple Rounds ke liye ready raho** – Maine interview ke 6-7 rounds diye. Har round me mere patience, confidence, energy, knowledge aur calmness ka test hua.
- **Sirf bolo mat, dikhao** – "Main hospitality mein acha hoon" kehne se zyada impactful tha guest feedback aur real examples unhe interesting tarike se share karna. Which was unusual.
- **Pehle khud pe vishwas karo** – Agar tum khud pe doubt karoge, toh saamne wale ko dikh jaayega. Pehle mujhe bhi laga main Burj ke laayak nahi hoon. Lekin jab interview ka time aaya, maine apna mindset badla, aur sab kuch badal gaya.

### Interview Master Karne Ke Tips

- **Company ke baare mein research karo** – Unke values, work culture aur expectations samjho.
- **Answers nahi, stories prepare karo** – Apne skills ko real-life examples ke through dikhao.
- **Practice karo, lekin robotic mat bano** – Natural, confident aur engaging sound karo.
- **Body language pe dhyan do** – Smile karo, eye contact rakho aur energy dikhao.
- **Smart questions pucho** – Interview two-way hota hai. Company aur role ke baare mein genuine curiosity show karo.

**Tips jinhone mujhe 15 interviews crack karne me help kiya hai -**

1. **Dress to win** - Aise ready hoke jaao jaise tum us hotel ko kharidne ja rahe ho. Dress well. Smell good. Look sharp.
2. **Jo hoga dekh lenge -** Zyada ummeed mat rakho. Main samajh sakta hu tumhare paas job nahi hai, paise ki zarurat hai lekin agar tum desperate rahoge toh waise bhi apna best nahi de paoge. Isiliye mock interviews ki practice karo and chillax.
3. **Work hard on yourself and know your worth** - Apne upar bohot kaam karo so that tumhe itna confidene ajaye jisse tumhe feel ho ki agar main is jagah kaam karne gaya toh meri life toh better hogi hi lekin inka business bhi grow karega.
4. **Woh mat batao jo CV me likha hai -** Aapki life itni interesting banao ki samne wala jab aap se sawaal kare toh use mazedaar cheezein sunne ko mile. Aap mano mera ek hotel me selection is base par hua ki mujhe GHOOMER dance karna aata hai. Karenge kabhi baat is bare me bhi, yaad dilana :)
5. **Wear a genuine smile, always** - Duniya ko khush log pasand hai. Aur log khush logo ke around rehna chahte hai.
6. **Tell me about yourself -** Iss sawaal ka ek acha sa jawaab ready rakho hamesha. Koi neend se uthakar bhi puchle toh aapke muh se confidently acha sa jawab nikalna chahiye.
7. **They want to hire good people, not toppers -** Samjho agar unko sirf toppers hi chahiye the toh woh top 5 colleges ke top 5 candidates laakar interview karlete na. Par unhe kuch aur chahiye.
8. **It's their business -** Simple sa funda samjho. Unke paas ek business hai jisko woh grow karna chahte hai. Kya aap woh insaan ho jo unki business grow karne me help kar sakta hai? **Ya is sawal ka jawab do** - Agar aapko ek insaan hire karna ho business grow karne ke liye toh '*kya aap khudko hire karenge*'? Agar haa toh kyu aur nahi toh kyu nahi. Agar aap sach bologe khudse toh aapko jawab mil jaega.

## Activity: Craft Your Perfect Introduction (Interview Style)

**Objective:** Interview mein 60–90 seconds ke andar apne aap ko confidently introduce karo — aise ki saamne wala impress ho jaye, aur tum naturally apne strengths, achievements aur goals ko highlight kar sako.

**Step 1: 4 Easy Steps Mein Structure Banao**

**1. Who You Are (Main Kaun Hoon?)**

Apna naam, current role ya education aur thoda background mention karo.

**Example:**

"Good morning, mera naam Jai Pareek hai, main ek hotel management graduate hoon, aur mujhe communication aur people management main bohot interest hai."

**2. What You've Done (Maine Kya Kiya Hai?)**

Apne key experiences ya achievements share karo — jo uss job ke liye relevant ho.

**Example**:

"Maine Taj aur Oberoi Hotels ke saath kaam kiya hai, jahan maine guest relations, communication aur team coordination mein apni skills sharpen ki."

**3. What Makes You Unique (Mujhme Kya Alag Hai?)**

Ek strength ya value batao jo tumhe dusron se alag banati hai.

**Example**:

"Meri speciality hai – jaldi adapt karna aur alag-alag background ke logon ke saath meaningful connection banana."

**4. Why You're Here (Main Yahan Kyun Hoon?)**

Apne goals ko is opportunity se link karo — kyun tum yeh job chahte ho.

**Example**:

"Main apne customer experience aur problem-solving ke passion ko ek dynamic team main use karna chahta hoon, jahan main grow kar saku aur value add kar saku."

**Step 2: Ab Apna Intro Likho!**

My Introduction:

____________________________________________________________

____________________________________________________________

____________________________________________________________

____________________________________________________________

____________________________________________________________

**Step 3: Practice Karo (2 Baar Daily)**

- Timer set karo 90 seconds ka.
- Apna intro bol ke record karo.
- **Recording suno**: Kya tum clear, confident aur natural lag rahe ho? Smile aur eye contact ka feel aa raha hai?

First impression strong banao — tumhare introduction se hi interviewer decide karta hai ki wo tumhe dhyan se sunega ya nahi.

Chapter 10

# THE TWIST IN DUBAI

Dubai jaane se pehle mujhe pata tha ki main papa ko nahi bata sakta. Taj Mumbai se pehle maine 4 jobs chhodi thi, aur Singapore bhi ek aise reason se chhoda tha jo unhe silly laga tha. Khair ab toh mujhe bhi sensible nahi lagta hai par theek hai. Life main aisi stories bhi honi chahiye.
Mujhe pata tha agar maine Dubai ke baare main papa ko bataya, toh unka jawab naa hoga.

Wo meri Mumbai wali life se khush the — celebrities se mil raha the, Taj ke bade hotel mein kaam kar raha tha. Par ab Dubai toh jana tha, isliye, maine decide kiya ki is baar unhe bataye bina hi nikal jaunga aur waha pohochte hi call kardunga.

Main Dubai land hua raat ke 3-4 baje. Sabse pehle SIM card liya aur papa ko call kiya. Mann nahi lag raha tha bhai. Galat kaam kiya tha. Unhone pehli baar mein nahi uthaya — mujhe laga, unhone socha hoga koi telemarketing ka call hai, kyunki unhe pehli baar kisi foreign number se call aa raha tha.

Fir maine mummy ko call kiya aur kaha, "Phone papa ko do."
Papa ne phone uthaya, "Hello, kya hua? Itni subah-subah kyun call kiya?"
Maine kaha, "Papa, main Dubai mein hoon."

Ek lamba pause hua.

Aur fir unhone phone kaat diya.
Mere papa ka background law se tha, very powerful personality. Kam bolte the, lekin har shabd mein wazan hota tha.
Maine phirse 5-7 baar call kiya back to back, lekin unhone nahi uthaya. Aakhir maine mummy ko kiya aur request ki, "Ek baar aur phone pakda do bass unhe."
Is baar jab papa ne uthaya, sirf ek shabd bola — "Hmm."
**Maine kaha**, "Papa, aap mujhe dusri job ka naam sunte hi mana kardete. Isiliye nahi bataya. So sorry.
**Unhone kaha**, "Woh foreign hai, wahan tujhe koi nahi jaanta. Agar kuch ho gaya toh? Main yaha se kuch kar bhi nahi paunga'

Maine kaha, "Kuch nahi hoga mujhe papa. Inhone mujhe Dubai me accommodation diya hai, khana unki taraf se hai, hotel ke liye transport hai, ticket visa bhi unhone hi diya hai plus acchi salary — sab kuch mil raha hai yaha." Aur yeh mera sapna tha papa.

Main unhe sab kuch explain karta gaya, unke sawalon ke jawab deta gaya aur dheere-dheere unka mood theek ho gaya.
Kuch saalon baad mujhe pata chala ki wo apne close logon ko call karke bade excitement ke saath bata rahe the ki maine kya kiya tha — full proud ke saath.

Papa ko batane ke baad mujhe finally Dubai aane ki excitement feel hone lagi. Uske pehle tak main poori flight me bohot nervous tha, bura feel kar raha tha ki maine papa ko bataya nahi.
Usually sirf mere bhai Chinu ko pata hota tha ki main kya karne wala hu. Isbar uske liye bhi surprise tha toh thoda load tha mujhe.

Dubai jab me aaya.. isbaar cheezein alag thi.
Jaise hi land kiya, ek representative mujhe receive karne aaya. Mujhe Jumeirah ke office le gaya documentation ke liye,
Uss moment mujhe 100% confirm ho gaya — yeh sab genuine hai.
Isbar hum hotel ki ek luxury car main accommodation ja rahe the.
Aur woh drive... main har second enjoy kar raha tha — kyunki main Dubai main me tha!
Hum Sheikh Zayed Road se guzar rahe the aur woh lambi lambi buildings dekh kar mere mann me aaya ki ekbar is area me zarur rehne aunga.
Hum accommodation pohoche and it was really nice.
Full hotel wali vibe. Hotel wala bed. Super comfortable home.

Representative ne kaha ki 2 din baad aapko hotel jana hai aur woh mujhe welcome karke chala gaya.

Dekho bhai jo sapna pehle hi sone nahi de raha tha woh ab 2 din ke liye kya sone dega.
Main raat bhar properly so nahi paaya — itna excitement tha.

Main subah utha, ready hua, aur nikal gaya Burj Al Arab ko door se dekhne. Aur jo jo suna tha Dubai me woh sab dekhne ka plan kiya.

Believe nahi kar pa raha tha ki main ye hotel real me dekh raha hu.
Abhi tak toh sirf photos me hi dekhi thi.
Aur ye view real me kaafi zyada sundar tha. Hotel ka view,

2 din Dubai explore karne ke baad, raat me ghar aake soya kyuki agle din mujhe **Burj Al Arab**, The only 7-star. The dream of almost all the hoteliers me job ke liye jana hai.

Subah jaldi uth gaya, hotel ki pick-up vehicle ka wait nahi kiya, seedha cab liya aur nikal gaya Day 1 ke liye.
Itna kisse control hota hai yaar?

Jaise-jaise cab chal rahi thi, hotel mere nazdeek aa raha tha.

Main window se bas usse hi dekh raha tha — fully mesmerized.
Maine driver se bola, "Bridge par hi drop kar do please." Kyunki main waha 2 min khade hokar us hotel ko paas se dekhna chahta tha. Plus mujhe pata nahi tha ki andar kaise jana hai.

Main cab se utra... aur 10 minute tak bas wahin khada hotel ko dekhta raha. Kya view tha yaar... main explain nahi kar sakta.

Main promise karta hoon — agar aap kabhi dekho na us building ko saamne se, toh samajh jaaoge main kya feel kar raha tha.

Security check-in aur documentation karne ke baad main andar gaya aur waha main pighal gaya.
Itna sundar bhi kuch banaya ja sakta hai kya yaar?
Itna surreal feel ho raha tha.

Phir mera induction hua.
Kaafi nationality ke logon se connect hua. Kuch friends bane.
Bohot kuch seekha unse aur phir kuch dino me same routine start hogaya.
Go to work - come back home - sleep - get up - go to work.

Mujhe around 2 mahine apne dream hotel me kaam karte karte ho chuke the. Lekin honestly, main khush nahi feel kar raha tha
Mujhe laga meri growth ruk gai hai, maine seekhna band kardiya hai.
Main poore hotel par toh comment nahi kar sakta par mere department mein staff training ki bohot zarurat thi. Karenge kabhi baat is baare me.

Main agar comparison karoon Taj se toh main Taj ke guest service ko choose karunga. (as an employee baat kar raha hu. As a guest toh abhi experience karna baaki hai)

Haan, duniya ka best hotel hai — infrastructure wise.
Lekin Taj jaisi hospitality nahi thi waha.

Plus mujhe samajh aa gaya tha,
Agar kisi jagah meri growth nahi ho rahi toh main waha reh nahi sakta hu. Mujhe kuch aur dekhna hota tha jaha life mujhe challenge kare, aur main ek behtar version me upgrade hojau.

Ek raat, main aise hi walk kar raha tha, dimag ko clear karne ke liye... tabhi phone baja. **Unknown number.**
Maine phone uthaya—aur ek lady ki awaaz aayi, achi si accent me:
"Is this Jai?"
Maine kaha, "Yes, speaking."

Unhone kaha, "This is Mrs. Lubna Moosa. How's Burj treating you?"
Main andar se confuse tha, lekin maine apne aap ko compose karke bola, "Yeah, things are good ma'am. Long time. How are you?"

Phir unhone kaha, "I have an opportunity for you."
"I'm starting a business and I need your help."

Mrs. Lubna ko 2015 mein maine kaafi time tak hotel me serve kiya tha toh unse ek positive bond bann gaya tha. Plus India me mera network accha hone ke kaaran maine unke businesses me bhi unko help kiya tha. So hamari business related baatein hoti thi, lekin saath business karne ke liye call aana was a surprise.

Main honest ho gaya, bola, "Ma'am, dekho mujhe ye hotel chhodne ka mann horaha hai lekin ek business start karne jitna na experience hai aur na itna paise"

Unka jawaab mere liye life-changing tha—"Mujhe tumhari capabilities pata hai. Let me know whenever you are ready. I have an investor and humein planning start karna hai"

Woh mere liye ek acha push tha
Plus meri Burj ki journey me bhi Mrs. Lubna ka bada role tha
Uss din mujhe realize hua *Integrity and honesty* ek bohot important cheez hai. Meri Mrs. Lubna ki nazar main ek acchi **rapport** banne ke kaaran unhone mujhe is opportunity ke liye choose kiya.

Main 50% ready hogaya tha hotel industry chhodne ke liye par ye ek bada decision tha aur mujhe ek aur zyada bada push chahiye tha.

Ek din hotel ke banquet hall mein ek bada event tha, aur waha team ko extra help chahiye thi.

Meri shift abhi khatam hi hui thi, lekin maine volunteer kiya —
"Main help kar lunga event me. Ghar jaakar bhi toh rest hi karna hai."

Main guests ko serve kar raha tha, tabhi meri nazar ek insaan par padi jo stage par apni journey share kar raha tha.

Uski lambi si speech me usne bola, "Maine apni job chhodi... ek bada risk tha apna business shuru karn par ab main apni terms pe zindagi jee raha hoon."

Uss moment... mere andar kuch hil gaya.
Mujhe samajh aa gaya — mujhe kya karna hai.
**"Ab mujhe counter ke doosri side ki life jeeni hai."**

Life kabhi kabhi aapko jo chahiye uske liye signs deti hai
Mera maanna hai ki woh signs aap tab hi accept karein jab aap 'paas aur fail' dono results ke liye ready ho.
Event ke baad, bina time waste kiye main HR ke paas gaya aur resign daal diya.
**Kya ye ek stupid decision tha?** Agey batata hu

Maine resign kar diya — uss hotel se jiska main saalon se sapne dekhta tha. Baad mein mujhe pata chala — mujhe 5000 Dirhams fine dena padega jo ki india ka 1 lac rs. hota tha, kyunki UAE mein contract poora kiye bina resign karne par yeh rule tha.
India me toh main aise hi chhod jata tha.

Lekin honestly — mujhe fark nahi pada.
Hotel industry ko maine alvida keh kar — ek naye sapne, ek naye mission ke saath agey badha.

**Note**: *Jab main aapko stories bata raha hu na toh isme bohot zyada main explain nahi kar sakta. Jo bhi main decisions le raha tha isme bohot saare factors involved hai. Pages zyada na ho isiliye short me explain kar raha hu. Kabhi seminars ya trainings me detail me bataunga.*

Hotel se bahar nikla apni learnings ki potli lekar aur pehle toh hotel ko khoob der tak ache se dekha, aur kaha ki ab guest banke aunga. Phir Mrs. Moosa ko phone kiya aur bola **"I am in."**

She was happy and fortunately she was in Dubai also.

Main unse aur unki family se mila. Unki mumma, unke bacche, husband aur unka bhai. Maine kaam ko samjha aur ek **Food Import Export Business** start karne ki planning ko start kiya.

Kuch din baad, maine flight li aur main pohocha — **Mauritius**.

## IS PROCESS ME EK SKILLS MERE BOHOT KAAM AAI..

## Goal Evaluation

Apne Goals Ka Sahi Hisab-Kitab

Goal evaluation ka matlab hai ye assess karna ki jis raaste par aap chal rahe ho, kya woh aapke long-term goals se match karta hai? Isme reflection, comparison, aur zarurat padne par changes karne ki himmat chhupi hoti hai.

**Goal Evaluation Kyun Zaroori Hai?**

- **Time waste hone se bachaata hai** – Aap samay unn cheezon main nahi lagate jo aapko sach main khushi ya fulfilment nahi deti.
- **Adapt karne ka chance milta hai** – Jaise-jaise aap grow karte ho, aapke goals bhi badalte hain. Evaluation se aap raasta badal sakte ho, bina regret ke.
- **Motivation badhata hai** – Jab aapko dikhta hai ki aapki mehnat ka result mil raha hai, toh commitment automatically strong ho jaata hai.

**Kaise Develop Karein Goal Evaluation Skill?**

- **Regularly reflect karo** – Kya aap khush ho jahan aap life main ho? Kya aap yahi chahte the hamesha?
- **Progress measure karo** – Milestones set karo, aur dekho kya aap us direction main aage badh rahe ho.
- **Feedback lo** – Mentors, colleagues, ya kisi trusted insaan se baat karo. Kabhi-kabhi doosre log aapko aapka true reflection dikhate hain.
- **Change se daro mat** – Agar andar se lagta hai ki yeh raasta galat hai, toh pivot karne mein koi burai nahi. Life ek journey hai — perfect path dhoondhna part of the process hai.

## Activity: Check Karo Apna Goal ka GPS

**Kya Aap Sahi Track Par Ho?**

**Goal Evaluation**

Ye Kyun Karna Hai?

Kabhi-kabhi hum goals set toh kar lete hain, lekin yeh sochte hi nahi:

- Kya yeh goal ab bhi mere liye important hai?
- Kya main sahi steps le raha hoon isse achieve karne ke liye?
- Kya kuch change karne ki zarurat hai?

**Step 1: Ek Current Goal Likho**

**Example**: "Mujhe agle 3 mahine mein ek achhi company mein job chahiye."

Aapka Goal: ____________________________________________

**Step 2: In 6 Sawaalon se Karo Evaluation**

- Kya yeh goal ab bhi mere liye important hai? Kyun?
  Yes / No – Kyun? ______________________________________
- Kya yeh aapke sapno se match karta hai?
  Yes / No – Kyun? ______________________________________
- Kya main actively kaam kar raha hoon iske liye?
  Pichhle 7 din mein maine kya kiya?
  Actions taken: ______________________________________
- Mujhe abhi kya rok raha hai?
  Dar? Skill ki kami? Distractions?
  Challenges: ________________________________________
- Ek chhota change kya kar sakta hoon jo mujhe paas le jaaye?
  Action step: ________________________________________
- Agar main aise hi chalta raha, toh kya goal achieve hoga?
  Yes / No – Kyun? ______________________________________

**Step 3: Har Hafte Ek Check-In Set Karo**

Ek din choose karo (jaise Sunday shaam) jahan aap apne goal ko review karo.

- Kya main sahi track par chala?
- Kya kaam nahi kiya?
- Kya change karna hai next week ke liye?

**Apne liye ek reminder line likho:**

______________________________________________

______________________________________________

______________________________________________

______________________________________________

**Example:** Main sirf goals set nahi karta, main apna direction check karta hoon aur zarurat padne par path change karta hoon."

Ye activity aapko self-aware banati hai, time waste hone se bachati hai, aur galat raaste par jaane se rok sakti hai.

**Note:** Kyuki hamari Self-reflection activities karne ki aadat nahi hai, kisine inki importance batayi nahi toh humein ye time waste lagta hai. Par ye aapko kitna productive bana sakti hai aapko iska idea bhi nahi hai.
So please, aaj se ye activities karna shuru kardo.

## Courage

Dar Ke Aage Growth Hai

Courage ka matlab hai dar ka saamna karna, risk lena, aur uncertain situations mein bhi action lena.
Yeh comfort zone ke bahar jaakar wahi cheezein karne ki himmat hai jo aapke liye truly matter karti hain.

**Courage Kyun Zaroori Hai?**

- **Bold actions lena possible hota hai** – Chahe nayi country shift karna ho, career change karna ho ya business start karna ho, courage ke bina growth mushkil hai.
- **Confidence build hota hai** – Har baar jab aap courage dikhate ho, aapka self-belief strong hota hai.
- **Fear se nikalne mein help milti hai** – Fear of failure, fear of rejection ya fear of unknown aapko rok sakte hain, lekin courage aapko aage badhne ka push deta hai.

**Courage Kaise Build Karein?**

- **Start small** – Chhoti chhoti risks lo jisse confidence aaye.
  **Example**: Meeting mein apni baat rakhna, naye experience try karna.
- **Failure ko growth ka part samjho** – Setbacks ko quitting ka reason mat banao; use learning ka chance samjho.
- **Khud par bharosa rakho** – Apni abilities aur instincts par trust build karo.
- **Brave logon ke saath raho** – Unn logon se seekho jo risk lete hain aur jeet te hain.

**Main ek cheez me believe karta hu -**

Agar koi insaan aap jaha pohochna chahte ho us raaste par aapse thoda sa bhi agey hai na. Aap uske samne ek student bann jao.
Woh kuch na kuch aapko aisa sikha dega jo aapko grow karne me help karega.

## Decision Making – Sahi Faisla, Sahi Raasta

Decision making ka matlab hai multiple options me se best option choose karna, based on available information, intuition aur reasoning.

Yeh skill aapki life ke chhote se bade har decision main kaam aati hai—career, relationships, money, ya daily life.

**Decision Making Kyun Zaroori Hai?**

- **Efficiency badhata hai** – Jab aap quick aur informed decisions lete ho, time waste nahi hota.
- **Stress kam hota hai** – Overthinking aur decisions delay karne se anxiety badhti hai.
- **Better results milte hain** – Acche decisions se aap challenges ko smartly handle kar paate ho.

**Decision-Making Skills Kaise Develop Karein?**

- **Information gather karo** – Decision lene se pehle sabhi options ke baare me research karo.
- **Pros & Cons likho** – Har option ke fayde aur nuksaan note karo. Comparison se clarity milti hai.
- **Instincts par trust karo** – Kabhi kabhi gut feeling bhi sahi direction dikhati hai, especially uncertain situations me.
- **Past se seekho** – Pehle jo decisions liye the unhe analyse karo —kya kaam kiya, kya nahi? Usse future decisions better honge.

**Goal Evaluation, Courage aur Decision-Making Ka Connection**

- Goal Evaluation batata hai ki aap sahi direction me ja rahe ho ya nahi.
- Courage deta hai action lene ki strength.
- Decision Making guide karta hai ki next step kya hona chahiye.

Teeno skills life ke har turn pe aapka guide bante hain. Jab aap sahi decisions lete ho, dar ke aage badhte ho, aur goals review karte ho —tabhi growth hoti hai.

## Activity: The Power of Quick Choices

### Ab Sochna Nahi, Karna Hai!

**Purpose**: Aapko everyday life me quick aur confident decisions lena sikhaana—overthinking se bachane ke liye.

**Step 1: Ek Chhota Decision Choose Karo Jo Aap Delay Kar Rahe Ho** (Chhoti cheez ho lekin real ho)
**Example**: Kya mujhe subah jaldi uthna chahiye ya ek book padhna chalu karni chahiye?
Aapka decision: ______________________________

**Step 2: 10-10-10 Rule Lagao**
Apne aap se 3 sawaal poochho:

- 10 minutes me iska result kya hoga?
- 10 months me?
- 10 years me?

**Step 3: Best vs. Worst Case Socho**

- Agar maine ye decision abhi liya, toh best kya ho sakta hai?
- Worst kya ho sakta hai?
- Kya main worst case handle kar sakta hoon? Yes / No

**Step 4: Abhi Decide Karo (Timer Lagao – 60 Seconds)**
Final decision:

______________________________

Pehla action step ab 24 ghante me lena hai: (first step likho)

______________________________

Quick Reflection
Decision lene ke baad kaisa laga? ____________________

"Success sochne ki speed se nahi, kaam karne ki speed se aati hai."

Chapter 11

# AFTER LEAVING HOSPITALITY

Main hospitality chhod kar Mauritius jaane wale decision se khush toh tha lekin mere andar ka ek middle class ladka ye bol raha tha ki bhai 'jis cheez ki tune itne saal padhai ki, mehnat karke experience liya, yaha tak aaya jaha tak bohot kamm log aa paate hai, hospitality me ek successful career banaya..
Usko tu aise hi chhod raha hai'?
Mere pitaji bhi thode confused the.

**Kya main dara hua tha?** - Ha bilkul tha
**Kya mere paas koi plan tha agar business nahi chala to?**
Nahi bilkul nahi tha

**Toh phir me ye kya karne ja raha tha?**
Pata nahi... Main sirf apne dil ki sunn raha tha aur uss samay jo sahi lag raha tha woh kar raha tha.

**Kya aapko bhi aisa koi decision lena chahiye?**
Agar aap woh insaan ho jo fail hone par kisi ko blame nahi karte aur apne actions ki 100% responsibilities lete ho toh lena chahiye.
Nahi toh rehne do.
Jo blame game khelta hai uske liye risk itni badi risks lena sahi decision nahi hai.
Aur aapko bhi aise insaan ke saath kaam nahi karna chahiye.
Mere andar se ek awaz arahi thi,
Jisne bhi kuch bada kiya hai apni life me, usne badi risks li hai
Aur mere liye ye ek badi risk hai.
Agar mein fail hua toh phirse hospitality me start kar sakta hu
Burj nahi par India me koi toh hotel mujhe job dedega
Lekin agar me businessman bann gaya toh mere parivaar me business mindset aajayega jo abhi tak nahi hai.

## Integrity

Integrity ka matlab hai hamesha sacch bolna, ethical tareeke se kaam karna, aur apne actions me consistency rakhna—even tab bhi jab koi dekh nahi raha ho ya situation tough ho.

**Key Components of Integrity:**

- **Transparency** – Hamesha sach aur transparent rehna, na woh sab chhupana jo batana chahiye aur na jhoot bolna.
- **Consistency** – Har situation me apne principles par tike rehna.
- **Accountability** – Apne actions ki zimmedaari lena, blame shift nahi karna.
- **Moral Courage** – Jab mushkil ho tab bhi apne values ke saath khade rehna.
- **Fairness** – Sabke saath respect aur equality se pesh aana, chahe situation kaisi bhi ho.

**Why Integrity Matters:**

- **Trust Build karta hai** – Jo log integrity dikhate hain, unpe log bharosa karte hain.
- **Reputation strong hoti hai** – Values aur actions me consistency se respect milti hai.
- **Inner Peace milti hai** – Jab aap apne beliefs ke saath aligned hote ho, to guilt aur doubt nahi hota.
- **Dusron ko inspire karta hai** – Aapka integrity dusron ke liye example bann sakta hai.

Decision-making bohot easy hota hai – Jab values aur goals clear hote hain, to decision lena asaan aur ethical hota hai.

## Activity: The Mirror Test

### Kya Main Sach Mein Apne Values Par Jeeta Hoon?

**Step 1: Mirror Questions**

Aaj ke din ke end me mirror ke saamne khade ho jao aur khud se poochho:

- Kya maine aaj kuch aisa bola jo main asli me mean nahi karta? (jaise – fake promise diya, baat badha kar bol di?)
- Kya maine sach chhupaya taaki mushkil se bach jaau ya achha dikhu? (jaise – kisi aur ko blame kiya, zimmedari se bache?)
- Agar meri family ya mentor meri har ek action dekhte, ya mere upar camera laga hota to kya main theek feel karta? (jaise – kaam me, online, ya doston ke saath kaise behave kiya?)

**Apne honest jawab likho:**

Mujhe kis cheez par garv hua: ____________________________________

Mujhe kis baat par doubt ya guilt feel hua: _________________________

**Step 2: Integrity Ka Test – 1 Din Ka Challenge**

Kal ek baar comfort ke bajaye sachai ko choose karo.

**Examples**:

- Kaam ya school/college me apni galti maan lo, chhupao mat.
- Gossip ya jhoot se door raho, chahe sab kar rahe ho.
- Jo promise kiya tha, wo nibhao—even agar thoda mushkil lage.

"Integrity wahi hai jab aap sahi kaam tab bhi karte ho jab koi nahi dekh raha." – C.S. Lewis

**Self Check:**

Kya maine aaj comfort ke bajaye sach bola?

□ Haan □ Nahi

Kya main apni baat par tika raha, chhoti baaton me bhi?

□ Haan □ Nahi

Din ke end me maine khud ke baare me kaise feel kiya?

________________________________________________________________

## How to Develop Integrity

- **Imandaar raho, chahe situation tough ho** – Galti maan lo aur 100% zimmedari uthao.
- **Apne values ke saath khade raho** – Chhote se faayde ke liye apne ethics compromise mat karo.
- **Jo wada kiya, wo nibhao** – Commitment pura karo so that tumhare logon ko lage ki tum dependable ho.
- **Imandaar logon ke saath raho** – Jo log honest hote hain, unka asar tumhari integrity ko bhi strong banata hai.

**Integrity ke Examples (Real Life):**

- Ek wallet milna jisme paisa bhara ho, aur bina kisi ke dekhe uske owner ko wapas dena.
- Kaam me galti hona aur chhupane ke bajaye usse admit karna aur sudharna.
- Jab pressure ho tab bhi apne principles pe compromise na karna —even agar personal faayda ho raha ho.

Dekho Jhooth bolna ek aisi cheez hai jo shuruaat mein chhoti si baat lagti hai, lekin dheere-dheere yeh aadat bann jaata hai. Aapko khud bhi kabhi-kabhi pata nahi chalega ki aap kab jhooth bol rahe ho.

Lekin aapke samne wala? Woh mehsoos kar leta hai. Uska aapke upar bharosa dheere-dheere tootne lagta hai jo aapko pata nahi chalega. Aur ek baar bharosa toot gaya... toh usse dobara jeetna almost namumkin ho jaata hai.

Jhooth temporary comfort de sakta hai, lekin long-term main yeh aapki credibility, aapki image, aur aapke rishton ko silently khokhla kar deta hai.

Jhooth bolke jeetne se behtar hai, sach bolke haar jaana.

Yaad rakhiye, duniya aapke shabdon se zyada, aapki vibe aur intention ko feel karti hai. Jhooth chhupaya ja sakta hai—lekin mehsoos zarur hota hai.

## Rapport Building – Connection Banane Ka Art

Yeh skill hoti hai logon ke saath achha, positive connection banane ki. Jab log tumse easily connect karte hain, toh conversations smooth hoti hain aur trust jaldi banta hai.

**Rapport Building Kyu Zaroori Hai?**

- **Naye mauke milte hain** – Strong relationships se naye business, career, aur growth ke chances badhte hain. Jaisa mere sath hua.
- **Teamwork improve hota hai** – Jab log trust karte hain, toh better cooperation hota hai.
- **Baat-cheet asaan hoti hai** – Jab rapport strong ho, toh conversation natural aur productive bann jaati hai.

**Rapport Banaane Ke Easy Tarike:**

- **Dhyan se suno (Active Listening)** – Puri attention do aur sach mein interest dikhao.
- **Common baat dhundo** – Koi shared experience ya hobby jo connection banaye.
- **Empathy dikhao** – Doosre ke emotions ko samjho aur respect do. Business karte time bhulo nahi ki hum insaan hai.
- **Follow-up karo** – Ek chhoti message ya call se connection strong bana rehta hai.

**Real-Life Example (From Your Story):**

Jab maine Mrs. Lubna ko bina dare bataya ki mujhe kya feel hua uss meeting main aur eventually woh sahi nikla—yeh Integrity thi. Aur kyunki mera unke saath with time rapport strong build ho raha tha, isliye unhone mujhe business ka chance diya.

**Lesson:**

Rapport building aur integrity dono aise skills hain jo sirf doors hi nahi kholte, balki long-term strong relationships banate hain—personal life me bhi aur professional life me bhi.

## Activity: 3-Minute Magic Connection

Trust aur comfort ka connection banaane ka aasaan tareeka – chahe saamne wala stranger ho ya koi jaana-pehchaana.

**Step 1: 3F Formula – Find, Feel, Follow**

Find Common Ground (Kuch common dhoondo).

Poocho ya notice karo:

- Hometown, food choices, movies, cricket, hobbies

**Example**: "Aap bhi Rajasthan se ho? Main Kishangarh se hoon!"

Feel Their Energy (Unki vibe samjho)

Observe karo – kya woh shy hain, energetic hain, ya formal?

Unke tone se gently match karo – isse comfort feel hota hai.

**Example**: Agar saamne wala calmly bol raha hai, toh apni speed bhi thodi slow karo.

Follow with Curiosity (Dilchaspi se baat aage badhao)

Open-ended questions poochho:

- "Aap is field me kaise aaye?"
- "Apne kaam ka sabse accha part kya lagta hai?"

Dhyan se suno.

**Step 2: 1-Day Challenge**

Aaj 3 alag-alag logon se baat karo:

- Ek friend
- Ek stranger (shopkeeper, classmate)
- Ek aapse koi bada (teacher, relative)

Sabke saath 3F Formula use karo.

Likho – kya accha kaam kiya:___________________________________

Likho – kya tough laga:________________________________________

*"Log yaad nahi rakhte tumne kya kaha, woh yaad rakhte hain tumne unhe kaisa feel karwaya." – Maya Angelou*

**Self Check:** Kya saamne wale ne smile kiya ya khul ke baat ki?

□ Yes □ No

Kya maine genuinely suna?

□ Yes □ No

Kya woh dobaara mujhse baat karna chahega/chahegi?

□ Yes □ No (If not, try again properly)

Chapter 12

# MAURITIUS

Main uss darr se door bhagna chahta tha ki maine accha bhala successful career chhod toh diya hai ab main fail na hojau.
Toh main bohot kaam karne laga.

Mauritius business mein apna sab kuch daal diya. Mujhe lagta tha din mein 24 nahi, 50 ghante hone chahiye.
Main itna busy tha ki time ka pata hi nahi chalta kab subah ho rahi hai aur kab raat.

Har din naye hotels, supermarkets, hypermarkets jaata, apne products pitch karta. Business seekhne laga, team ko train kiya, sales wala banda agar deal close nahi kar paya toh main karne pohoch jata tha, kya behtar ho sakta hai bass yahi poore time dimaag me chalta tha.
Mujhse jo ho paa raha tha main sab kar raha tha kyuki koi plan B nahi tha mere paas aur na safety net.

By God's grace and our Karma, hum kuch hi mahino main profit kamaane lage.
Meri din-raat ki mehnat ka result finally mujhe milne laga.

Phir humne ek new product launch karne ka decide kiya aur uske liye humein ek model chahiye tha. I suggested ki ek chhota baccha ho jo mango kha raha hai. Cover par uski picture lagate hai.

Team ne kaha ki aapko hamare mango product ka brand ambassador aur model hona chahiye.

Waisa hi hua.. kuch hi dino me poore Mauritius main meri picture ke sath pamphlets, banners, newspaper me advertisements print the. Humne khoob kaam kiya, aur hum bohot grow karne lage.

## Ek Sapne Jaise 7 Din – Flic en Flac, Mauritius

Kaafi mahino ke nonstop kaam ke baad, humne ek break lene ka decide kiya. Aur mujhe aaj bhi woh week yaad hai...
Mauritius ka Flic en Flac area—jahaan ek hi road par line se khade hain Hilton, Sofitel, Sugar Beach jaise bohot saare 5-star hotels.

Main har ek hotel mein ek ek raat ruka.
Ek din Hilton, agle din Sofitel, uske baad Sugar Beach, aise 7 hotels for 7 nights.
Check-in kiya... 1 din resort explore kiya... poolside coffee, khana, beachside sunset.
Next morning, bag uthaya, seedha doosre hotel main walk-in.
No planning, no taxi, no agenda—
Bas main, mera bag, aur ek naya luxury experience.

Aisa lag raha tha jaise main kisi movie ka hero hoon... ya shayad khud apne sapne main jee raha hoon.
Wahi moments hote hain jo yaad ban jaate hain.
Aur unhi yaadon se lagta hai—haan, maine kuch toh sahi kiya hai

## Ek aur maze ki baat batata hu

Mujhe swimming nahi aati. Lekin Mauritius aakar scuba dive kaise miss kardu?
Hilton me puchne gaya ki Scuba Dive kab aur kaise kar sakta hu
Unhone pucha swimming aati hai?
Main confidently bola 'haa aati hai'. Jo ki jhooth tha.
Unhone kaha aaj shaam ko training ke liye aajao aur kal dive karwa denge. I said 'cool'.
Shaam ko main pool side par gaya, unhone diving suit pehnaya.
Training start hui, suit main kya-kya hai, kaise use karna hai usko.
Main sab kuch seekh raha tha, signs, oxygen kaise lena hai tank se and all. Par mera main focus bass 1 cheez par tha. Agar doobne lago toh paani se bahar kaise aana hai.
Unhone 3 ghante me unke hisaab se sab kuch sikha diya aur bola kal aap 12 baje yahin milo.

Next day apan full ready hokar pohoche.
Ab dekho unko pata hai ki mujhe swimming aati hai, lekin apan ko toh pata haina ki nahi aati toh kuch toh safety settings ON karni padegi na.
Waha 2 aadmi the aur 1 lady. Main gaya lady ke paas aur usko bola ki mujhe karni toh hai scuba dive par mujhe bohot darr lag raha hai, ye mera first time hai toh please aap mere aas paas hi rehna.
Utni hi der me same cheez ek ladki bhi bol gai ki usko bhi darr lag raha hai first time hai isiliye.
Trainer badi pyaar se boli 'I understand, you don't worry'.
Toh bhaiya apan ko apni Katrina mil gai hai aur jaan bachne ka jugaad hogaya hai. Ab banate hai Zindagi Na Milega Dubara.

Ab hum 2 ghante deep sea side me gaye speed boat se aur ek jagah boat rok di gai. Full shanti, dur dur tak sirf paani.
Main Hrithik Roshan wali feel lena chah raha hu lekin darr ke kaaran nahi aa pa rahi.
Ekdum se ek awaz aati hai, GET READY, IT'S TIME TO JUMP.

Bhai apna poora confidence ek second main apne ko chhod ke nikal liya. Ab woh oxygen tank na bohot bhaari hota hai aur suit aur mask bohot weird.
Hum ready hogaye aur boat ke side par humein ulta bethna ko bola gaya. Jaise hi main waha betha, unhone kaha ki ulte hi paani me gir jao.

Dekho bhaiya, training hoti hai 4 feet ke swimming pool main jaha aapko kabhi bhi dar lage toh niche khade ho sakte ho. Yaha main jaise hi paani me gaya, actually, paani me gira, sab blank hogaya. Aisa lag raha ki koi aur duniya main aa gaya hoon. Suddenly mere paas se fish, turtle sab nikalne lag gaye. Apni toh haalat tight hogai.

Training me sikhaya tha ki dheere dheere saans lena so that cylinder me oxygen der tak chale aur pair dheere-dheere chalana.
Main toh darr se sab kuch ulta karne laga. Phir madam aayi, unhone meri aankhon me dekha ekdum jaise Katrina ne Hrithik ki aankhon me dekha tha, aur ishaara kiya 'take it easy, dheere dheere saans lo'. Tab mujhe woh rule yaad aaya and main thoda normal hua.

Ab dekho is kitaab me sirf ye hi nahi bataya ja raha hai ki kya kya karna hai. Isme ye bhi bata raha hu ki kya-kya nahi karna hai jeevan me aapko. Agar swimming nahi aati toh Scuba Dive nahi karo.
Bhai kyuki mujhe aadat nahi hai itna paani me rehne ki, mere dono legs dukhne lag gaye. Main itna thakk gaya thodi der me ki mera mann kar raha hai ki chhod bhai jaan jaaye toh jaaye mujhe toh niche jaakar khada hona hai. Aur swim nahi kiya ja raha tha mujhse.

Maine training me seekha tha ki suit se hawa kamm kaise karte hai so that aap niche ja sako. Maine bina kisi permission ke niche jana chalu kardiya.
Pressure se kaan dard hone lage aur eye glasses main poora khaara paani bhar gaya.
Par mujhe toh khada hona tha toh main niche jaata gaya. Aur finally jab pair rakhne ka chance aaya toh pair fisal gaya aur coral ki mujhe zor se lagi.
Utne me meri trainer ki nazar mujhpar padi ki bhai gaya kaha ye.
Woh daud ke.. matlab jaldi se tair kar mere paas aai aur usne phirse meri aankhon me dekha. Par isbar mujhe katrina ki aankhon se ek badi wali gaali nikalti sunayi di.
Phir jitna time bacha tha usne pure samundar me mujhe haath pakad kar scuba diving karwai.
Jaisa bhi tha par ye meri life ka ek best experience tha.
Mujhe bachpan se bola gaya tha paani se dur rehne ko lekin is experience se mera water activities me interest develop ho gaya.

Next page par photo dekho. Sirf 2 minute photo ke liye usne mera haath chhoda tha. Baaki poore time mujhe tochen kiya gaya tha.

Scuba dive ke baad maine Mauritius mein Surfing seekhi, paddle boating aur Kayaking seekha. Photography ka professional course complete kiya. Wildlife Safari experience ki.

Waha mujhe ek cheez samajh aai ki apni education aur experiences par aap jo paisa kharch karte ho woh expense nahi balki apne upar ek investment hota hai. Tab se main apni income ka ek bada hisaa apni education aur travel par spend karta hu.

Aapko agar is fast paced environment me relevant rehna hai toh aapko apne liye ye investment karna padega.

Business start karne ke baad, hamari traveling kaafi badh gai thi. Main Dubai, Mauritius, India ke beech hi ghumta hota tha.
Facebook par jab traveling ka post daalta tha toh log comments karte the ki 'bhai, pass banwa liya hai kya?'
Kuch time baad ek car lease par bhi le li thi. Ye meri life ki pehli car thi jiski key hamesha mere paas rehti thi. Kabhi bhi leke nikal lo.

Is business ke sath maine social media ka kaam bhi start kardiya aur ek aur taraf se income chalu hogayi.
Yaad hai pehli baar jab main Dubai aaya tha toh meri iccha thi Sheikh Zayed Road par rehne ki? Burj ki car me se dekha tha.
Is dauraan maine 54th floor par ek room rent kiya—Dubai ke sabse posh areas me se ek. Jitna me job me pure mahine kaam karke kamata tha usse zyada yaha ek room ka rent tha. Phir kuch din baad main ek hotel apartment me shift hua. Jo ladka hotel me guests ko dekh ke shock hota tha wahi woh 1 saal ek 5-star hotel me raha.
Metro se chalne wala insaan, ab cabs use karne laga. Har din bahar khaana, luxury ka har wo maza jo afford kar sakta tha, le raha tha.

Mujhe lag raha tha—Burj Al Arab me kaam kiya hai, 2 businesses karta hu... ab mein duniya me kuch bhi kar sakta hoon.
1 saal humne bohot acha kaam kiya. Full luxury life jee.
Waha jo 40 saal se ek brand thi usko shelf se hatakar humne hamari jagah banai jo ki impossible tha.

Sab sahi chal raha tha.. Main zyadatar Mauritius rehne laga. Dubai kuch hi din aata tha.
Subah se raat tak kaam karta tha.. behte bethe weight badhne laga.

Unfortunately, financial ke alawa life ke har aspect me meri growth ruk chuki thi. Aur ek point ke baad financial growth bhi excite nahi kar rahi thi. Aisa lag raha tha bhaagne daudne wala insaan ek jagah ruk chuka hai.
Jaha main rehta tha uss area me log raat me 8 baje so jate the, so koi social life bhi nahi thi. Main poore din kaam karta tha aur raat me akele room me beth kar subah hone ka intezaar.

Mujhe lagne laga ki ye main kya kar raha hu?
Iss age ko maine aise hi jane diya toh baaki cheezein kab karunga, kaise seekhunga?

I started missing Dubai. Dubai jahan main ek time par 5 nationalities ke beech hota tha. Experiences and life ko explore karta tha.

Kuch mahine aise hi nikle, lekin phir life me **ek dhamaka hua.**

Business me issues aane lage.
Jaha hum badi plannings kar rahe the, wahi cheezin slow hone lagi.

Main pehle hi soch raha tha waha se nikalne ka aur mujhe finally ek reason mil gaya wapas Dubai jaane ka.
Bass Mrs. Lubna ko chhodne ka mann nahi tha kyuki woh meri mentor thi aur India ke bahar meri family.

Humne ek mature discussion kiya, decide kiya ki abhi ye business kisi aur ko hand over karte hai aur future me kabhi kuch aur start karenge.

Aur mein dubara Dubai aaya, phirse ek nai shuruaat karne.

Business se income ruk chuki thi lekin expenses same hi the
Kuch hi mahine huve aur paisa khatam ho hone laga kyu jo life me jee rahe tha usko ab afford nahi kar pa raha tha.

Yaha ek badi learning ye thi ki jab paisa ho toh usko manage karna bhi seekho. Maine ye nahi seekha tha.

Sasti jagah dhoondhne laga rehne ke liye, Sheikh Zayed Road par hi. Khane ke paiso tak ki dikkat ho gayi kuch dino me, dosto se udhaar lena pada sirf daily expenses nikalne ke liye.

Ek raat mujhe clearly yaad hai— jo insaan return me change nahi leta tha, woh apne room me 1 dirham ka coin dhoond raha tha sirf ek water bottle kharidne ke liye. Lekin mil hi nahi raha tha.
Aakhir me bathroom se nal ka paani peena pada.

Wo meri zindagi ka ek sabse low point tha, jahan kal tak main luxury me tha, aaj paani kharidne ko 1 Dirham nahi tha.

Maine apni poori life me kabhi bhi apni problems ghar me share nahi ki lekin ye mujhe batana pada kyuki mujhe emotional support chahiye the. Maine Mrs. Lubna ko bhi nahi bataya kyuki woh apne aap ko iska zimmedaar maan leti jo ki sacch nahi tha.

Papa ne mana kiya tha job mat chhod.
Lekin maine unko bola tha ki papa, job main kabhi bhi kar sakta hu.
Lekin business risk lene ke liye mere paas baad me time nahi hoga.

Mere parents baar-baar call karte the—
"Wapas aa jao, ghar aake kuch naya shuru karlo."
Mujhe bhi pata tha, ghar aake sab aasaan ho sakta hai.
Rehna, khana aur ek nayi shuruat easily ho sakti hai.

Lekin andar se ek awaaz keh rahi thi—
"Agar abhi wapas gaya, toh shayad kabhi khud ko upar uthaa nahi paunga."

Mujhe ek cheez realise hui...
Yeh ek pattern ban gaya hai meri zindagi ka.
Main mehnat karta hoon, phir success milti hai.
Cheezein chalne lagti hain, sab appreciate karte hain, aur mujhe bhi accha lagne lagta hai.
Phir ek waqt aata hai... sab kuch repetitive lagne lagta hai.
Roz wahi kaam, wahi routine... aur phir andar se awaaz aati hai —"Kuch toh badalna chahiye, aur experiences lene chahiye."
Aur phir me kuch naya karne ka sochne lagta hu
Aur purana kaam haath se jaane lagta hai
Aur main waapas ground zero pe hota hoon...
Shuruwaat se shuruwaat.

**Maze ki baat batau?**
Mujhe farq nahi padta.
Mujhe yahi zindagi jeene me maza aata tha. Khushi milti thi.
Bass ab apne finances set karna chahta hu taaki kahi rukna na pade.
Logo ko shayad lagta tha main immature hu, casual leta hu life ko, serious nahi hu career ko lekar, lekin baat ye hai ki mujhe yahi sab khush rakhta hai. Jo mann hua woh karliya, job change karli, business badal liya, jaha mann kiya waha chala gaya.

Mujhe school ke exams me zyada kuch aata nahi tha toh ek hi copy me sab kuch likhta tha. Lekin agar ye life end hone ke baad bhagwan ne mujhse pucha liya **'haa bhai Jai, tujhe ek zindagi di thi maine insaan ki, kya kya karke aaya hai?'**
Maa kasam itni supplementary sheets bharunga na ki bhagwan ka dimag kharab hojaega. Aur woh hass ke mujhe bolenge 'zindagi toh tu hi jee ke aaya hai yaar'.
Main sach bata raha hu, bohot saare experience toh main book me likh hi nahi raha hu kyuki aapko lagne lagega ki show off kar raha hai ya fek raha hai.

Accha aap khud imagine karo ki 'aapke paas paisa khatam hogaya'
Ab aap kis thought se zyada pareshan ho:

1. Paisa nahi aapke paas. Ya phir,
2. Logo ko pata chal gaya mere paas paisa nahi hai toh woh kya sochenge mere baare me. 35-40 saal ka hogaya abhi bhi paisa nahi hai iske paas. Berojgaar aadmi.

Bhai log, suno. Main aapko galat guide nahi kar raha.
Na hi bol raha hoon ki paise mat kamao, job chhod do, society se ladd jao, rebel bann jao. Nahi. Paisa kamana bohot zaruri hai.
Main khud ab financial education par kaam karunga. Mujhe 30 tak life seriously nahi leni thi, sirf experience karni thi.
Main bass yeh keh raha hoon — society ke remote pe chalna band karo. Apna remote apne haath me lo.

Zyaadatar log khush nahi hai. Isliye nahi kyuki unki zindagi buri hai. Balki isliye, kyuki unhone apni zindagi jeena hi band kar di hai.
Kisi ko engineer nahi banna tha — bann gaya.
Koi gay hai — aur ladki se shadi karke guilt mein jee raha hai.
Koi family business chala raha hai — sirf isliye kyuki himmat nahi hui apna khud ka raasta choose karne ki.
**Yaar a*ise jiyoge toh jiyoge kab*?**

Main sirf woh karta hu jisme mujhe harr din ka swaad aata hai. Zinda feel hota hai. Jo dil se nikalta hai... jisme kick milti hai... jisme main khush hu. Haa bass ab calculated risks leta hu kyuki ab family bhi saath haina. Aur pehle se zyada grow kar raha hu.
Burj Al Arab me manager nahi bann paaya jo society me zyada acceptable sound karta, but theek haina, abhi main ek educator hu, content creator hu, author, businessman hoon, log mujhse mil kar saath pictures lena chahte hai. Bade brands mere saath kaam karna chahte hai. Ye miss hojata na manager banta toh.

Kaam ke saath-saath khushi ko bhi priority dena start karo.
Ek baar jee ke dekho... apni marzi se.
Kya pata, zindagi tumse maafi maangne lage — itna ignore karne ke liye.

World Heath Organization ke according, 60% log job ya business main burnout feel karte hain — kaam zyada hone ki wajah se nahi, jo woh kaam kar rahe hai usse disconnected feel karne ki wajah se. Log jo kar rahe hai usme woh khush nahi hai.

**Lesson?**
Paisa kamana zaruri hai, lekin khud ko khone ki keemat par nahi.

# Goal Setting

Goal setting ka matlab hota hai – apne sapne ko ek clear aur realistic objective mein badalna, aur usse achieve karne ka proper plan banana. Ye skill aapko batati hai kya chahiye, kaise milega, aur kab tak milega.

**Key Components of Goal Setting**

- **Clarity (Spashtata):**

Goal ko simple aur measurable terms me define karo.
**Example**: "Next 1 months me 20% coures complete karna hai."

- **Purpose (Maqsad):**

Goal aapke values aur vision ke saath align hona chahiye. Sirf dusron ko dekh ke mat banao.

- **Action Plan (Yojana):**

Goal ko chhote-chhote tasks mein divide karo aur deadlines banao.

- **Accountability (Zimmedari):**

Apne progress ko track karo, aur zarurat pade toh strategy badlo.

- **Motivation:**

Apne "Why" ko yaad rakho—kyun chahiye ye goal?
Ye yaad raha toh focus bana rahega.

**Kaise Develop Kare Goal Setting Skills?**

- **SMART Goal Use Karo** – Specific, Measurable, Achievable, Relevant, Time-bound.
  **Example**: "Main 3 mahine mein 5 kg weight lose karungi."
- **Goals likh lo** – Likhe hue goals clear hote hain, aur commitment badhata hai.
- **Bada goal = chhoti steps** – Ek hi baar mein sab nahi hota, small wins par focus karo.
- **Har week progress check karo** – Kya kaam kar raha hai? Kya change karna hai?
- **Flexible raho** – Life unpredictable hai. Zarurat pade toh goal ya plan adjust karo.

"Jis goal ko likha nahi, woh sirf ek sapna hai. Jis goal pe action nahi liya, woh sirf ek idea hai."

## Types of Goals (Goals ke Prakar)

**Short-Term Goals (Chhote Goals):**
Jo 1-3 mahine me achieve ho sakein.
**Example**: Ek course complete karna, ek nayi diary kharidna.

**Mid-Term Goals (Beech ke Goals):**
Jo 1-2 saal me poore ho sakte hain.
**Example**: Apna business shuru karna, iPhone, laptop ya DSLR kharidna.

**Long-Term Goals (Lambe Goals):**
5-10-20 saal ka plan.
**Example**: Apna dream house lena, Lamborghini kharidna, dusra passport lena, etc.

**Types Based on Life Areas**

- **Personal Goals (Khud se jude goals):**

Self-improvement, health, relationships ya well-being se related.
**Example**: Fit hona, better communication seekhna, apne family ke saath time spend karna.

- **Professional Goals (Career ke goals):**

Job growth, skills ka development, ya financial success ke around.
**Example**: Ek high-paying job lena, apna business badhana, naye clients laana.

**Lesson:**
Kabhi kabhi goal change karne ke liye courage chahiye hota hai.
Jo goal life ko fulfil kare, wahi sahi goal hai.
Master These Skills
✓ Self-motivation
✓ Goal-setting
✓ Self-awareness
Yeh skills sirf career me nahi, puri life me success laati hain.
Satisfaction sirf paise se nahi—growth aur purpose se milta hai.

## Activity: The 3-Level Goal Map

**Apna Sapna Set Karo!**

**Step 1: Write Your BIG Dream (Bada Sapna Likho)**

Agle 3-5 saal mein ek bada goal jo aap achieve karna chahte ho.
(Be bold – job, business, lifestyle, fame, fitness, kuch bhi!)

**Example**: Main apne sheher ka ek successful business owner banna chahta hoon.

**Aapka Sapna:** ____________________________________________

**Step 2: Break It Down – 3 Levels Goal Map**

Yearly Goal (1 Saal ka Goal)

Ek saal mein kya achieve karna hoga jo aapko sapne ke kareeb le jaaye?

**Yearly Goal:** ____________________________________________

Monthly Goal (Iss Mahine ka Focus)

Iss month mein kis pe kaam karna chahiye?

**Monthly Goal:** ____________________________________________

Weekly Goal (Chhote Chhote Kadam)

Iss week mein kya 2-3 chhote kaam kar sakte ho jo aage le jaaye?

**Weekly Goal:** ____________________________________________

**Yearly Goal: Apna business launch karna with 50 customers**
**Monthly Goal:** Product final karna, marketing seekhna
**Weekly Goal**: 5 logon se feedback lena, logo design karna, etc

**Step 3: Deadline Set Karo (Tareekh Fix Karo)**

Apna bada sapna kab tak pura karna hai?

**Date**: ________________________

**Step 4: Aaj Ek Kaam Karo (Start Now!)**

Ek chhota step jo aap Aaj le sakte ho?
(Even chhota kaam chalega – likhna, call karna, research, plan banana)

**Aaj ka Action:** ____________________________________________

**Self-Check: (Apne Aap Se Poochein)**

□ Kya mera goal clear aur measurable hai?
□ Kya maine realistic steps likhe hain?
□ Kya maine aaj apne goal ke liye kuch kiya?

"Goal bina plan ke sirf ek sapna rehta hai." – Antoine de Saint-Exupéry

## Activity: Find Your WHY Fuel

Apne goal ke peeche ka asli reason samjho – jo aapko tough times me bhi chalata rahega.

**Step 1: Kya Chahiye Zindagi Me?**
Ek goal likho jo aap achieve karna chahte ho.
**Example**: Main ek high-paying job chahata hoon kisi bade city me.
Aapka Dream: ____________________________________________

____________________________________________________________

____________________________________________________________

**Step 2: 5 Baar 'WHY' Puchho**
Apne dream ka reason samjho – 5 baar 'kyun' puchho.
Example:
→ Main high-paying job chahata hoon. Kyun?
→ Family ko achha support de sakoon. Kyun?
→ Kyunki unhone mere liye sacrifice kiya hai. Kyun?
→ Unko acchi life dena chahta hoon. Kyun?
→ Mujhe zimmedaari ka ehsaas hai. Kyun?
→ Unko proud feel karwana chahta hoon. Kyun?

**Aapka WHY Ladder:**
Kyun chahiye ye? → __________________________
Kyun important hai? → ________________________
Kyun? → ___________________________________
Kyun? → ___________________________________
Kyun? → ___________________________________

**Step 3: Motivation Statement Banao**

Ek powerful line likho jo aapko yaad dilaye kyun rukna nahi hai.

**Example**: "Main kabhi give up nahi karunga kyunki mujhe apni family ko proud feel karwana hai."

**Aapka Statement:** ___________________________________________

___________________________________________________________

**Step 4: Ek Chhota Action Lo (Aaj Hi)**

Aaj apne goal ke liye ek chhota step lo.

**Aaj ka Action:** ______________________________________________

___________________________________________________________

Har subah 2 minute ke liye aankhein band karke apne dream life ko imagine karo. Feel karo jaise wo sach ho gaya hai.

**Self-Check:**

□ Kya mujhe pata hai mera dream kyun matter karta hai?
□ Kya main apna motivation statement daily padh raha hoon?
□ Kya maine aaj koi ek action liya?

## Time Management

Master Your Time, Master Your Life
Time ek aisi resource hai jo kabhi wapas nahi milti. Sabke paas din ke 24 ghante hote hain, lekin unka use kaise karte ho – wahi farq laata hai.

Time Management ka matlab hai apne tasks aur priorities ko smartly organize karna taaki din ka best use ho aur stress bhi na ho.

**Time Management Kyun Zaroori Hai?**

- Stress kamm hota hai, last-minute bhaag-daud nahi hoti
- Productivity aur efficiency badhti hai
- Family, health aur personal growth ke liye time milta hai
- Goals jaldi achieve hote hain

**Time Ka Sahi Use Kaise Karein?**

- **Prioritize Tasks (80/20 Rule)**

Har task important nahi hota.
Pareto Principle kehta hai ki 80% results aate hain 20% efforts se.
Jo tasks sabse zyada impact karte hain, unpe focus karo.

- **Plan Karo Apna Din Pehle Se**

Har din ek plan ke saath start karo.
Chahe to-do list ho ya time-blocking, pata hona chahiye ki agla step kya hai. Yeh time bachata hai aur focus bana rehta hai.

- **Pomodoro Technique Try Karo**

Chhoti-chhoti bursts me kaam karo:
**25 mins focused work**
**5 mins break**
**4 baar repeat karo, fir ek lambi break lo**
Isse mind fresh rehta hai, aur burnout nahi hota.

- **Multitasking Se Bacho**

Ek time pe ek hi kaam karo. Tasks switch karne se efficiency kam hoti hai aur quality bhi girti hai. Focus banao, kaam jaldi aur behtar hoga.

- **Har Task Ke Liye Deadline Banao**

Jis kaam ki koi deadline nahi hoti, wo kabhi khatam nahi hota. Chahe koi aur deadline na de, khud ko ek deadline do – urgency create hoti hai aur track pe rehte ho.

- **Distractions Ko Control Karo**

Social media, notifications, bekaar meetings – yeh sab time khate hain. Socho tumhein sabse zyada kya distract karta hai aur usse control karo.

- **'Do Not Disturb' mode use karo**

– Messages check karne ka specific time set karo

– No Kehna Seekho. Har kaam "Yes" kehke lena zaroori nahi. Jo tumhare goals se match nahi karta, use politely mana karo.

"Har cheez ke liye haan" bolne se time bhi chala jata hai aur energy bhi.

**Breaks Lo & Achi Neend Lo**

- Brain ko rest chahiye hota hai. Zyada kaam karne se productivity badhne ke bajaye gir sakti hai.
- Short breaks
- Proper sleep = Better focus & energy

**Reminder**

- Time management ka matlab zyada kaam nahi, balki important kaam sahi tarike se karna hai.
- Smart plan banao, focus banao aur apna time control karo – zyada achieve karoge, kam stress me rahoge!

## Activity: 24-Hour Audit

### Time Ka Hisaab-Kitaab

**Step 1: Track Karo Apna Din – Har Ghante Ka Record**

Agle 2 din, har ghante kya kiya, likho.
Honest raho – koi dekh nahi raha.

| Time | Kya Kiya |
|---|---|
| 6 AM – 7 AM | Got ready |
| 7 AM – 8 AM | Gym/Yoga |
| 8 AM – 9 AM | Prayers/meditation |
| 9 PM – 10 PM | Office work |

Aise hi har ghante ka likho jab tak so nahi jaate.
***Phone ke notes ya ek notebook me likhna easy hota hai.***

**Step 2: Analyze Karo – Time Kaha Ja Raha Hai?**

2 din ke baad, 3 cheezein highlight karo:

- **Time Waste** – Scrolling, gossip, aimless net, etc.
- **Productive Time** – Work, study, skill learning
- **Neutral Tim**e – Eating, travel, etc.

**Step 3: Set Karo 3 Non-Negotiables**

Roz ki 3 important cheezein jo tumhe karni hi karni hai growth ke liye.

**Example**:

- 30 min ek new skill seekhna
- 20 min exercise
- 1 hour apne dream/goal pe kaam

**Step 4: Apna Kal Ka Plan Banao – Hour by Hour To-do List**

Raat ko sone se pehle, kal ka plan likho hour-by-hour.

**Self-Check:**

□ Kya maine apna time honestly track kiya?
□ Kya main bekaar cheezo me hours waste kar raha hoon?
□ Kya maine kal ka din plan kiya?
□ Kya maine apne 3 non-negotiables follow kiye?

## Delegation – Kaam Karwana, Smart Tareeke Se

Delegation ek powerful skill hai jo har leader aur business person ko aani chahiye. Ye kaam thopna nahi hota—it's about trust karna aur doosron ko zimmedaari dena, taaki tum important cheezo pe focus kar sako.

Lekin zyada log delegation se darte hain, kyunki sochte hain:
"Mujhse jaldi ho jaayega, kyu kisi ko doon?"
"Mujhse achha koi karega nahi." "Galat ho gaya toh?"

**Sach kya hai?**
Tum sab kuch akela nahi kar sakte. Agar grow karna hai—chahe business ho ya personal life—delegation seekhna hi padega.

**Delegation Kya Hai?**
Delegation matlab kisi aur ko task dena aur uske result ke liye responsible rehna.

**Yeh kya karta hai:**

- Time aur energy bachata hai
- Team ke skills grow karwata hai
- Productivity badhata hai, tum focus kar sakte ho big tasks pe

**Kaise Delegate Karein – Smart Tareeka**
**1. Sahi Insaan Chuno**
Jo task kar sake, skill aur interest dono ho.
Agar naye hain, to guide karne ke liye ready raho.

**2. Expectations Clear Karo**
Task, deadline, aur result kya chahiye—sab clearly explain karo.
Zaroori resources/training bhi do.

**3. Ownership Do**
Micromanage mat karo.
Unhe responsibility do – apne tareeke se kaam karne do.
Unki creativity aur decision-making ko respect karo.

Jab doosre log kaam karte hain, tum leader bante ho, labour nahi.

**Checkpoints Set Karo, Har Time Check Mat Karo**

Task de diya toh peeche padna zaroori nahi.
Sirf important milestones pe follow up karo.
Jab zarurat ho, tab support aur feedback do.

Appreciate Karna Na Bhulo
Unke effort aur results ko recognize karo.
Agar mistake ho jaye toh blame mat karo—learning ka chance do.

**Delegation Mein Galtiyaan Jo Nahi Karni Chahiye**

- **Kaam Thopna Bina Samjhaaye** – Task dekar bhaag mat jao, guide karna bhi zaroori hai.
- **Har Cheez Mein Taang Adana (Micromanage Karna)** – Har choti cheez check karoge toh unka motivation khatam ho jaayega.
- **Kaam Jaldi Wapas Le Lena** – Agar struggle kar rahe hain, toh help karo—task ko cheen mat lo unse.
- **Credit Na Dena** – Credit team ka kaam hai, sirf khud ki tareef mat lo.

**Delegation Superpower Kaise Hai?**

✓ Tum zyada kaam kam samay me kar paate ho.
✓ Team ki confidence aur skills dono grow hote hain.
✓ Tum strategic aur creative kaam pe focus kar pate ho.
✓ Poora system smooth aur efficient chalne lagta hai.

"You can do anything, but you can't do everything."
– Smart leaders delegate, toh tum bhi seekho kaam karwana, kaam mein doobna nahi.

## Teamwork

The Power of Working Together
Teamwork ka matlab hota hai jab log milke ek common goal achieve karte hain. Ye hota hai collaboration, communication aur trust ka game.
Ek strong team sirf talented logon ka group nahi hota—it's about how well they work together.

**Teamwork Kyun Zaroori Hai?**
✓ **Zyada Achieve Karna** – Ek well-coordinated team solo kaam se zyada fast aur efficiently kaam karti hai.
✓ **Creativity Badhata Hai** – Alag-alag perspective se naye ideas aur better solutions milte hain.
✓ **Trust & Support Banta Hai** – Jab team members ek dusre pe rely karte hain, toh belongingness aur motivation badhti hai.
✓ **Stress Kam Hota Hai** – Jab kaam divide hota hai, toh ek hi banda sab kuch nahi karta.
✓ **Leadership & Communication Skills Grow Hote Hain** – Team mein kaam karke log apne lead karne, delegate karne aur clearly express karne ka skill develop karte hain.

**Effective Teamwork Ke Key Elements**

- **Clear Communication** – Openly bolo, actively suno, aur ensure karo ki sab ek hi page par ho.
- **Defined Roles & Responsibilities** – Kaun kya karega yeh clear hona chahiye—confusion kam, efficiency zyada.
- **Mutual Respect** – Har team member ke strengths aur kaam ko value karo.
- **Conflict Resolution** – Ladai-jhagde hote hain, lekin samajh aur compromise se handle karna team ko aur strong banata hai.
- **Shared Goals** – Jab sab ek hi goal pe kaam karte hain, teamwork naturally ho jaata hai.

"Teamwork makes the dream work, but a vision becomes nightmare without a team."

## Chapter 13

# GIRL OUTSIDE METRO STATION

How I decided to take ahead my training journey?

Condition thodi behtar ho chuki thi, main social media, trainings aur events me freelancing karne laga tha.
Ek din main Dubai me ek metro station se bahar nikal raha tha jab kisi ne mujhe awaaz di, “Excuse me, can you take a photo, please?”

Maine dekha ek young lady thi kuch uske friends ke saath.
“Sure,” maine kaha, aur unki photos lene gaya.
Photos lene ke baad, usne casually baat karna start kiya,
“Aap Dubai mein kya kar rahe ho?”
Maine kaha, “Kuch mahino pehle hi Mauritius se wapas aaya hoon, freelancing karta hu events me.”

Maine thodi apni past journey share ki. Usne dhyan se meri baat suni aur pucha,
“Aap hotel industry se ho aur training bhi ki hai toh customer service training karna chahte ho?”
Maine kaha, “Sure, Maine hospitality me 5-6 saal kaam kiya hai”
Usne bola, “Apna CV bhej do.”
Mujhe laga waise hi bola hoga, kyunki aisa aksar hota hai—log CV maangte hain, phir response nahi dete.

Phir bhi, maine bhej diya.
3 din baad, main movie dekhne jaa raha tha, tickets le chuka tha, mera flatmate wait kar raha tha. Tabhi ek phone aaya,

"Kya tum abhi interview ke liye aa sakte ho?"
Main confused tha—movie skip karun ya nahi? Par andar se awaaz aayi—"Jaa, try kar opportunity aai hai toh."
Main interview ke liye chala gaya.
Wahan ek gentleman mile, unhone kuch baatein ki aur phir bola, "When can you join? (Kab join kar sakte ho?)"
Main thoda hairaan ho gaya aur pucha —"Aap interview nahi loge?"
Woh muskuraake bole,
"Interview ho chuka hai aapka. Jo lady aapko metro station ke baahar mili thi, woh hamari group of companies ki CEO hai – Ms. Mehreen Raj."

I was happy and also confused.
Thodi der baad Mehreen office me aai aur mujhe pata laga ye toh koi badi profile hai.
Maine meri salary expectations share ki. Unhone kaha ok.
Main samajh gaya, mata ji ne ek aur kanya bhej di hai life ka naya chapter start karne ke liye.
Maine pucha aap ek conversation par mujhe hire kaise kar sakte ho
She said 'Aapka CV dekha, humein jo chahiye tha aap uske liye best candidate ho, aur baat karne se aapki strengths samajh aagai'.
and then mujhe Dubai main Training Manager ki position mil gayi aur life phirse track par aane lagi.
Company se thoda advance lekar mein phirse acche apartment me shift hua, subah uth kar accha view dekhne laga.
Mera role tha – ek group of companies ke staff ko customer service aur hospitality skills sikhana.

Uss moment pe mujhe feel hua – insaan insaan se milta hai kisi reason se, aur opportunities kahaan se milengi, kabhi pata nahi chalta. Aapko sirf prepared rehna hai, ek accha First Impression banane ke liye.

Ye job milne ke kuch hi din baad mujhe ek aur job offer aaya **Las Vegas, USA** se. Front office department ke liye. 4500 USD Salary, accommodation, transport, food, insurance, everything covered. Par ye baat maine kisi ko nahi batai aur us job ke upar maine apni training journey ko choose kiya.

## The Art of First Impression

Pehli mulaqat mein hi accha impression banana ek kala hai – jisme aap sirf kuch hi seconds mein saamne wale ko impress karte ho.

Aapka appearance, behaviour, communication aur body language milke yeh tay karte hain ki saamne wala aapko kaise yaad rakhega.

**Benefits**

- **Nayi opportunities milti hain** – Jaise meri story me Mehreen se ek casual mulaqat life-changing bann gayi. (agey batata hu)
- **Trust build hota hai** – Strong first impression se log aapko yaad rakhte hain aur dusron ko recommend bhi karte hain.
- **Confidence badhta hai** – Jab aapko pata hota hai ki aap apne aapko acche se present kar rahe ho, toh har interaction smooth ho jaata hai.

**First Impression Kaise Sudhaarein?**

- **Posture aur body language pe dhyan dein** – Seedhe khade ho, eye contact banaayein aur handshake firm ho.
- **Dress appropriately** – Occasion ke hisaab se kapde pehnein jo aapki personality ko suit karein. Hamesha well-dressed raho.
- **Genuine interest dikhayein** – Bas apne baare mein na bolein, saamne wale se connect karne ki koshish karein.
- **Dhyan se sunein** – Nods, facial expressions aur relevant responses se dikhayein ki aap sunn rahe ho.
- **Positive aur open attitude rakhein** – Log unhi se attract hote hain jo warm aur enthusiastic hote hain.

"Pehla impression last impression bann sakta hai – isliye har mulaqat ko apna best shot do."

**Examples of Mastering First Impressions:**

1. **In an Interview:** Time par pahuchna, formal dressing, smile ke saath greeting karna, aur ek firm handshake dena.
2. **At a Networking Event**: Confidently apne aap ko introduce karna, active listening karna, aur business cards ko poise ke saath exchange karna.
3. I**n Social Settings:** Naam yaad rakhna, logo ko comfortable feel karwana, aur conversation mein positive contribution dena.

**Activity:**

Apni first impression practice karo apne friend ya mentor ke saath. Unse pucho ki tumhara appearance, body language aur communication kaisa lag raha tha. Unse feedback lo—kaunsi cheez positive thi aur kaha improvement ki zarurat hai.

***"Aapko kabhi bhi doosra moka nahi milta first impression banaane ka." — Will Rogers***

Chapter 14

# THE LEAP INTO ENTREPRENEURSHIP

Main jab Training Manager ke role mein kaam karne laga, aur yeh experience meri life ka ek bahut hi enriching phase ban gaya.
Is role ke saath-saath, maine company ke liye Business Development aur social media ka kaam bhi handle karna shuru kiya.
Isi dauraan, meri mulakat kuch sharp-minded logon se hui Dubai mein, jinke saath main connect hua via Mehreen, our CEO—the same lady jisne mujhe hire kiya tha. Unse influence hokar unhi ke sath maine apna ek E-commerce business build karna shuru kiya.

**Mera daily schedule kuch aisa tha:**
8 AM se 6 PM – Job
7 PM se 1 AM – Apna business
Friday job off hota tha toh morning to night business trainings.

Yahin se mujhe pehli baar global business aur "work from anywhere" ka concept samajh aaya.
**Life kaafi exciting thi –**

- Do jagah se paise aane lage the (Job aur business)
- Successful logon ka circle tha aur unse bohot kuch seekhne ko mila – work-from-home father ka concept, life kaise jeena chahiye, aur bhi bohot kuch.

**Mujhe lag raha tha sab perfect chal raha hai.**
Lekin 2019 mein ek twist aaya – haha! Ab aap samajh rahe ho na.
Company ne decide kiya ki unhe ab Training Manager nahi chahiye. Unhone pucha ki kya main kamm salary me kaam kar sakta hu?
Mere liye woh possible nahi tha.
Ek pal ke liye toh darr laga – Fix salary nahi aayegi toh manage hoga kya Dubai me? Kharcha toh mast wala hai. Kaise manage karunga?

Lekin kuch waqt baad maine realize kiya –
"Yeh toh mere liye ek opportunity hai" Ab main apne business pe pura focus kar sakta tha, aur apna kuch bada build karne ka time aa gaya tha.

Mehreen emotional thi kyuki hum best friends bann chuke the. Woh nahi chahti thi main waha se jaau par usko apna CEO role bhi nibhana tha. Though main uss company ka social media handle karne wala tha, company se connected rehta par physically waha nahi rehne wala tha.
Ek point par mujhe aisa laga jaise meri training journey ka end ho gaya hai... lekin saath hi kuch naye darwaze khul gaye.
Kyuki hamara business shaam ko chalta tha, toh din ke time mere paas kaafi freedom thi. Yeh meri life ka ek aur major turning point tha. Lekin ek aur challenge saamne tha.

Dubai mein rehne ke liye visa chahiye hota hai, aur meri job khatam hone ke baad mera visa cancel ho gaya tha.

Ab mere paas do options the –

- Ya toh India wapas jau aur waha trainings karu
- ya phir koi raasta nikaalun Dubai rukne ka.

Aur tab, jaise koi magic ho gaya. Mujhe pata chala ki mera ek friend hai Mouzam, jiski Dubai mein apni company hai, uske through main visa le sakta hoon. Aur kuch hi din baad finally main ek Unskilled Labor Visa par Dubai me rehne laga. (Electrician Assistant)

Maine turant decide kiya – India nahi jaunga, main yahin rukunga aur apna kuch bada build karunga.
Aur yahin se meri **freelancing** journey start hui.

Kuch samay ke liye ek aur business meri life me aaya tha, jiske liye sab mana kar rahe the lekin mera dil kiya karne ka aur maine woh kiya. Us phase ne mujhe life ki bohot badi learnings di. Aaj main agar work from home father hu aur life ko apni choices se jeeta hu toh uska reason mere woh mentors hai jo is opportunity ke kaaran mujhe mile the.
Woh business tha ek Network Marketing business.

Mujhe pata tha India me ye business badnaam hai, par main toh curious child hoon, mujhe toh ye bhi try karna tha.
Maine join karne se pehle kuch logo se pucha par sabne mujhe mana kiya. Even mere pitaji ne tak mana kardiya tha par maine unhe kaha 'try karke dekhte haina', and he said, 'dekhle tu.'
Thoda research kiya tha pata chala kaafi saare successful logon ne apni journey me ye business kiya hai.
Mujhe Dubai me kuch aise log mile jinke jaisa main banna chahta tha. Leaders jinhone corporate me kaafi success paai, koi Harvard dropout, koi Palm Jumeirah me villa khareed kar reh rahe hai, Rolls Royce, Tesla, Cadillac, Ferrari drive kar rahe hai aur kaafi khush hai.
Mujhe pata chala ki woh sab milkar ye business kar rahe hai aur maine decide kiya ki **'business ka toh pata nahi par inke saath roz uthne bethne se life change ho sakti hai.'**

Join kiya aur kaafi growth hone lagi meri. Jo mentorship waha mili woh aur kahi nahi mili. Main NM business ko promote nahi kar raha hu, bass ye keh raha hu ki agar aapko successful aur sorted log mil jaaye na jinke saath aap kisi bhi reason se samay bita sako, us mauke ko chhodna mat. Paisa wapas ajayega, samay nahi ayega.

Mujhe aisa lagta tha ki 'yaar jo main seekh raha hu woh sab logon ko seekhna chahiye' toh maine apne close logon ko jisme mujhe potential dikhta tha unhe kaafi push kiya ye business karne ke liye. Kuch ne mujhe join kiya aur kuch ne mujhe galat samjh kar ignore.
Jisne yaha kaam kiya aur ache se trainings li woh aaj kuch na kuch accha kar rahe hai life me, aur jisne nahi kiya woh abhi tak mujhe galat samjhe bethe hai. Mera goal un log se paisa kamane ka nahi tha, woh main waise bhi kama raha tha. Mera goal tha apne logon ko woh opportunity dena jo mujhe ek behtar insaan bana rahi thi.

Ye main aapko isiliye bata raha hu kyuki, Life me kabhi aapko kisi ek random insaan se push mile ga, ya koi opportunity aaegi. Usko samajhna zaroor par kisi ke galat batane ke kaaran chhod mat dena. Mujhe ye opportunity ek stranger se mili thi and I am truly grateful to that person. **2 number ka lage business toh chhod dena.**

**Key Learnings** - Maine Networking aur Relationship building seekhi. Samjha ki Coaching ki importance kya hai life me, ek bada vision hona important kyu hai aur kaise aapki strategic thinking aapko failure me bhi opportunity dekhne me help karti hai.

# Networking & Relationship Building

Logon se milna, connections banana, aur unse meaningful dosti aur professional relationships develop karna hi asli networking hai.
Yeh ek 2-way street hoti hai—sirf lena nahi, dena bhi hota hai.
And its never TAKE AND GIVE, it's always GIVE AND TAKE.

**Mere Liye Networking Ka Kya Matlab Tha?**

- Mujhe job opportunities mili Mehreen ke through.
- Mujhe ek visa ka solution mila Moazam ke zariye.
- Mujhe e-commerce business bhi ek connection ke through mila.
- Mauritius ka raasta bhi aise hi open hua.
- Aur sirf maine receive hi nahi kiya hai, mere through bhi kaafi logo ko jobs ya business opportunities mili hai. Jab aap dene laayak bann jao tab usse zyada return karo jitna aapne receive kiya hai. Ye hi right process hai.

**Networking Se Kya Seekha?**

- Jab aap logon me genuine interest lete ho, toh connections strong bante hain.
- Pehle value do, fir return me kuch expect karo, ya na karo.
- Relationships ko time ke saath nurture karo—bas ek baar milke bhulna nahi. Aur kaam nikalte hi gayab bhi nahi hona. Kabhi ek message, kabhi ek helpful link, kabhi ek coffee meet.

## Networking Kaise Build Karein?

- **Logon ke stories mein interest lo** – Unki journey, unka passion, unke goals samjho.
- **Clear bolo ki tum kya karte ho** – Apne goals, skills ya needs ko asaani se express karo. Follow-up karo.

Connection banaana ek baar ka kaam nahi hai, relationship build karne ke liye regular touch aur right intent chahiye.
Yaad rakho – Apne network ka asli power tab dikhta hai jab mushkil time aata hai.
Mere liye, wo visa wala time ek bada challenge tha... aur ek dost hi solution bana.

## Networking Kyu Zaroori Hai?

- **Opportunities Open Hoti Hain**

Jobs, business partnerships, mentorship ya collaborations—connections se milta hai sab.

- **Support System Banta Hai**

Aise log milte hain jo tumhare growth mein help karte hain—mentors, peers, ya advisors.

- **Naya Seekhne Milta Hai**

Jab tum different backgrounds ke logon se milte ho, tumhare sochne ka nazariya expand hota hai.

- **Tumhara Influence Badhata Hai**

Industry ya apni community mein tumhari value aur reach dono badhti hai.

- **Confidence Boost Hota Hai**

Jab tum logon se baat karte ho, acche logo se relationship build karte ho, tumhara confidence level bhi next level chala jaata hai.

## Networking Ke Types:

### Professional Networking

Colleagues, industry experts ya potential employers se connection banana. Kaise? – Events attend karo, LinkedIn use karo, ya workplace par acchi conversations karo.

### Social Networking

Friends, acquaintances ya common interest wale logon se bond banana. Kaise? – Shared hobbies, social events ya communities ke zariye.

### Strategic Networking

Kisi goal ko achieve karne ke liye specific logon se connection banana—business expand karna ho ya koi collaboration.

### Networking in Real Life – Examples

- Seminar attend karo? Speakers se milo, contact exchange karo.
- LinkedIn pe like-minded professionals ya mentors se connect ho jao.
- Kisi online ya local professional group join karo jo tumhare career ya interest se judi ho.

## Activity: Apna Network Fresh Karo!

**Step 1: 3 Log, 3 Messages**
Apne circle mein se 3 log identify karo jinke saath tumne kaafi time se baat nahi ki hai.
Unko ek thoughtful message bhejo ya ek catch-up call schedule karo.
**Goal**: Relationship ko dobara ignite karna – bas ek "Hello" se shuru karo!

**Mere 3 log:**

1. ______________________________
2. ______________________________
3. ______________________________

**Step 2: Ek Networking Event Attend Karo**
Iss month ek networking event attend karo – virtual ya in-person.
Aur target rakho – kam se kam 5 naye logon se milna, baat karna.
**Tip**: Sirf milna nahi – interest dikhao, unka naam ya story yaad rakho.

**Event Idea**: Seminar, workshop, industry meet-up, ya LinkedIn webinar.

**Remember**:
***"Your network is your net worth." — Porter Gale***
Jo log tumhe jaante hain, wahi tumhari growth ke doors open karte hain. Toh seed lagao, relationship grow karo — results khud milenge.

# Vision and Strategic Thinking

Badi soch + sahi planning = long-term success

### Kya hai Vision aur Strategic Thinking?

Ye skill hoti hai badi picture dekhne ki, future trends samajhne ki, aur ek aise plan par kaam karne ki jo aapko lambi race ka ghoda banaye. Har din chhote actions lena, bade goals se align karna aur time ke saath adapt karte rehna—ye hi vision ke saath kaam karna.

### Kyu Important Hai?

- **Long-Term Success** – Shortcuts se nahi, vision se badi kamyabi milti hai.
- **Smart Decisions** – Soch samajh ke risk lena aur mauka pehchanana aasan hota hai.
- **Adaptability** – Situation badle toh direction adjust karo, lekin goal pe focus bana rahe.
- **Innovation** – Aaj se aage sochna hi naye ideas aur growth ka raasta hai.

### Mere Journey Mein Kaise Kaam Aaya?

Job ko end goal nahi, ek stepping stone maana. Job ke time network banaya, jisse baad mein business main help mili.
Jab job gayi, usse setback nahi, opportunity banaya – freelancing aur business pe shift.
**Job + business + networking** – teenon ko balance karke, freedom ki tayyari ki.

### Kaise Develop Karein Ye Skill?

- **Think Big** – Sirf aaj ka nahi, agle 5-10 saal ka goal socho.
- **Plan Backwards** – "Kaha pahunchna hai?" se shuru karo, phir waha tak jaane ke steps likho.
- **Stay Informed** – Industry trends dekho, books padho, successful logon se seekho.
- **Be Flexible** – Vision clear rakho, lekin raste flexible ho sakte hain.

"Duniya ki sabse badi companies ek idea se bani. Badi soch aur sahi planning, kisi bhi level pe kaam karti hai."

## Activity: "Apna Future Kagaz Pe"

**Step 1: Aankhein Band Karo Aur Visualize Karo**

Ek shaant jagah par baitho. Aankhein band karo aur socho – aaj se 5 saal baad tumhari life kaisi hogi?

Sochne wale points:

- Tum kahan reh rahe ho?
- Kaam kya kar rahe ho?
- Tumhara din kaise shuru hota hai?
- Tumhare aas paas kaun hai?
- Jab subah aankh khulti hai, tum kaisa feel karte ho?

5 minute tak imagine karo – bold socho, clear socho.

**Step 2: Apna Vision 5 Lines Mein Likho**

Ab jo tumne dekha, usse 5 sentences mein likh daalo.

**Example**: Main Goa ke ek sundar sea facing apartment mein rehta hoon, apni khud ki training and marketing company chalata hoon. Main roz subah excited ho ke uthta hoon aur apne parivaar ke saath quality time bitata hoon. Main ek best selling author, best content creator, coach, husband, son, father aur brother hoon.

Main saal me 4 baar international travel karta hu aur international events me bolta hu, aur logo ko unki zindagi badalne me help karta hu. Main apni dream Lambo Urus car drive karta hu, apni choice ki life jeeta hu aur gratitude me rehta hu.

Main healthy, confident aur financially settled hoon. Log mujhe respect dete hain aur kehte hain ki maine unki life main value add ki hai.

Idea laga?

**Ab tum likho:**

________________________________________________

________________________________________________

________________________________________________

**Step 3: Apna Ek Symbol Choose Karo**

Koi ek cheez choose karo jo tumhare sapne ko represent karti ho – **Example**: ek car, ek city ka naam, ek job title, ya ek house ka photo. Uss symbol ko apne phone wallpaper, desk ya wall pe rakh lo – har din yaad rahega.

Tumhara Symbol: ________________________________________

**Step 4: Ek Action Lo – Iss Sapne Ke Taraf**

Ab likho ek chhoti si action jo iss week tumhe apne vision ke kareeb le jaaye.

**Example**: Ek course shuru karna, ek mentor se milna, subah jaldi uthna.

**Tumhara Action Step: ____________________________________**

**Self-Check:**

□ Kya mera vision clear hai ya vague?
□ Kya main excited feel karta hoon jab ise padhta hoon?
□ Kya cheez mujhe rokti hai action lene se?

***"Tumhara vision tabhi clear hoga jab tum apne andar jhakoge ki tumhe chahiye kya. Ye process jitna delay karoge utna nuksaan me rahoge'.***

## Coaching & Mentorship

Dusron ko guide karna, unka saath dena, aur unka best nikalna—yeh hi hai coaching aur mentorship ka magic.
Coaching aur mentorship ka matlab hai apna gyaan, experience aur learnings dusron ke saath share karna—taaki wo grow karein, challenges ko beat karein, aur apna best version ban sakein.

**Kyun Zaroori Hai?**

- **Growth Unlock Hota Hai** – Log apni potential pe kaam karte hain aur nayi heights chhoote hain.
- **Leadership Skill Banti Hai** – Team ko guide karna seekhte ho, strong leader bante ho.
- **Strong Bond Banta Hai** – Coach aur mentee ke beech ek trust aur respect ka relation banta hai.
- **Lifelong Learning Hoti Hai** – Jab dusron ko sikhate ho, khud bhi aur zyada seekhte ho.

**Mere Life Mein Coaching & Mentorship Ka Role**

- Jab main Training Manager tha, tab maine kai professionals ko grow karne mein help kiya.
- Dubai ke mentors ne mera mindset hi change kar diya—business, life aur work ethics ke baare me.
- Unn sab successful logon se seekh ke maine better decisions liye, aur apne businesses build kiye.
- Team building aur leadership ka experience ne ek behtar trainer banaya.

**Kaise Badhayein Coaching & Mentorship Skills?**

- **Khud Example Bano** – Jo advice de rahe ho, khud usse follow karo. Log tumhare actions se inspire hote hain.
- **Dhyan Se Suno** – Samjho ki samne wale ka goal kya hai, struggle kya hai. Bina samjhe advice mat do.
- **Growth Push Karo** – Feedback do—jo improve kar sakein, aur motivate karo ki wo apna best de.
- **Seekhte Raho** – Achhe coach hamesha student rehte hain.

**Coaching ke sath ek aur important skill aayi hai - Feedback.**

## Feedback – Tarakki Ka Mirror

Feedback ka matlab hai — aapko koi bata raha hai ki aap kya accha kar rahe ho, aur kya behtar kar sakte ho. Ye process hoti hai appreciation + suggestion ki, jo aapko improve karne mein madad karti hai—skill ho ya mindset.

**Why Feedback Matters – Kyun Zaroori Hai?**

- **Improvement aata Hai** – Apne skills ko aap polish kar paate ho
- **Self-Awareness Badhti Hai** – Khud ke blind spots dikhte hain.
- **Relationship Strong Hoti Hai** – Open feedback se trust aur collaboration badhta hai. Jab feedback lete ho, to criticism se ghabrate nahi—usko use karke grow karte ho.

**Meri Life Mein Feedback Ka Role**

- **Dubai ke successful logon se feedback mila**—mera business mindset sharp hua, mujhe meri kamiyaan pata chali.
- Training Manager ke role mein, maine bhi feedback diya aur liya—isse meri team bhi grow hui.
- Constructive criticism se mujhe samajh aaya ki kaise ek employee se ek entrepreneur banna hai.
- **Pehle feedback personal lagta tha**—ab samajh aaya, ye growth ka tool hai, attack nahi, aur aapko ye samajhne ke liye maturity chahiye hogi.

**Kaise Banayein Feedback Skill Strong?**

- **Feedback Maango** – Mentor, boss, ya client se pucho: "Aapko kya lagta hai, main behtar kya kar sakta hoon?"
- **Open Mind Rakho** – Feedback se hurt nahi hona, use opportunity ki tarah dekhna.
- **Jab Do, To Clear Do** – Bas "Accha kaam kiya" mat kaho. Bolo kya accha tha aur kya improve kar sakta hai.
- **EQ Use Karo** – Aise bolo ki saamne wala encourage ho, discourage nahi.

Use sandwich method to give feedback
**Appreciation - Feedback - Appreciation**

## Activity: "Feedback Mirror

Khud Ko Dekho, Khud Ko Grow Karo"

**Part 1: Self-Reflection – Pehle Khud Ko Jaano**

In 3 sawaalon ke jawab honestly likho:

- Ek cheez jo main acchi tarah karta hoon jab main kisi ke saath kaam/padhai karta hoon:
- Ek area jahan mujhe lagta hai main improve kar sakta hoon:
- Ek time jab mujhe feedback mila aur usne mujhe grow karne main madad ki:

**Part 2: Feedback Circle – Do Logo Se Pucho**

Do log jinpe aap trust karte ho (friend, colleague, ya family), unse pucho:

"Ek cheez jo main achha karta hoon aur ek cheez jahan main behtar ho sakta hoon"

**Write Their Response:**

Person 1 – Naam: ____________________

- Strength (Taqat): _________________________________
- Improvement (Behtar ho sakta hoon): ______________

Person 2 – Naam: ____________________

- Strength (Taqat): _________________________________
- Improvement (Behtar ho sakta hoon): ______________

**Part 3: Ab Aap Do – Feedback Do 2 Logo Ko**

Kisi friend ya family ko bolo: "Main ek cheez batana chahta hoon jisme tum awesome ho, aur ek jahan tum aur better ho sakte ho—agar open ho to sunne ke liye."

Be kind + Be specific + Rude mat hona.

**Part 4: Reflection – Kaisa Laga?**

Feedback lena kaisa laga?

Feedback dena kaisa laga?

Apne baare mein kya naya seekha?

"Feedback is the breakfast of champions." – Ken Blanchard

Chapter 15

# COMFORT ZONE

Ek waqt aaya jab main job se bhi paisa kama raha tha aur business se bhi. Main phirse wahi luxury me jeene laga tha. Dedh do lakh rupaye mahine ka bina matlab udana, saving na karna, unnecessary logo ko gifts dena. Mere paas business me chhoti si team thi, jo meri baat sunti thi, mujhe respect deti thi. Dheere-dheere woh ego bankar dimaag pe chadhne laga, main comfortable hone laga— aur uska asar mere kaam par padne laga. Business mein problems aane lagi.

**Tab mere mentor ne ek din mujhe call kiya aur poocha:**
"Jai, woh kaunsa kaam hai jo tujhe bilkul pasand nahi?
Jo tu kabhi nahi karega, chahe tu bilkul berozgaar ho?"
**Maine turant jawab diya:**
"Credit card sales wale nahi pasand mujhe. Woh kaam sahi nahi lagta"

Kuch din baad, main UAE ki ek badi financial company – Majid Al Futtaim – ke saath kaam kar raha tha.
Kya kaam tha? **Credit cards bechna.**
Meri mentor ne mujhe wahi kaam karne ko kaha jo mujhe sabse zyada napasand tha.
Ohho rejections? Duniya ke saare 'NOs' mujhe mil rahe the. Har roz.
Uss samay main sochta tha – "Main yeh kyun kar raha hoon?"
Dil se nafrat thi mujhe is kaam se. Par us process me main "Surrender' karna seekh raha tha. *Mentor ne bola karne ka toh karne ka.*
Yeh experience ne meri duniya ko dekhne ka nazariya badal diya.
Business aur sales ko dekhne ka tareeka hi alag ho gaya.
Mujhe samajh aaya: **Life me kuch bada karna hai toh SALES SEEKHNA ZARURI HAI.** Sales sirf numbers nahi hai, logon ka trust jeetna hai
Business sirf profit nahi hai, mindset ka game hai.
Aur kabhi-kabhi, jo kaam hum avoid karte hain, wahi hume sabse zyada sikhaata hai. Ek mahine baad maine aise aise accounts ko credit cards diye jinka bank balance millions of Dirhams me tha. Aur ek cheez dekhne ko mili, ki agar aapko logon ke paas zyada paisa dikh raha hai, car, ghar.. Zaroori nahi hai unke paas sach main itna paisa ho. Mostly big shots jinko maine cards ke liye approch kiya, unke cards reject hogaye because unke upar bohot loans already the aur EMIs bounce ho rahi thi.

**Lesson:**
Jis cheez me tum sabse zyada uncomfortable ho, uss cheez ko pehle karo. Tumhe jeetne se koi nahi rok payega. Meri income phir se grow hone lagi.

## Surrendering

Surrendering ka matlab hota hai apne ego, control, aur zid ko chhodkar process par bharosa karna.
**Hum aaj baat karenge Mentorship lete samay surrender ki.**

Mentorship ke dauraan surrender ka matlab hai apne ego ko side par rakhkar seekhne ke liye khud ko open rakhna. Bahut baar hum mentorship lete toh hai, lekin andar hi andar resist karte hain—mentors ke feedback ko judge karte hain, unn par doubt karte hai, ya unki baat maan ne ke bajaye apni hi soch ko priority dete hain.

**Lekin jab aap truly surrender karte ho, tab:**

- Aap maante ho ki mentor ka experience aapse zyada hai aur kisi reason se aapne unko choose kiya hai.
- Aap apni har baat prove karne ki jagah sunne aur samajhne par focus karte ho.
- Aap feedback ko personal attack nahi, growth ke tool ke roop mein lete ho.
- Aap results pe obsess nahi karte—process pe trust karte ho.

**Example:**
Tumhara mentor kehta hai:
"Stop chasing 10 things. Pick one and go deep."
Tumhara ego kehta hai: "Mujhe sab kuch ek saath karna hai."
Surrender ka matlab hai: "Mujhe apne mentor pe trust hai. Result jo bhi aaye, mujhe ek baar unka process follow karna hai."

**Why It Matters?**

- Mentorship sirf knowledge lene ka process nahi hai, transformation ka process hai.
- Jab tak aap surrender nahi karoge, aap seekhne se zyada resist karoge.
- True growth tab hoti hai jab aap apni conditioning ko tod kar naye perspectives accept karte ho.

"Surrendering in mentorship doesn't mean giving up control of your life—it means giving yourself the gift of guidance.

**Ek story sunata hu, bahut simple story hai, lekin iska message deep aur timeless hai—especially jab hum surrender aur mentorship ki baat karte hain.**

Ek bohot intellegent student ek famous Monk ke paas jata hai life skills seekhne ke liye.
Wo Monk se milte hi kehta hai, “Sir main kaafi kuch pehle se hi jaanta hoon, par mujhe aapse aur gyan lena hai—please mujhe guide karo.”
Monk muskurate hain, aur kehte hain:
“Pehle chai pee lete hain.”
Wo student ke cup mein chai daalne lagte hain...
Cup bhar jaata hai... lekin monk chai daalte hi jaate hain...
Chai cup se bahar girne lagti hai
Student ghabrakar kehta hai:
“Arre! Cup toh full hi hai, isme aur chai nahi jaegi!”

Monk shaant ho kar kehte hain:
“Bilkul waise hi tumhara mind bhi already full hai—apni baatein, assumptions, knowledge, ego, aur 'main sab jaanta hoon' waali soch se.
Jab tak tumhara cup empty nahi hoga, tum kuch naya nahi seekh paoge.”

**Moral:**
"Sikhne ke liye pehle dimag ko khaali karna padta hai."
Surrender karo. Apna ego aur preconceived notions side me rakho aur ek student bann jao. Tabhi mentorship ka asli faayda milega.

Ab saath milkar ek activity karte hai.

## Activity: Let Go to Grow

**Part 1: Kya Tum Kisi Cheez Ko Pakad Ke Baithe Ho?**

Socho ek situation jahan tum stuck ho, frustrated ho, ya overwhelmed feel kar rahe ho.

Uss situation ko short me likho:

Ab apne aap se pucho:

- Iss situation ka kaunsa part mere control mein hai?
- Kaunsa part mere control ke bahar hai?

**Part 2: The Surrender Letter (Apne Liye Ek Chhoti Si Chitthi)**

Ek short letter likho jisme tum surrender kar rahe ho unn cheezon ko jo tumhare control mein nahi hain.

**Start like this:**

"I surrender the need to control... [yahaan likho specific cheezein] I trust my mentor aur sab kuch waise hi hoga jaise hona chahiye, main sirf uss par focus karunga jo main kar sakta hoon."

Write here: ____________________________________________

**Part 3: Anchor Phrase – Bharosa Ka Ek Line**

Ek phrase ya line choose karo jo tumhe yaad dilaye ki surrender power hai.

**Examples**:

- "I trust my mentor and his processes."
- "What's meant for me will find me through these trainings."
- "I let go and let life flow."

Apni line likho yahaan: ____________________________________

Har baar jab tum anxious feel karo, yeh line khud se bolo.

**Part 4: Action Through Surrender**

Ek chhoti si action likho jo tum shanti ke saath le sakte ho—bina control ki chinta ke:

**Action**: ________________________________________________

**Reflection**

Apna letter aur line likhne ke baad kaise feel hua?Agar tum zyada surrender karne lago, to tumhari life mein kya badlega?

"Surrender is not giving up, it's giving in to a greater wisdom."

# Sales Skills

## Har Conversation main Kaam Aayenge

Sales skills wo ability hai jisse tum kisi customer ka need samajh ke unhe convince karte ho ki unka problem tumhara product ya service solve kar sakta hai. Yeh sirf sales job ke liye nahi, zindagi ke har part mein kaam aata hai—negotiation, influence, persuasion sab kuch sales se juda hai.

**Key Components of Sales Skills**

1. **Communication**
   - Apni baat clearly aur confidently rakhna.
   - Customer ko dhyan se sunna (active listening) – kya chahiye unhe, kya problem hai.
   - Apni baat unke style me present karna – har kisi ka approach alag hota hai.
2. **Relationship-Building**
   - Pehle trust jeeto, fir product becho.
   - Unke saath connection banao jisse wo repeat customer ban sakein ya referrals dein.
   - Genuine interest dikhao unke problem aur unke goals mein.
3. **Product Knowledge**
   - Apne product/service ko andar tak samjho.
   - Features nahi, benefits highlight karo.
   - Customer ke doubts aur objections ko confidently handle karo —facts ke saath.
4. **Problem-Solving**
   - Customer ke pain points pakdo.
   - Unke problem ka solution kaise ho tumhare product se— clearly samjhao.
   - Objection aaye to react mat karo, samjho aur empathize karo.
5. **Negotiation**
   - Win-win solution dhoondo—customer bhi khush ho, tum bhi.
   - Price ke neeche mat jao bina value samjhaaye.
   - Flexible raho, lekin apne product/service ki value mat girao.

***'People want to buy but they don't want to be sold.'***

### Time Management in Sales

- **Leads ko priority ke hisaab se handle karna** – sabse pehle unpe kaam karo jinke convert hone ke chances zyada hain.
- **Follow-ups time pe karna** – "bhool gaya" ka excuse sales mein kaam nahi aata.
- **Customer interaction aur paperwork (admin tasks) ke beech balance banana** – sirf kaam karna nahi, smart kaam karna hai.

### Emotional Intelligence

- **Customer ka mood aur emotion samajhna** – kya woh confused hai? Kya wo interested hai? Uss hisaab se approach change karna.
- **Jab rejection mile, panic nahi karna** – calm raho, seekho aur next step lo.
- **Apne emotions ka control rakhna** – overconfidence ya fear dono se sales miss hoti hai.

### Closing Skills

- **Samajhna kab sale close karni hai** – zyada push kiya to customer nikal jayega, right push kiya to sale gayi.
- **Confidently bolo** – "Let's go ahead and get this started."
- **Scarcity ya urgency ka use karo** – "Offer sirf 2 din ke liye valid hai."

### Why Sales Skills Matter

- **Business Grow Hota Hai** – Sales se revenue aata hai, customer base banta hai.
- **Communication Improve Hoti Hai** – Apni baat confidently aur clearly bol paate ho.
- **Relationships Bante Hain** – Trust build hota hai, log loyal bante hain.
- **Rejection Handle Karna Aata Hai** – Har 'no' se seekhte ho aur strong bante ho. Life ke har aspect me ye aapki help karta hai.
- **Har Jagah Kaam Aata Hai** – Chahe relationship ho ya job interview, sales skills har field mein kaam karti hain.

***'People buy people, people don't buy products.'***

## Examples of Sales Skills in Action

Kisi client ko product pitch karna by showing how it solves unki problem. Discount negotiate karna, lekin business ka profit bhi safe rakhna.
Customer ko upsell karna by explaining how ek extra feature zyada value dega unke liye.

**Activity to Improve Sales Skills**

- Create a 1-Minute Sales Pitch
- Pick koi bhi product ya service jo tumhe pasand hai – phone, laptop, fitness plan, anything.

**Apni pitch mein include karo:**

**Hook** – Dhyan kheenchne wali line
**Example**: "Kya aap bhi apna phone roz baar-baar charge karte ho?"

**Benefit-Focused Explanation** – Product kya fayda dega
**Example**: "Ye phone ek baar charge hone ke baad 2 din tak chalega, woh bhi bina hang hua."

**Call to Action** – Customer kya kare
**Example**: "Isko ek baar try karo aur khud feel karo difference."

**Now Do This:**

- Record yourself – 1 min pitch
- Watch it – Kya tone clear thi? Hook effective tha? Convincing lage?
- Improve and re-record if needed.

"Great salespeople are relationship builders who provide value and help their customers win." — Jeffrey Gitomer

## Activity: "Sell Me This Pen – With a Twist"

**Part 1: Understand the Customer**

Pick any item near you – pen, bottle, notebook, etc.

**Step 1: Ask yourself:**

Customer kaun hai? (Student / Office worker / Homemaker / Artist / Traveller)

Unko kya chahiye? (Affordable / Stylish / Durable / Reliable / Time-saving)

Write your customer profile: ______________________________

**Part 2: Highlight the Value – Not Features**

Write 3 benefits jo iss customer ke kaam aayenge. (Features mat likhna – sirf fayda)

**Example** (Pen):

- Exams ke time smooth writing, tension-free.
- Interviews mein professional dikhata hai.
- Jaldi dry hone wali ink, time bachaata hai.

**Your turn – 3 benefits:**

1. ______________________________________________
2. ______________________________________________
3. ______________________________________________

**Part 3: The 1-Minute Pitch**

Ab ek short sales pitch likho – focus karo value aur customer ke benefit pe. **Example**:

"This pen sirf likhne ke liye nahi hai – ye aapke baare me baat karta hai interviews ya meetings main. Ink smooth hai, time save hota hai aur looks professional.

Ye pen nahi – success ka tool hai."

**Now, write yours below :**

## Part 4: Objection Handling

Customer bole: "Bohot mehenga hai."
Ab aisa jawab do jo value pe focus kare.

**Example**:
"Main bilkul samajh sakta hoon, lekin iss cost main aapko presentation aur confidence milta hai, plus stress-free important moments.  Ye ek investment hai Mr. Pareek, sirf product nahi."

Aap **FEEL FELT FOUND** technique bhi use kar sakte ho.
**Feel** - Main samajh sakta hu aap kya feel kar rahe ho
**Felt** - Maine bhi jab ek expensive pen kharida tha, mujhe yahi sab thoughts aa rahe the.
**Found** - Par jab maine kharid kar woh pen use kiya toh mujhe bohot benefits huve. Aur mujhe realize hua ki I found a solution. Mujhe ek perfect pen dhundhne me bohot problems aati thi. Jo accha dikhe mere paas, accha chale (add your experience)

**Your own response (write below):**

______________________________

______________________________

______________________________

______________________________

**Reflection**:
Kya seekha value vs product bechne mein?
Pitch karte waqt kaisa feel hua?

***"People don't buy products;***
***they buy solutions to their problems."***

## Let People Gossip

Gossip failures aur free logon ka favorite past time hai. Aur apne paas waste karne ke liye time nahi hai toh hamara kaam hai uss par se dhyaan hatana aur apni growth par focus karna – bina kisi ke negative comments ya opinions se affect hue. OK?

**Why It's Important?**

- **Dusron ke opinion se azaadi** – Decisions khud ke liye lena seekh jaate ho.
- **Inner strength banti hai** – Apne journey pe trust karna aata hai.
- **Fear of failure kam hota hai** – Jab log kya kahenge chhod dete ho, tabhi bade risks le paate ho.

**Kaise Master Karein Ye Skill?**

- **Self-awareness develop karo** – Apna purpose clear rakho, aur apni self image strong rakho, taaki log kya bolte hain usse farak na pade.
- **Samjho kya sikhne layak hai aur kya sirf noise hai** – Acchi advice lo, baaki ignore karo.
- **Detach rehna seekho** – Log kya bol rahe hain, wo unki soch hai – tumhari nahi.
- **Apne goals pe focus rakho** – Tumhara result sabse bada jawab hoga.
- **Yaad rakho** – Log hamesha bolenge – success pe bhi, failure pe bhi. Toh tum wahi karo jo tumhare liye best hai.

Jo log tumhare peeche baatein karte hain, samjho woh tumhare peeche hain. Agar unke paas kuch accha karne ko hota toh woh bechare kar rahe hote, tumhari baat thodi karte.
Unn par daya karo aur unko acchi acchi energy bhejo. Bechare nasamajh hai, unko nahi samajh aa raha ki woh apna aur apne parivaar ka kitna nuksaan kar rahe hai.

## Chapter 16

# THE HUSTLE AND HIGH PROFILE EVENTS

Business ke saath saath main freelance events, social media handling and trainings dene laga. Iss process me mujhe samajh aaya ki network ke through new opportunities dhoondhni hongi.
Main social media ke zariye logon se milne laga, roz LinkedIn se 1 ya 2 naye log se meeting karta tha. Restaurants me random logo se baat cheet karta tha, aur jahan bhi lagta tha ki accha kaam nikal sakta hai – wahan jaake door knock kar diya karta tha.
Ghar baar chhod kar Dubai sirf aish karne ke liye nahi aaye hai na, Kaam karna hai, life behtar karni hai toh hustle toh karna padega. Comfort Zone chhodna padega.

Dheere dheere sab kuch set hone laga. Mauritius mein jab main kaam karta tha, toh har mahine mujhe 10 din Dubai rehna hota tha. Uss time mere paas accha paisa bhi tha, contacts bhi, toh maine socha is time ka best kaise use karu? Toh maine ek event management course join kiya tha – intention simple tha: jab bhi Dubai aau, ek accha social circle ho, interesting events me jaana mile. Thanks to Dalida who was managing that institute, ye iccha bhi poori hui.
Us course ki learning and contacts mere ab kaam aane lage.
Mujhe Dubai ke kuch sabse high-profile events mein kaam karne ka chance mila.

2019 mein maine events industry mein kadam rakha. Aur maine jitna time yaha bitaya woh bohot fruitful tha.
Maine celebrity manager ke taur pe kaam shuru kiya –
Formula 1 Racing, Sensation Music Awards, Bollywood Awards, International Screen Awards jaise bade events main. Maza tab aaya jab main Pakistan Screen Awards 2020 ka Celebrity Manager bana.
Sirf hum 3 log poora celebrities department manage kar rahe the.
Meri dost Sabrina ke kehne par maine haa toh kardiya lekin jab celebrities aana chalu huve toh 90% logo ko main janta bhi nahi tha. Kabhi bethenge toh bataunga kya kya gadbad hui thi.
Agar aap YouTube search karenge **PISA Awards 2020 Red Carpet,** toh main dikh jaunga aapko waha chill karta hua. (08:45).
Uss process me almost har bade celebrity se mulaqat hui.
Main Dubai ke royal weddings, Interpol conferences, Dubai's first space mission live screening, Dubai Motor Show jaise bohot ache ache events ka important part raha.

Yeh sab experiences ne mujhe unn logon ke beech laa khada kar diya jinke saath milna kabhi uss Kishangarh ke bacche ke liye possible hi nahi tha – aur entertainment & events industry ki real duniya ka exposure diya. Meri kuch badi learning yaha hui jaise ki, **People management, conflict resolution aur teamwork.**

## People Management

People management ka matlab hai logon ko acche se samajhna, unhe motivate karna, aur team ke saath milke goals achieve karna. Isme communication, emotional intelligence, aur leadership jaisi skills include hoti hai.

**Why It's Important?**

- Jab aap alag-alag personalities ke logon ke saath kaam karte ho (specially high-pressure situations me), toh ye skill zaroori hoti hai.
- Strong relationships aur networking build karne me madad milti hai – jo long-term success ke liye kaafi important hai.
- Efficient planning aur execution possible hota hai, especially jab kaam tight deadlines ya big events ka ho.

**Kaise Develop Karein – People Management Skills**

- **Samajhiye alag-alag type ke logon ko** – Har kisi ka nature alag hota hai, unke according apna approach adjust karo.
- **Clear aur confident communication** – Chahe instructions dene ho ya misunderstandings solve karna ho, bolne ka tareeka matter karta hai.
- **Tasks delegate karna seekho** – Har kisi ke strengths pe focus karo aur kaam ussi ke according baanto.
- **Pressure me shaant rehna** – Jab cheezein out of control lagti hain, log unhi leaders ko follow karte hain jo calm rehte hain.

***"Team chalti hai vision se, grow karti hai leadership se, aur jeet-ti hai trust se.".***

## Conflict Resolution

Conflict Resolution ka matlab hai jab do ya do se zyada logon ke beech disagreement ho jaaye, toh uss tension ko suljhana samajhdari, respect, aur communication se.
Conflict hona normal hai—har relationship me hota hai. Lekin usse kaise handle kiya jaata hai, wahi decide karta hai ki relationship strong hoga ya break ho jayega.

**Common Reasons for Conflict:**

- Miscommunication
- Ego clash
- Lack of listening
- Unclear expectations
- Past baggage ya assumptions

**Steps to Resolve Conflict Like a Pro:**

**1. Pause Before You React**

Gussa aaya? Pehle 10 second ka break lo.
React mat karo—**respond karo**. Calm mind se baat karo.

**2. Listen to Understand, Not to Win**

Samne wale ki baat dhyan se suno bina interrupt kiye.
**Pucho**: "Tum aisa kyun feel kar rahe ho?"

**3. Express Without Blame**

"Tu hamesha aisa karta hai" se baat bigadti hai.
Try this instead: "Jab aisa hota hai, mujhe yeh feel hota hai..."

**4. Find Common Ground**

Dono ki problem suno. Dekho ki solution kis baat se bann sakta hai jo dono ke liye fair ho.

**5. Forgive and Let Go**

Baar baar galti batane se problem solve nahi hota.
Kabhi-kabhi chhoti baaton ko chhodna bhi zaroori hota hai.

**Conflict Resolution ka Golden Mantra:**

"We are not against each other. We are against the problem."
Jab aap yeh mindset leke baat karte ho, tab relationship strong hota hai.

***"Jitna jaldi fire ko bujhaoge, utna kam nuksaan hoga."***

## Activity: “Resolve the Roommate Fight”

**Scenario:**
Aap ek room share karte ho 2 roommates ke saath jab aap city mein kaam ya study kar rahe ho. Ek din, dono ke beech badi fight ho jaati hai:

- Anand chahte hain ki lights jaldi off ho kyunki wo subah 5 baje uthte hain.
- Ansh chahte hain ki lights midnight tak on rahein kyunki wo late tak padhte hain.
- Tension badh chuki hai, aap bhi affect ho rahe ho.
- Aap decide karte ho ki aap dono ki fight calmly resolve karoge. Toh aap kya karenge?

**Step 1: Dono Ki Suno**
Anand aur Ansh gussa kyun hai?
2 concerns likho.

Anand ke concerns:
1. ______________________________
2. ______________________________

Ansh ke concerns:
1. ______________________________
2. ______________________________

**Step 2: Common Ground Dhoondo**
Ek aisi cheez jo dono chahte hain ya jisme dono adjust kar sakte hain.
**Example**: Dono apne kaam ya exams ke liye accha perform karna chahte hain.
Aapka answer: ______________________________________

**Step 3: Ek Win-Win Solution Suggest Karo**
Aisa solution socho jo dono ki respect kare.
**Examples**:

- Anand desk lamp use kare.
- 11 PM ke baad quiet hours ho.

Aapka solution: ______________________________________

**Step 4: Shaanti Se Baat Karo**
Ek calm sentence likho jo aap dono se kahoge.
**Example**:
"Dono ki baat sahi hai, chalo aisa solution nikalte hain jisse sab comfortable rahein."
Aapka sentence: ______________________________________

**"Conflict mein humein jeetne ki zarurat nahi, samajhne ki zarurat hoti hai."**

## Chapter 17

# KNOWING HOLLYWOOD

Dubai me business ke regarding meri LinkedIn ke through ek ladki se baat hui. Jis kaam ke liye connect kiya tha woh kaam toh hua nahi, par hamari energy match hui aur hum kabhi kabhi baat kar lete the call ya messages par.

Ek din kuch baat ho rahi thi toh usne mujhe bola, "Mere paas ek project hai jo tumhari personality se perfectly match karta hai, interested ho toh batana"
Mujhe curiosity hui, maine information li aur main interview ke liye chala gaya – honestly, zyada idea nahi tha ki opportunity kya hai.

Jab main wahan pahucha, toh shock ho gaya – saamne Hollywood ki ek badi casting director thi, jo ek business development professional hire karna chahti thi Dubai me projects ke liye.
Aur ye koi normal casting director nahi thi – Fast & Furious 7, Star Trek, 6 Underground jaisi badi films ke liye casting ki thi unhone.
Main interview dene gaya and bohot acchi conversation hui.
Unhone job role samjhaya aur kaha kab start kar sakte ho,
Maine kaha 'Abhi'.

Woh 5-6 mahine bade mazedaar nikle. Ab socho agar main abhi bhi training wali job kar raha hota toh kya main kabhi ye duniya experience kar pata?
Bilkul nahi. ***So, jo hota hai acche ke liye hi hota hai.***
Experience mind-blowing tha. Hollywood ki duniya ko andar se dekhne ka mauka mila – kaise casting hoti hai, kaise behind-the-scenes kaam hota hai, kya lagta hai ek blockbuster film banane me – sab dekha aur samajhne ki koshish ki.

Yaad hai main apne work desk par ek laptop ki photo laga kar rakhta tha jo mera ek dream tha lena.
MacBook Pro (Touch Bar wala)
Job join karte hi mujhe kaam karne ke liye woh laptop diya gaya :)
Woh ek aisa moment tha jab laga – universe is so kind, sab kuch align ho rakha hai, bass aap apne karma karte raho.

## Creativity & Innovation

Creativity ka matlab hai naye ideas, naye tareeke, aur naye solutions sochna.
Aur Innovation ka matlab unn ideas ko real life mein use karke kuch impactful create karna.

**Why It's Important (Kyu Zaruri Hai)?**

- Problem-solving easy ho jata hai – Challenges ka unique tareeke se solution milta hai.
- Especially film aur entertainment industry mein, out-of-the-box socch hi game changer hoti hai.
- Jab aap naye perspective ke saath aate ho, log notice karte hain – you stand out.

**Kaise Develop Kare Creativity aur Innovation?**

- **Alag-alag environments aur cultures explore karo** – Inspiration kahin se bhi mil sakti hai. Interview me creative baatein main isiliye kar paaya kyuki roz main alag-alag logo se alag-alag topics par conversations karta rehta tha.
- **Open-minded raho** – Naye experiments se hi naye ideas aate hain.
- **Trends observe karo** – kya chal raha hai aur usme aap kya naya laa sakte ho?
- **Different socho** - Har kaam ka ek fixed tareeka nahi hota. Socho: "Kya isse aur better kar sakte hain?"

Creativity aur Innovation wahi log laate hain jo risk lene ke liye taiyaar hote hain.

Jab aap same thinking chhod kar kuch hatke sochte ho – wahin se nayi possibilities shuru hoti hain.

# Etiquette

## (Professional Conduct & Social Intelligence)

Etiquette ka matlab hai woh tareeka jisse aap professional aur social settings mein baat karte ho, behave karte ho, aur logon se interact karte ho. Tameez, tahzeeb aur samajhdari.

Yeh ek invisible skill hai jo aapko classy aur well-mannered insaan banati hai—chahe aap office me ho, party me ya social media par.

**Why Etiquette Matters?**

- Aapke etiquette se aapki upbringing aur values reflect hoti hai
- Ye aapko ek accha first impression banane me help karta hai
- Acche etiquette ke kaaran log aapko respect karte hai
- Aapke relationships healthy rehte hai aur professionalism dikhai deta hai

Chahe aap kisi business meet mein ho ya event mein kisi celeb ke saath —
Aapka conduct, tone, aur body language hi aapki pehchaan banaata hai.

## Types of Etiquette & How to Master Them

### Professional Etiquette

Yeh woh tareeke hote hain jo aapko ek workplace ya business setting mein follow karne chahiye.

### Kyu Zaruri Hai?

- Aapka credibility aur respect banta hai professional circles mein.
- Colleagues, clients, aur bosses ke saath strong relationships banane mein help karta hai.
- Misunderstandings aur conflicts avoid hote hain office ya meetings mein.

### Key Aspects

- **Punctuality** – Time pe pohchna meetings aur deadlines ke liye. Dusron ka time respect karo.
- **Workplace Communication** – Polite, short aur professional emails/messages bhejo.
- **Meetings & Calls** – Dhyan se suno, notes lo, aur beech mein interrupt mat karo.
- **Dress Code** – Office ya industry ke dress rules ko follow karo. Pehle impression se pehchaan hoti hai.
- **Confidentiality** – Company ke sensitive information ko kahin share na karo.

### Small Thing, Big Impact:

Agar meeting mein koi bol raha hai, to phone mat check karo aur beech me mat bolo.

Bas dhyan se suno aur jab turn aaye tab calmly respond karo — yeh chhoti si baat, aapko alag level pe le jaa sakti hai.

## Dining Etiquette

Kaise khane ke table par apna best impression banana hai – chahe business ho ya social dinner.

**Kyu Zaruri Hai?**

- Jab aap clients, colleagues, ya VIPs ke saath acchi tarah se khana khate ho, positive impression banta hai.
- Formal dinner me awkward moments avoid karne me help karta hai.
- Aapki politeness aur cultural sense dikhata hai.

**Key Aspects**

- **Cutlery Ka Sahi Use** – Western dining me fork left hand mein, knife right hand mein.
- Khana tab shuru karo jab sabko serve ho jaye. Jaldi mat dikhao.
- **Muh mein khana aur baat nahi** – Chhote bites lo, muh band rakh ke chabao. Respectful lagta hai.
- **Napkin Kaise Use Karein** – Baithte hi lap par rakho, aur mouth ko dab karo, pocho nahi.
- **Excuse Kaise Le** – Table chhodte waqt bolo, “Excuse me for a moment.” Chupke se uthna avoid karo.

Business lunch mein messy food mat order karo jaise spaghetti ya over-saucy dishes. Aur soup slurp mat karo – log judge karte hain!

**Time nikalo, aur ek accha sa dining etiquette ka session lo aur jitna ho sakta hai utna seekho.**

## Email & Digital Etiquette

Jab aap emails, social media, ya kisi bhi digital platform pe baat karte ho – kaise likhna hai, kaise behave karna hai, aur kaise apna professional image banana hai.

**Kyu Zaruri Hai?**

- Texts ya emails mein tone ko galat samjha ja sakta hai – etiquette confusion se bachata hai.
- Online reputation agar strong hoti hai – toh log aapko seriously lete hain.
- Clear aur respectful communication hoti hai – time bhi bachta hai.

**Key Tips:**

- **Greeting ka dhyan rakho** – "Dear Mr. Sharma" bolo, "Hey" nahi.
- **Email short aur clear likho** – lambe aur confusing emails bore karte hain.
- **ALL CAPS mat likho** – lagta hai chillaa rahe ho!
- **Jaldi reply karo** – zyada late karna unprofessional lagta hai.
- **Soch kar post karo** – online duniya mein aapki image sab kuch hai. Aapko bina jaane log aapke online behavior se aapki image bana lete hai.

**Example:**

"Hey, let's meet tomorrow."

"Dear [Name], Can we meet at 3 PM tomorrow for a quick catch-up?"

## Workplace Etiquette

Office mein woh chhupe hue rules jo aapki respect aur growth dono decide karte hain.

**Kyu Zaruri Hai?**

- Office environment positive aur respectful rehta hai.
- Unnecessary conflicts se bacch jate ho.
- Career growth fast hoti hai – log aapko respect dete hain.

**Key Tips:**

- **Shared space ka khayal rakho** – pantry ya meeting room mein gandgi mat chhodo.
- **Gossip mat karo** – office politics image kharab karti hai.
- **Boundaries samjho** – jab koi busy ho, disturb mat karo.
- **Meetings mein phone silent rakho** – distractions avoid karo.
- **Credit do** – kisi ne help ki, toh unka naam lo seniors ke saamne.

**Example:**

Agar kisi colleague ne project complete karne mein madad ki, toh unki contribution mention karo jab boss ke saath discuss karo.

## Cultural Etiquette

Alag-alag cultures ke customs aur traditions ko samajhna aur respect karna.

**Kyu Zaruri Hai?**

- Galti se kisi ko offend karne se bachoge.
- Cross-cultural relationships strong bano.
- Global business mein zyada chances milte hain.

**Key Tips:**

- **Greetings alag hote hain** – Japan mein bow karte hain, Middle East mein handshake har time nahi hota.
- **Business customs samjho** – kuch cultures direct bolte hain, kuch diplomacy ko value dete hain.
- **Religious sensitivities ka dhyan rakho** – kuch gestures ya topics inappropriate hote hain.
- **Meal customs respect karo** – India mein left hand se khana galat mana jata hai. France mein table pe haath rakhna normal hai.
- **Dress code samjho** – International fine dine restaurants mein aap sliders ya sandles me nahi ja sakte ho.

**Example:**

Japan mein business card dono haathon se dena aur lena hota hai. Waha business card ko ek extension of the person maana jata hai. Isliye uska istemal, dena-lena, aur sambhalna bohot hi graceful aur serious tareeke se hota hai.

Ise **Meishi Koukan** kehte hai.

Yeh sirf card dena nahi hota—yeh ek formal ritual hota hai jo respect, professionalism, aur business culture ka hissa hai.

Card dono haath se do ya lo, usey read karo, apna head thoda sa bow karo to show respect aur agar meeting me ho toh card ko table par apne saamne rakho.

Yaad rakhna card par kabhi kuch nahi likhna, ise disrespectful mana jata hai waha.

## Telephone & Video Call Etiquette

Phone ya Zoom call pe baat karte waqt kaise professional aur clear lagein – yeh skill har kisi ko chahiye.

**Kyu Zaruri Hai?**

- Baatein clearly samajh aati hain – communication perfect hota hai.
- Professional impression padta hai – log impress hote hain.
- Body language nahi hoti, toh galat samajhne ka risk kam hota hai.

**Key Tips:**

- **Clearly aur politely bolo** – Na bahut tez, na bahut dheere.
- **Baat short aur point pe rakho** – Dusron ka time respect karo.
- **Mute rakho jab nahi bol rahe ho** – Background noise se distraction hota hai.
- **Camera mein dekh ke baat karo** – Virtual eye contact se connection banta hai.
- **Interrupt mat karo** – Doosra bol raha ho toh usse finish karne do.
- **Video off nahi rakho -** Kisi reason se video off karna hai toh inform karo ya permission lo. Respect the speaker.

**Example:**

Agar meeting reschedule karni hai, toh last moment cancel mat karo – sabko pehle se inform karo.
Chhoti cheezon se, bada farq padta hain. Call pe aapka tone, timing, aur tareeka – sab log yaad rakhte hain.

## Cyber Etiquette & Security Awareness

Online safe rehna bhi important hai.

- Passwords strong rakho, phishing se bacho.
- Fake news ya spam forward mat karo.
- Respect privacy – Apni bhi aur dusron ki bhi.

**Kyun Ye Skills Zaroori Hai?**
Jab India shift kiya, sab kuch online ho gaya:

- Networking face-to-face nahi, DM aur Zoom par.
- Business aur brand ka management – Instagram se.
- Presentations aur collaborations – Virtual duniya se.

Digital duniya mein aap agar sahi tarike se communicate karna seekh gaye toh bohot agey jaoge.

Tumne note kiya hoga na hamare bade buzurg bolte hai, 'pata nahi kya kya karte rehte hai phone me, chat, video call wagerah'.

Agar tumne abhi ye jo chal raha hai woh sab nahi seekha toh agle 4-5 saal me tum bhi abba dabba jabba hojaoge.

Sab kuch bohot fast change ho raha hai, tech bohot speed me grow kar raha hai, AI aur AR duniya chalane wale hai.
Jaise school me jo seekhna hamare zyada kaam nahi aa raha waise hi aap jo abhi kar rahe woh kuch time me relevant shayad nahi rahe.
Please roz kuch naya seekho, grow karte raho samay ke saath, apne aap ko update karte raho.

## Master Etiquette – Set Yourself Apart!

Professional ya social setting – acche etiquette aapko alag banati hai. Yeh sirf rules follow karne ki baat nahi hai — yeh hai respect, samajh, aur adaptability dikhane ki skill.

Business ho ya networking – log aapko seriously lete hain. Casual interaction mein bhi aap positive impression chhodte ho. Har jagah fit hone ka confidence milta hai.

Chahe office meeting ho ya dinner table – jab aap etiquette master kar lete ho, toh log aapko yaad rakhte hain aur respect karte hain.

**Men, additional tip for you**

Open the lid before doing your business and aim right.
(You see the circle? Yes, there!)
Check the pot before stepping out of the washroom.

Chapter 18

# THE DREAM OF BEING ON TV

Yaad hai actor banne wala sapna? Jo meri maa chahti thi kabhi poora na ho. Woh finally poora hua... Kaafi Unexpected Tareeke Se!

Ekdin main ek restaurant mein baitha tha, aur saamne 2 log YouTube ke baare mein kuch baat kar rahe the. Maine kuch mahino pehle hi YouTube start kiya tha.
Jaise hi woh banda conversation khatam karke restaurant se bahar nikla, main bhaag kar gaya aur politely usse pucha,
"Bhai, mujhe social media ke kuch tips de sakte ho? Maine apna YouTube channel chalu kiya hai. Maine suna aapko baat karte huve"

Valeen bhai ne badi kindness se kuch suggestions diye, aur bola,
"Apna YouTube link bhejo mujhe. Dekhta hu."
Aur maine unko bhej diya.

Kuch din baad, mere paas ek lady ka call aaya, Maria.
"Kya aap is date ko free ho? Mujhe ek TV commercial shoot karna hai aapke saath."
Main toh shock ho gaya. Dil mein khushi ka toofan, lekin muh se nikla, "Aap sure ho? Maine aisa kabhi kuch kiya nahi hai."
She smiled and said, "Maine aapke videos dekhein hain. Mujhe pata hai aap kya kar sakte ho."

Shoot ka din aaya. Jaise hi main set par pohocha – mere liye lights, camera, makeup artist, sab ready the– ekdum dream jaisa feel.
Wahan ek director mile – Farid Jillani. Very intellegent.
Unhone badi patience se mujhe guide kiya, process sikhaya.
Pehla shot dene mein toh halat kharab hogai. Kitne retakes huye, mujhe khud yaad nahi. Darr lag raha tha kahin director mujhe nikaal na de set se. Lekin unhone bola,
**"Koi baat nahi Jai, keep going. Hojaega"**
13 ghante me humne do TV ads shoot kiye.

Aur maine ek aur cheez seekhi – *Delegation* – aap agar kaam ko insaan ke strengths ke according delegate kardoge toh, aapki life easy hojaegi.
Set par harr insaan ko apna kaam asigned tha, koi kisi ke kaam me interfere nahi kar raha tha, isiliye hum ek hi din main itna result nikaal paaye.
Wo din main kabhi nahi bhool sakta. Maine uss experience par ek video bhi banaya – taaki wo yaadein hamesha mere saath rahein. Mere YouTube par hai woh video. Resources me aapko mil jeaga.

Shoot khatam hone se pehle, Farid bhai ne mujhe do short films aur kuch aur TV Ads ka offer diya.
Lekin, meri India waapis jaane ki planning thi, isliye wo projects nahi ho paaye. Main abhi bhi touch me hoon unke saath, kya pata future me short films bhi ajaye bhai ki.
Kuch toh bada hoga waise mujhe pata hai.

Par sacch kahu toh us din jo feel hua – woh lights, woh set, make up artist specailly mere liye, woh cameras ke saamne khade hone ka ehsaas – meri zindagi ke sabse memorable moments mein se ek ban gaya. Full hero wali vibe mil gai.
**Us din mujhe phirse ek cheez realize hui**
*Kisi cheez ko agar tum shiddat se chaaho toh poori kaaynaat tumhe usse milane ki koshish me jutt jaati hai.*

Iss process me main apne aap ko thank you bol raha tha ki maine apni presentation skills par kaam kiya hua tha.

## Presentation Skills

### Aise Bolo Ki Log Sunein... Aur Yaad Rakhein

Zindagi mein presentation kaafi important hoti hain – chahe aap idea pitch kar rahe ho, speech de rahe ho, video bana rahe ho ya meeting lead kar rahe ho.

Par honestly, bahut log public speaking se darte hain.
Good news? Presentation skills seekhi ja sakti hain!
Ek zabardast presentation sirf kya bolte ho par depend nahi hoti – kaise bolte ho pe zyada depend karti hai.

**Presentation start karne se pehle ek baat socho:**

- Kis se baat kar raha hoon?
- Unhe kya matter karta hai?
- Main unka kya problem solve kar raha hoon?

Jab aap apne audience ko samajhte ho, tab aapka tone, content, aur examples direct unke heart se connect hote hain.

**Presentation Ko Structure Do – Simple Format**
Ek accha structure audience ko engage karta hai.
**Ye 3 steps follow karo:**

- **Opening** (Hook)

Start with a strong hook – ek interesting kahani, sawal, ya shocking fact jo sabka dhyaan kheench le.

- **Body (Main Points)**

Key points explain karo – examples, data, ya short stories ke through.
Less is more – clarity is power.

- **Closing (Takeaway & Call to Action)**

End with a powerful summary aur ek clear message/action:
"Agar aaj aap sirf ek baat yaad rakhein, toh woh yeh hai..."

## Confidence Se Bolo

**Perfect Nahi, Powerful Bano**

Confidence ka matlab perfect hona nahi hai—iska matlab hai apne words pe believe karna.

**Stand Tall**

Seedhe khade raho – acchi posture se aap confident dikhte bhi ho, feel bhi karte ho.

**Eye Contact**

Audience ke alag-alag parts ki taraf dekho – sab connected feel karenge.

**Filler Words Avoid Karo**

"Um... Uh..." ki jagah short pauses lo – professional sound aayega.

**Pace Control Karo**

Dheere-dheere aur clearly bolo – jaldi mat karo! Har word ka impact banao.

**Agar aap ek PPT use kar rahe hai toh,**

Slides aapka support hain, poora show nahi. Use them smartly:

- **Simple** – Kam text, zyada images
- **Readable** – Bada font, clear contrast
- **Engaging** – Charts, infographics, ya short video daal sakte ho (jab zarurat ho)

Nervousness? Normal Hai!

**Even bade speakers nervous feel karte hain. Par handle kaise karein?**

- **Practice x 3**

Mirror ke saamne bolo, record karo, ya kisi dost ko sunao.

- **Deep Breathing**

Saans andar – saans bahar – heartbeat control mein aayega.

- **Nervous Energy = Excitement**

Khud se bolo: "Mujhe ye topic pasand hai, main isme best hoon.

## Audience Ko Banao Part of the Show

Log wahi presentation yaad rakhte hain jo fun aur interactive ho – sirf boring bolne se kaam nahi chalega!

- **Sawaal Puchho**

"Iss situation ka solution kya ho sakta hai?"
Audience sochegi, connect karegi.

- **Relatable Story Sunao**

Apni ya kisi aur ki kahani batao – log emotions se connect karte hain.

- **Thoda Humor Chalega**

Jahaan fit ho, halka-phulka joke ya funny line daalo – energy behtar hogi room ki.

- **Polls ya Quick Activity**

"Haath uthao jinko ye experience hua ho..."
Audience ka involvement hona = attention pakka!

**Strong Ending Zaroori Hai**

Apne audience ko ek punch do – jo unke dimaag mein chipak jaaye.

- Powerful Quote

"Kamyabi unhi ko milti hai jo bolte nahi, kar ke dikhate hain."

- Call to Action

"Ab aap kya karoge? Ek chhoti action lo, aur apni journey shuru karo."

- Ya koi sawaal ya fact ke saath unko chhod kar jaao

Approximately 75% of the global population experiences some degree of fear or anxiety when speaking in public, according to research.

Baat Perfection Ki Nahi Hai—Connection Ki Hai.
Practice karo, apna style banao, aur audience ka dil jeet lo.
Kal log kisi aur ko sunn rahe the. Agli baar woh kahenge—'Uske session mein jaana hai!'

Chapter 19

# EXPLORING DIFFERENT PATHS

Events, e-commerce, trainings aur entertainment duniya ke saath-saath, maine ek FMCG company aur ek Mystery room game company ke liye freelance business developer ke taur par bhi kaam kiya.
Har din ek naya challenge, har din ek nayi learning.

Main apne aap ko har waqt push karta tha – naye skills seekhna, naye logon se milna, aur aise areas mein kaam karna jo mere comfort zone ke bahar the.

Issi journey mein ek skill ne mori ek dost bankar mera saath diya woh hai – **Small Talk Mastery.**

Chhoti baatein?
Haan, lekin in chhoti baaton ka bada impact hota hai—networking ho, sales ho, ya relationships banana ho.

# Small Talk Mastery

Chhoti baatein, bade connections.
Small talk ek aisi skill hai jisse aap halka-phulka conversation karke logon se connection bana sakte ho. Ye ek door kholne wali chaabi hai—jo deeper conversations aur relationships tak le ja sakti hai.

**Kyun Zaroori Hai?**

- **Networking mein kaam aati hai** – First impression strong banta hai. Zaruri nahi hai kisike paas zyada time nahi ho.
- **Sales** aur business development mein persuasion badhta hai.
- **Awkward silences door ho jaate hain** – baat karna natural lagta hai.
- **Time bachaata hai** – Aap impactful baat kamm samay mein kar paate ho.

**Kaise Master Karein Small Talk?**

- **Quick Introductions ka Funda** – Naam, kya karte ho, aur ek interesting fact – bass, short aur impactful.
- **Logo ki energy samjho** – Shy hai ya outgoing? Formal hai ya chill? Tone uske hisaab se adjust karo.
- **FORM Method use karo**

**F – Family**
**O – Occupation**
**R – Recreation (Hobbies)**
**M - Message (that you want to convey)**

**Example: Main ek Coach hu aur kisi se baat kar raha hu.**
"Apka hometown kaha hai?", "Apka kaam kaise chal raha hai?", "Free time mein kya karna pasand karte ho?", "Maine bhi is industry ke logon ko trainings di hai?"

- **Suno actively** – Sirf bolne ka nahi, samajhne ka bhi art hai. Jo saamne wala keh raha hai, uspe react karo.
- **Concise bolna seekho** – Baat ko jaldi aur clear karne ki practice karo.

Jab small talk naturally ho jaati hai, to sales, networking, aur even interviews super easy lagte hain.

## Activity: "Small Talk Challenge

**Step 1: Start Small – Seedha aur Simple Topics**

Pehle kuch easy topics choose karo, jinke baare mein baat karna aasaan ho: **Examples**:

- Aaj ka weather
- Favorite food ya restaurant
- Latest movie, web series ya book (as per his/her interest)

**Apne 3 topics likho:**

1. ______________________________________________
2. ______________________________________________
3. ______________________________________________

**Step 2: The 2-Minute Rule – Baatchit ki Shuruaat**

Kisi naye ya kam jaane-pehchaane insaan se baat shuru karo (office, neighborhood, event ya party mein).

**Goal: 2 minutes tak chhoti baat karni hai kisi ek topic pe.**

Conversation Starters:

- "Aaj ka weather notice kiya? Kitna [hot/cold] hai na?"
- "Koi acchi web series dekhi recently ya book padhi?"
- "Yahan ka best restaurant kaunsa hai, aapka favorite?"

**Step 3: Keep the Conversation Flowing – Baatchit Ko Behne Do**

- **Open-ended sawaal pucho** – Jo sirf 'yes'/'no' mein na ho.
- **Apne baare mein thoda share karo** – Connection banega.
- **Actively suno** – Eye contact rakho, smile karo, aur sir hilao (nod) to show interest.

**Step 4: Reflect & Improve – Thoda Socho, Thoda Sudharo**

Baatcheet ke baad yeh sawaal khud se pucho:

- Kya maine saamne wale ko comfortable feel karwaya? Kaise?
- Baat natural flow mein thi ya thodi zabardasti wali?
- Kya accha kaam kiya? Next time kya better kar sakta hoon?

"Small talk impress karne ke liye nahi hoti, saamne wale ko valued feel karwane ke liye hoti hai."

Chapter 20

# When COVID hit

Jab COVID aaya, main ek aise apartment mein reh raha tha jiski window se mujhe clear Sheikh Zayed Road dikhti thi, plus Burj Khalifa ka iconic nazaara.
Sheikh Zayed Road, Dubai ki ek main artery hai—jahaan skyscrapers, luxury hotels, aur badi-badi global companies ke headquarters hain. Yahi jagah Dubai ke modernization ka symbol hai—hamesha logon se, traffic se aur energy se bhara hua.
Lekin 2020 main, sab kuch achanak badal gaya.
Pandemic ne Dubai ke fast-paced life ko ekdum pause pe daal diya. Main COVID ke baare me sochta tha ki kuch din ka aur hai ye jo bhi ho raha hai, theek hojayega. Dubai par kuch impact nahi kar sakta. Main yahan safe hu.

Ekdin Sheikh Zayed Road par ek bhi car nahi thi. 12 lanes main ek bhi car nahi, jaha se laakhon cars poore din me pass hoti hai. Saare stores band hone lag gaye. Hospitality sector—jo Dubai ka sabse bada pillar hai—bahut badi hit le chuka tha. Tourism bhi almost ruk gaya. Offices remote work par shift ho gaye, aur duniya ki jo sabse busy streets me se ek hai, woh ekdum se sunsaan ho gai.

Maine news dekhi toh mujhe thoda sa darr lagne laga, ajeeb sa feel ho raha tha, jaise koi nightmare ho.
Main naturally ek positive insaan hoon. Main negativity me khud ko drag nahi hone deta. Toh maine news ke sab sources ko side me rakha, duniya se disconnect kiya apne aap ko aur phirse apni life aur career par focus karne laga.

Ek din, mere mentor ne casually bola,
"Kyu na tu tab tak India me business expand karne pe focus kare jab tak Dubai ka haal theek nahi hota? Waise bhi 1 mahine se ghar se bahar nahi nikla hai, rules itne strict hain. India chala jaa 1 saal."

Bhai main na apna sapna jee raha tha, Bachpan wala. Aur maine kabhi wapas India shift hone ka nahi socha tha.
Shuruaat me toh maine iss idea ko reject kar diya.
Lekin kuch hafton tak jab main ghar mein akela band tha, negativity se surrounded, kahin ja nahi sakta tha, tab woh idea dhire-dhire samajh me aane laga.

Decision simple nahi tha. Aaj main casual tone me bol raha hoon, lekin uss waqt ye decision andar se mujhe tod dene wala tha.
Meri mentor samajh rahi thi mujhe parr unhe uss samay yahi mere liye sahi lag raha tha.
Bohot mind mapping aur strategic planning ke baad, maine decide kiya ki main India wapas jaunga. Aur main sure tha ki ek saal me phirse Dubai laut aaunga.

Jis din maine flight pakdi, aisa lag raha tha jaise apna ek hissa chhod raha hoon. Jaan nikal rahi thi meri Dubai se jaate waqt.

Lekin woh hota haina, aapki life ke kuch decisions aap nahi lete ho, Universe aapke liye le raha hota hai aur uske piche ek bada reason hota hai jiska aapko idea bhi nahi hota.
India move hone ka decision meri life ka ek bohot sahi decision raha. Shayad main agar ye decision nahi leta, meri mentor ki baat nahi maanta, toh lifetime regret karta.

## Strategic Planning

Socho Door Tak, Chalo Smartly

Strategic planning ka matlab hai apne goals ko clearly define karna, priorities set karna, aur ek strong roadmap banana jo aapko long-term success tak le jaaye. Chahe individual ho, business ho ya koi organization—ye skill sabke kaam aati hai. Isse aap smart decisions le sakte ho, resources ko sahi jagah laga sakte ho, aur changing situations ke hisaab se adapt kar sakte ho.

**Strategic Planning ke Key Elements**

✓ **Vision & Goals** – Kya chahiye life se? Clear likho.

✓ **Situation Analysis** – Abhi kaha ho? Kya strengths hai? Kya challenges hai?

✓ **Strategy Development** – Kya tareeka sabse best hoga goal tak pahunchne ka?

✓ **Action Plan** – Strategies ko chhote-chhote steps aur deadlines mein divide karo.

✓ **Execution & Monitoring** – Action lo aur dekhte raho ki kaise chal raha hai.

✓ **Flexibility & Adaptation** – Zarurat pade to plan ko tweak karo, naye mauke pakdo.

**Maine Strategic Planning Kaise Use Kiya**

Jab COVID-19 aaya, maine kya kiya?

- **Situation Assess Ki** – Dubai poori tarah band tha, business slow ho gaya tha.
- **Options Soche** – Dubai mein rukoon ya India jaa ke expand karu? Dubai me bahar nikal nahi sakta lekin mahine ka 10,000 AED basic expense tha, aur India me uske adhe se bhi kamm.
- **Decision Liya** – India shift hokar, business ko expand karne ka.
- **Action Liya** – Focus shift kiya, naye logon se connect kiya.
- **Adapt Kiya** – Long-term changes ke liye khud ko mentally prepare kiya.

Jahan log crisis dekh rahe the, maine wahan opportunity ko samjha. Ye possible hua strategic planning se. Jab aap soch samajh ke step lete ho, life ki uncertainty mein bhi growth possible hoti hai.

## Digital Communication Skills

Online Baat Karne Ka Tareeka Jo Kaam Aaye

Aaj ke digital-first zamaane mein, online communication ek basic skill nahi, ek career superpower hai. Email ho ya Zoom call, Instagram post ho ya WhatsApp message—kaise baat karte ho, wahi farq laata hai.

**Key Skills Jo Zaroori Hai:**

**1. Email & Professional Messaging**

Clear aur professional email likhna aana chahiye.

- Subject line short aur clear ho
- Tone respectful ho – "Please," "Thank you" use karo
- Format – Start, Body, Close (Kya chahiye, kyun, aur action kya hai)

Tools jaise Gmail, Outlook, aur Slack ka use aana chahiye.

**Example**: "Hope you're doing well. I wanted to follow up on..."

**2. Video Communication & Virtual Meetings**

Zoom, Google Meet, Microsoft Teams par confidently baat karna aana chahiye.

- Camera angle sahi ho, light clear ho, mic kaam kare
- Eye contact – Screen nahi, camera mein dekho jab koi important message dena ho.
- Body language – Smile karo, bored ya distracted mat dikho

**Pro Tip**: Background clean aur quiet jagah choose karo.

**3. Content Creation & Digital Storytelling**

- Video banao – YouTube, Reels, TikTok – relatable, engaging aur short.
- Design ya edit karo – Canva, Photoshop, VN, CapCut, InShot jaise tools ka use aana chahiye.

**4. Value + Emotion = Viral Content.**

Effective Texting & Messaging

- WhatsApp ya Telegram pe baat karna bhi ek art hai.
- Formal aur informal tone samjho.
- "Hi Sir, Hope you're well" vs "Bro, kya scene hai?" – Situation ke hisaab se baat karo.
- Spelling aur tone matter karta hai – Jab business baat ho, toh emojis aur short forms avoid karo.
- Ky kr rhe h.. (Aisa message likhna paap me count hota hai)

**5. Online Sales & Negotiation**

Product ya service bechna hai online?

- Value batao, benefit explain karo.
- Objections ko calmly handle karo – "Let me explain how it helps you."
- Close karo confidently – "Shall I go ahead and send the payment link?"

Aaj ka zamaana digital duniya ka hai. Har deal, dosti, aur decision online ho raha hai. Agar tumhe communicate karna aata hai screen ke zariye, toh duniya tumhaari hai.

Detail mein seekhna hai toh main isse related courses launch karne wala hu, stay tuned..

**www.jaivpareek.com**

## Chapter 21

# MOVING BACK TO INDIA

Jab main India wapas aaya, mere parents ki khushi ka thikana nahi tha. Maine 5 saal ghar walo ke saath holi, diwali, rakhi kuch nahi celebrate kiya tha. Meri maa, jo har baar mere jaane par roti thi—uska muskurana dekhkar, Dubai chhodna worth it lag raha tha.

Meri team Jaipur me thi toh maine Jaipur ko apna base banaya. Jaipur mere dil ke kareeb tha—maine yahan apna college kiya tha, jobs ki thi, city ki vibe awesome thi, roads acchi thi, traffic kam tha compared to bade metro cities.

Humne Jaipur mein ek ghar kharida. Nishank ko call kiya jo Delhi mein events ka accha kaam kar raha tha. Maine usse bola, "Apni job chhod de, aur mere saath Jaipur main aa ja kuch acha karenge saath me." Mera ek plan tha—humari family main ek business legacy banani hai. Hum hamesha se job karne waale log rahe hai—average life, average home, average car and bank balance.

Par main chahta tha ki ye sab change ho—na sirf mere liye, balki pure khandaan ke liye.

Mujhe Nishank ke liye bahut strong sense of responsibility thi, aur mera goal tha ki uska apna business ho, apna empire ho.

Pehle kuch mahine sirf humne maze kare kyuki bohot saalon baad dono bhai saath reh rahe the. Phir humne plan karna start kiya ki kaise hum business grow kar sakte hai. Sab kuch online ho gaya tha, to naye skills seekhne padd rahe the—YouTube, social media, digital world ka game. Kuch time baad humne dekha ki jo business hum kar rahe the, woh Nishank ke liye sahi fit nahi tha. Uska interest, uski energy wahan bloom nahi kar rahi thi. Humein feel hua ki uske liye kuch aur sochna padega, kuch aisa jisko karna usko accha lage aur uski growth ho. Har insaan ka apna ek path hota hai. Kisi ke liye jo sahi hai, woh dusre ke liye struggle ban sakta hai. As an elder brother, mera role tha usko samajhna aur uske liye sahi direction dhoondhna. Jaha sab log mere career choices par doubt kar rahe the, woh mere perspectives ko trust kar raha tha.

# Perspective

Mere sheher aur aas-paas ke towns me, kai logon ne meri journey dekh kar hotel management ko career ke roop mein chuna— accha laga dekh ke ki maine kisi tareeke se ek nayi soch shuru ki.

Mujhe yaad hai jab maine pehli baar hotel management karne ka decision liya tha?
Tab logon ka reaction isse bilkul alag tha.
Mujhe log bolte the -
“Tu Brahmin hai, tu waiter banega? Kuch accha hi kar le!”
(You’re a Brahmin, and you want to be a waiter? Do something meaningful)
Main sirf muskura diya aur socha—
"Bhai main front office department me jaane wala hu, lekin agar waiter bhi bann gaya to kya bura hai? Kaam koi chhota-bada nahi hota."

Fast Forward Kuch Saal Baad...
Wahi log jo kabhi judge karte the, ab call karke puchte hai:
“Beta, humare bacche ko hotel management karwana hai, kaha se karwaye?”
Wahi career jisko kabhi unhone “waiter ka kaam” bola tha, ab usme future dikh raha hai.

**Moral of the Story?**
Log badlenge. Soch badlegi. Lekin tum apna kaam karte raho.
Aaj jo log tum par hans rahe hain, kal tumse salah lenge.
Funny how perspectives changes, right?

## Soch Badlo, Duniya Badal Jaayegi

Zindagi ki sacchayi yeh hai ki cheezein kabhi waisi nahi hoti jaisi woh dikhti hain—woh hoti hain jaise hum usse dekhte hain.

Jiska nazariya badal gaya, uske liye wahi duniya ek nayi kahani ban gayi.

- Jab tumhara sapna chhota dikhe, to perspective badlo—shayad sapna nahi, tumhari soch chhoti hai.
- Jab log tumhe underestimate karein, to socho—shayad unhe tumhara potential nahi dikh raha, par tumhe khud pe bharosa hona chahiye.
- Jab duniya tumhe tumhare against lage, to perspective rakho ki—shayad yeh test hai, taaki tum aur strong ban sako.

**Perspective Kya Karta Hai?**

- Problem ko opportunity mein badal deta hai.
- Failure ko feedback bana deta hai.
- Judgement ko curiosity mein badal deta hai.

Jab log mujhe “waiter” kehke judge kar rahe the, maine unke shabdon ko challenge nahi kiya—maine unki soch ko chhod diya aur apna upar kaam karne laga.
Aaj wahi log mujhse salah le rahe hain.

"Duniya wahi dekhti hai jo tum dikhaate ho, lekin tum wahi dekhte ho jo tum sochte ho. Perspective tumhaare haath mein hai."

## The Wildest Rumour Yet

Ek aur story sunata hu. Bohot mazedaar hai.
**Imagine karo**: Aap naye naye videsh gaye ho, aapko road par ek bohot mast Mercedes dikhi, aur aapne uske paas khade hokar picture li aur facebook par DP laga di.

2020 me jab main India aaya toh kuch din mere hometown kishangarh me raha. Kaafi log mujhe social media par contact karke milne aaye usme se ek mere school time ka junior tha. Usne mujhse kaafi der baat ki aur jaate time sehmi si aawaz me mujhse pucha 'Bhaiya ek baat bataoge sacch sacch'. Maine bola 'haa bol na bhai'.
Bola, 'Aap Dubai me kya karte the.'
Maine bataya thoda bohot ki ye ye kiya.
Woh bola 'parr maine toh kuch aur hi stories suni hai. Lekin kyuki maine aapki motivational videos dekhi hai social media par toh bharosa nahi hua unn stories par'
Mujhe interest aaya aur maine kaha bata na, darr mat.
Woh bola 'aap naraz toh nahi honge na'. I said 'na bhai, bol na'.
Usne bataya ki mere hometown me kuch rumours hai ki,
**Jai ko ek Shaikh ne adopt karliya hai Dubai me, woh ek billionaire wali life jee raha hai. Kuch kaam nahi karta bass khata, peeta, travel karta aur sota rehta hai. Jo cars uske social media par dikh rahi hai, Mercedes jo DP me lagi hai woh sab us Shaikh ki hi hai, Jai ka kuch bhi nahi hai.**

**Phir ye baat uski mummy ko pata lag gai toh unhone use phirse India bula liya.**
**Toh woh abhi isiliye phirse India aagaya hai.**

Maine thodi der toh story ko suna, aur phir agle 10 minutes tak meri hasi hi nahi ruki.
Woh shock tha ki mujhe iss baat ka bura kyu nahi lag raha. Par main usko kaise samjhau ki main ghar chhodne ke baad kin cheezon se guzar ke aaya hu. Maine use kuch explain nahi kiya aur bola 'koi baat nahi'.

## Moral?

Jab tum upar uthna shuru karte ho, logon ko tumhari mehnat dikhna band ho jaati hai—unhe sirf result dikhai deta hai.
Aur jab result unki soch ke hisaab se nahi hota, toh woh tumhari ek nayi kahaani bana lete hain.
Par sach kya hai?
Tumhe pata hai tumhara struggle. Tumhe pata hai tumhara journey. Aur asal mein, wahi matter karta hai.
Baaki sab sirf noise hai. Baatein hai.

## Log is hadd tak gir jaate hai ki aapko idea bhi nahi

Maine aaj tak social media par meri 4 fake IDs padki hai.
Woh bhi kaise? Jab main thoda famous hone laga social media par toh mujhe ladkiyon ke messages aane lage 'block kardiya mujhe', 'aur kitni ladkiyon ko dhokha doge?'
Pehle toh mujhe samajh nahi aaya ki ye kya horaha hai, phir mujhe click hua ki koi kisi ke saath kuch galat na karde.

Jab main is case ke deep me gaya toh pata chala ye chaaron ladke the. Jisme se 3 ko main jaanta tha.

1. Mere papa ke friend ka ladka chala raha tha jisse me sirf 10 minute mila tha life me.
2. Dusra mera ek classmate tha jo mera accha friend tha lekin school ke baad usse zyada baat nahi hui thi. Married aur uske bacchi hai.
3. Mere ek relative cousin ka best friend jisse bhi me sirf ek baar hi mila tha, aur iske bhi ek daughter hai.
   Is bhai ne toh hadd kardi thi. Ek muslim ladki ko shadi ke liye propose kardiya tha mere naam ki shadi.com par ID bana kar. Thankfully usne Vini ko message kardiya ki 'aapka pati aapko dhokha de raha hai' toh humein uske baare me pata lag gaya.

4. Somebody unknown. Usko message kiya toh unse ID delete kardi. But mujhe shaayad idea tha woh kaun hai.

Kabhi milenge tab bataunga ki kaise kaise pakad me aaye le log.

## How to Handle Criticism Like a Pro?

"Log kya kahenge?" – Isko handle karna seekho

Criticism zindagi ka ek hissa hai. Chahe career ho, relationships ho ya personal growth—log judge karenge, feedback denge—kabhi positive, kabhi negative. Lekin baat ye hai, aap uss criticism ko handle kaise karte ho?

**Criticism ko pehchano -**

- **Constructive Criticism (Seekhne ka chance)**

"Presentation accha tha, lekin agar zyada examples hote to aur engaging hota."
**Use it** – Improve karo, aur agli baar aur accha karo.

- **Destructive Criticism (Bas neeche girane ke liye)**

"Tumse to kabhi kuch accha ho hi nahi sakta."
**Ignore it** – Ye sirf demotivate karne ke liye hota hai.

- **Self-Criticism (Apna dimaag hi dushman)**

"Main kabhi successful nahi ho paunga."
**Replace it** – "Main seekh raha hoon, main better ho raha hoon."

**Lesson -** Constructive se seekho, destructive ko chhodo, self-criticism par control karo.

**Criticism Ko Personal Attack Mat Samjho**
**Galat Reaction:** "Ye mujhe pasand nahi karte!"
**Sahi Soch:** "Ye mere kaam par feedback hai, meri value pe nahi."

**Ek baat hamesha yaad rakhna—**
Kuch log aapko sirf isliye criticize karte hain kyunki jo zindagi aap jee rahe ho, wahi unka bhi sapna tha. Lekin woh uss sapne ko jee nahi paaye... aur ab jab aap jee rahe ho, unka dard aur adhuraapan unhe chubhne lagta hai.
Aapko 4 logo ke saamne neecha dikhakar unhe temporary relief milta hai. Unka ego kehta hai, "Agar mujhe appreciation nahi mil raha, toh kisiko bhi nahi milni chahiye."
Yeh unki andar ki frustration hai—unresolved pain.
Aapki zindagi ki chamak kisi aur ke andhere se kam nahi honi chahiye. Shine anyway.

## Pause Before Reacting

**Pehla reaction?** – Defend karna ya argue karna.
**Smart reaction?** – Ek deep breath lo, suno, socho... phir response do.

**Example: Jab koi aapke kaam par aapko feedback de.**
**Instant Reaction:** "Tumhe kya pata mere kaam ka?"
**Smart Response:** "Interesting point hai. Aap bata sakte ho kya improve ho sakta hai?"
Yeh response dikhata hai maturity, confidence, aur emotional intelligence.

**Extract Value from Criticism**
Jab feedback chubhta hai, tab bhi usme ek hidden lesson hota hai. Khud se pucho:

- Kya yeh sach hai? (Honestly analyze karo)
- Kya main kuch seekh sakta hoon? (Every feedback is a chance to grow.)
- Kya action lena hai? (Improve karo, adapt karo, ya ignore—agar bekaar hai.)

**Example:**
**Feedback**: "Tumhara leadership style thoda zyada strict hai."
**Response**: "Shayad mujhe thoda flexible hona pade. Main observe karke adjust karunga."
Grace & Confidence Se Respond Karo

**Defensive hone ke bajaye, yeh lines use karo:**

- "Thank you for your feedback." – Simple, mature lagte ho.
- "Aapka perspective valuable hai, aur detail mein bataoge?" – Openness dikhata hai.
- "Main is par sochunga aur dekhunga kaise improve kar sakta hoon." – Positive energy maintain karta hai.

Jab tum criticism handle karte ho class aur confidence ke saath, log tumhe aur zyada respect karte hain.

## Kab Ignore Karna Hai – Yeh Bhi Seekho

Har criticism par reaction dena zaroori nahi hota.
Kuch log sirf jealousy, insecurity, ya negativity se bolte hain.
Agar koi rude hai aur koi value nahi de raha—let it go.

**Rule:**
Jo tumhe grow karne mein help nahi karta, uss par energy waste mat karo.

**Criticism Ko Fuel Banao**
Great leaders, athletes, aur entrepreneurs criticism ko fuel bana kar jeet te hain.
Break hone ke bajaye, usse apna mindset sharp karo aur grow karo.

**Criticism ko use karo:**

- Apne skills improve karne ke liye
- Apni thinking next level pe le jaane ke liye
- Aur jo doubt karte hain, unhe silently prove karne ke liye

**Handling Criticism = Superpower**
Jab tum criticism ko smartly handle karna seekh jaate ho,
koi tumhe rok nahi sakta. Master this, and you'll be unstoppable.

Chapter 22

# MANIFESTING MY FIRST CAR

## i20 – Ek College Ke Time Wali Iccha

College ke time 2011-2012 ki baat hai – maine kisi ki ek din i20 chala li, bohot badhiya lagi. Phir ekdin usse wapas chalane ko bola toh usne kaha bass bhai, chala li na ekbar.
Uss samay i20 was trending aur main toh afford nahi kar sakta tha. Usdin socha tha ki ek din mere paas bhi hogi ye car. Khud se promise kiya tha, jab bhi possible hua, yeh car zaroor lunga.

2020 mein jab India aaya mujhe car ki zarurat bhi mehsoos hone lagi. Ekdin facebook par ad dikha ki i20 ka naya model aa raha hai. Ekdum se woh purana sapna yaad aaya aur lene ka decide kiya. Aisa nahi tha ki usse behtar car nahi le sakta tha. Baat ye thi ki woh college wala jo Jai tha na, uss bhai ko khush karna tha.

Yeh ek brand new car launch hui thi market me, aur main dil se chah raha tha ki sabse pehle main hi loon.
Par twist yeh tha ki 7 din baad ek shaadi attend karni thi Indore me– aur har dealer keh raha tha: "Stock nahi aaya abhi."
Yaad hai maine aapko Law of attraction aur Manifestation ke baare me bataya tha. Meri life na us par hi chalti hai.

Main meri mumma ke paas gaya aur unhe kaha 'Maa, Indore toh apan meri **Brand New Fiery Red Top Model i20 me hi chalenge'.**

**SMART** Goal Setting
**S**pecific, **M**easurable. **A**chievable. **R**ealistic. Time Bound.

Woh hansi – socha ye kuch bhi bolta rehta hai.
Par maine universe aur meri maa ko apna plan bata diya tha.
Aur mujhe uss plan par 1% bhi doubt nahi tha.
Papa bole– 'arey kabhi practical bhi soch liya kar. Market me available hi nahi hai car, kuch hi din toh huve hai car ko launch huve'

Lekin maine accept karne se mana kardiya aur phir mumma ko dekh ke bola 'Maa, Indore toh apan apni i20 me hi chalenge'.

Back to back Ajmer, Kishangarh, Jaipur ke harr showroom ko calls, follow-ups – jo kar sakta tha sab kiya. Lekin sabne bola nahi hai.
Aur agar available hai to Top Model me Red available nahi hai.

Lekin apan ko toh jo chahiye tha wahi chahiye tha. Sapna haina, compromise kaise karlenge. Plus universe ko bol rakha hai, uske liye thodi kuch tough hoga.

Phir maine socha ye nearby cities me nahi mil rahi ekbar, thoda bahar try karte hai. Mere bhai Abhishek ko call kiya, uska network accha hai kaafi. Maine kaha bhai ek Red, i20 Top Model Asta O leni hai, Kisi Hyundai dealership me contact hai.
Woh bola 'ek hai yaar Vijaynagar me'. I was like 'Bhai Jaipur Ajmer me nahi mil rahi, udhar hogi kya?'. Usne bola 'dekhle ekbar'.
I was like 'chalo, puchne me kya jata hai'.
Ab top model itna zaruri kyu tha pata hai?
Kyuki isse pehle hamare paas ek Alto thi base model, aur maine soch liya tha kabhi koi car lenge toh usme kuch bhi kami nahi honi chahiye.
I called his friend and maine pucha 'bhai, i20 agai aapke paas?'
Woh bola 'haa bhaiya aagai'
Maine pucha 'Please bolo Red, i20 Top Model Asta O mere paas available hai'.
Woh bola 'Red, i20 Top Model Asta O mere paas available hai'

Ohuhuhu! main uss waqt hawa me udd raha tha
Usne kaha bhaiya bas ek hi car aai hai market me, woh bhi hamare owner ne apne liye mangwai hai,
Maine request ki bhai please ye mujhe dedo. Extra lelena bhali hi.
Usne kaha puchke batata hu owner se.
He called me back aur bola 'bhaiya lelo aap'

Maine bina ruke, soche samjhe usko token amount transfer kiya aur bola 'woh meri car hai, hilne mat dena uss jagah se, main lene aunga usko kuch din me'
Main papa ke paas gaya aur unko bataya ki car mil gai. Unhone kaha chalo abhi next step lete hai. Loan karwana tha mujhe.
Unke ek friend ko bank me call kiya, unhone bola aajao kal, loan process kardenge. Mere chharon taraf guitars baj rahe the, car aane wali thi. Manifest ho raha tha jo chaha maine.

Jaise hi 2 din baad hum bank jaane lage, ek naya jhatka aaya–
Bank manager jo loan dene wala tha, woh COVID positive nikal gaya, aur ab pata nahi office kab aayega.
Mere paas bache the ab kuch hi din shaadi me jane ke liye,

Meri maa ko samajh aa raha tha ki mujhe accha nahi lag raha, mera bohot mann ho raha hai car lene ka. Unhone mujhe dekha aur full mamta ko reload karke kaha ‘koi baat nahi beta, kuch time baad lelena, leni toh hai hi na car’.

Maine mumma ko bola **“Maa, Indore toh apan apni i20 me hi chalenge’.**
Isbar meri maa ki muskurahat main ek bharosa tha. Woh muskuraayi aur boli, theek hai teri iccha yahi hai toh, Bhagwan karega poori.

Mera ek dusra bhai Suraj Lawyer hai, unke banks me contact the. Maine unko call kiya aur bola bhaiya aisa aisa hai. Woh bole is bank me chala ja, ek manager milenge, main baat karleta hu.
Bina time waste kiye, usi time hum bank gaye, manager se mile aur MERI CAR KA LOAN PASS HOGAYA.

Toh bhai log, **‘Indore toh hum meri Brand New Fiery Red Top Model i20 me hi gaye the’**

Jab aap pehle wala page padhne lage the toh aapko niche car ki picture dikh gai hogai. Aur itni impossible situation me bhi aapko lag gaya hoga ki car toh aane wali hai Jai ki. Right?

**Chalo ek aur situation samjho**
Imagine karo India - Pakistan ka cricket match hai raat ko 8 baje
Aao aap ho cricket ke Die-heart fan. Kabhi match miss nahi karte.
Aap 6 baje jaldi jaldi apna kaam khatam karke office se ghar jana chah rahe ho. 7 baje nikalne lagte ho aur aapka boss kehta hai adha ghanta ruko, ek meeting khatam karke aata hu tumse kuch baat karni hai.
Boss 8 baje aata aur tumhe pata hai match chalu hoagaya hai.
10 baje tumhari meeting khatam hoti hai aur jaise hi tum ghar jaane ke liye office se bahar nikalte ho, road par log celebrate kar rahe hote hai. Patakhe jala rahe hote hai.
Aur aapko samajh aajata hai ki India match jeet chuki hai.

Ab aap gussa toh the par jeet ki khush me excited hokar ghar jaate ho match ke highlights chalu karte ho.
Last over chalu karte hi aapko dikhta hai 6 ball me 35 runs chahiye.
Jo ki super impossible hai.

Kya ab aapko haarne ka darr hoga?
Stress toh hoga thoda lekin ye darr nahi hoga na ke jeetoge ya nahi jeetoge. Kyuki result kya aana hai ye toh aapko pehle se hi pata hai.

Sirf usi tarah mere bhai, meri behen
**Life mein bhi apni ek highlight bana lo. Tumhari jeet ki highlight.**
Ab phir bhale hi beech me kitne bhi ups and downs aaye
Tum fail ho, gir jao, almost marr jao, gareeb hojao, sab khatam hojaye. Aapko future ki tension nahi hogi kyuki life ka match toh aapne pehle se hi jeet rakha haina.

## Activity - Learn this Manifesting Technique
## 369 Method (Nikola Tesla Inspired Manifesting)

369 method ek writing-based manifesting technique hai jo number repetition aur intention setting par based hai.

**Kaise Kare:**

**3 Times** – Subah uth kar 3 baar apni manifestation likho. (e.g. "Main apne sapno par kaam kar raha hoon.")

**6 Times** – Dopahar me usi sentence ko 6 baar likho.

**9 Times** – Raat ko sone se pehle 9 baar likho, aur likhne ke baad visualize karo.

Consistency is the key — Ise kam se kam 21 din tak daily karo.

**Manifestation = Thoughts + Feelings + Actions**

Sirf sochne se nahi hota. Sochne ke baad vibration create karo (feel it) aur phir small aligned actions lo — tabhi universe tumhare signals ko seriously lega.

***If you knew the magnificence of 3, 6 and 9, you would have a key to the universe." – Nikola Tesla***

Chapter 23

# FINDING LOVE AGAIN

PAPA JI - PAPA - JAI & VINI - MUMMA - MUMMY JI

---- In college, I went through a serious breakup that left me unsure if I ever wanted to settle down again.
Woh ek aisa break up tha, jisne meri duniya hila di thi.
Main itna hurt tha ki mujhe lagta tha – “Shaadi? Pyaar? Nahi bhai, yeh mere liye nahi hai.”
Darr tha. Negativity thi. Trust karne se darr lagta tha kisiko.

Papa mujhse jab bhi shadi ki baat karte the main phone cut kardeta tha.
Car se Indore jaate time mere papa ne mujhe 3-4 saal pehle ek ultimatum diya tha, woh yaad dilaya – **“22 January 2021, tere birthday tak agar tu ladki nahi dhundta, toh main dhund lunga aur usi se tujhe shaadi karni padegi”**
Mera birthday aane me zyada time nahi tha. Papa ye baat 22nd November 2020 ko kar rahe the. Par maine ye baat mazaak me taal di aur hum hamari new car me safar enjoy karne lage.
Main andar se jaanta tha... papa mazaak nahi kar rahe the par main shadi ke liye mentally ready nahi tha.

Suddenly January 2021 me kuch bohot strabge hua –
Ek aisi story shuru hui jisne mujhe phirse ek emotional insaan bana diya. Woh dil ke darwaze phir se khul gaye the. Detail me bataunga toh poori book isi se bhar jaegi isiliye detail me jaan na hai toh follow @viniandjai on social media.

Toh ji... Ek ladki meri life mein aayi.
Bilkul random. Bilkul unexpected. Aur bohot zyada pyaari. Sacch me.
Sirf kuch hi din me usne mere puraney cut huve taar phirse jod diye.
8 saal tak jo bhawnao ke gates maine lock kar rakhe the, usne khol diye, actually tod diye. Aur main gir gaya, pyaar mein. Poora. Bina rok-tok ke.
Papa bohot zyada khush the, main khush tha, aur universe jaise bol raha tha – “Beta, ab tera time aa gaya hai, jeele apni zindagi.”
4th Jan ko hum mile, 16th Feb ko papa ne khud hi hamari engagement fix kar di, aur humein invite kiya ki aajao tumhara roka decide karliya hai.
Papa ko Vini hamesha se bohot pasand thi. She is our relative par kyuki woh mujhse 6 saal chhoti thi toh kabhi maine socha bhi nahi tha aisa.

Agar aapka breakup hua hai toh suno, **‘Koi aapke saath hai toh woh aapka hai, aur chala gaya toh aapka kabhi tha hi nahi.;** Aagey badho, self growth par focus karo aur universe ko bass ek cheez bolke rakho ki ‘mujhe ek best life partner chahiye mere liye, jab aapko sahi lage tab dedena’. Never say ‘meri life me toh pyaar hai hi nahi.’

Chapter 24

# HEARTBREAK IS IMPORTANT

Dil tootne par bura isliye lagta hai... kyunki sirf aapka relationship nahi tootta, umeedein, yaadein, aur future ke sapne bhi toot jaate hain. Zyada scientific bolein toh heartbreak ek emotional trauma hota hai. Jab aap kisi se deeply attached hote ho, aapka brain dopamine aur oxytocin release karta hai—yeh dono "happy hormones" hote hain. Jab wo insaan chala jaata hai, yeh hormones suddenly release hona band ho jaate hain. Aur tab aapko physical dard jaisa feel hota hai, isi ko kehte hain "heartbreak hurts."

Mujhe is tough situation se jaldi bahar nikalne me jisne help ki thi woh hai 'self growth'. Maine instantly realize karliya ki abhi tak mera saara focus us insaan par tha, jo ki ab hai hi nahi. Isse better ab uss insaan par focus karte hai jo mere sath hamesha rehne wala hai**. Woh hoon main.**
Hum jab teenage wale pyaar me hote haina tab aksar humein kuch nahi dikhta. Family, friends, career, rules. Aur jaise hi breakup hota hai, yahi sab important lagne lag jata hai.
Maine sab chhod diya aur sirf apne career par aur apne loved ones par focus karne laga. College ke sath jobs karna iss event ka hi nateeja tha :D
Main bohot grateful hu ki mere saath woh incidence hua, nahi toh main apne aap ko kabhi seriously nahi leta aur grow nahi kar pata. Shayad aap ye book kabhi padh hi nahi rahe hote.

Aur rahi baat phirse pyaar hone ki...
Kabhi kabhi ek sahi insaan, sahi waqt par aata hai... humein fir se bharosa karna sikhata hai.
Aur woh insaan jo gaya woh bhi galat nahi tha, usko rights hai apne liye sahi galat choose karne ka. Toh usko acchi blessings do aur jo saath me acha samay guzara uske liye grateful raho. Us insaan ka aapke saath itna hi waqt likha tha.

Agar tum bhi wo ho jiska dil toot chuka hai, aur lagta hai ki ab bas... "Mujhse nahi hoga," toh yaad rakhna—

- Healing time leti hai—apne pace pe chalo, rush mat karo.
- Self growth, self love aur apni family par focus karo.
- Galat habits choose mat karo, zyada regret hoga.
- Positive thinking rakho. Jo hua hai woh aapke liye sahi hai, abhi shayad aapko samajh nahi aayega.Par baad me ajaega.

# Positive Thinking

Positive Soch Ki Taqat

Positive thinking ka matlab problems ko ignore karna nahi hai, balki unka saamna ek sahi mindset ke saath karna hai.
Yeh soch tumhe problems me solutions dhoondhne, stress kam karne, aur khud ko motivated rakhne me madad karti hai.
Agar tum ye nahi seekhe toh solutions me problems dhundne lagoge. Galat kya ho sakta hai pehle ispar focus karne lagoge.

**Positive Thinking Kya Hai?**
Positive thinking ek aadat hai jisme tum har obstacle me opportunity dhoondhte ho aur yeh maante ho ki acchi cheezein ho sakti hain.
✓ Complain karne ke bajaye solution pe dhyaan dena
✓ Failures me lesson aur opportunities dhoondhna
✓ Jo tumhare control me hai, uss par focus karna

**Example:**
✗ **Negative**: "Main fail ho gaya, ab kabhi success nahi milegi."
☑ **Positive**: "Main fail hua, par ab mujhe pata hai kya kaam nahi karta. Main phir se try karunga!"

**Positive Thinking Ke Fayde**
✓ **Stress Kamm** – Problems pe nahi, solutions pe focus karte ho.
✓ **Confidence Zyada** – Khud par aur apni ability par vishwas badhta hai.
✓ **Behtar Health** – Positive logon ka immune system strong hota hai.
✓ **Strong Relationships** – Optimistic log acchi energy attract karte hain. Aur log unke around rehna chahte hai.
✓ **Zyada Success** – Positive mindset se tum action lete ho aur mushkilon me bhi lage rehte ho. Iske kaaran aapko success milti hai.

Soch badloge, toh aapki duniya badal jaayegi.
Positive thinking tumhe har haalat me strong aur focused banaati hai. Easy nahi hoga shuru me positive sochna, magar possible hai.

## Positive Soch Kaise Laayein?

**Negative Thoughts Ko Reframe Karo**
❌ "Main ye nahi kar sakta"
✅ "Main ye kaise kar sakta/sakti hoon, kyuki ye mujhe karna hai?"

**Problem se solution ki taraf shift ho jao.**
✓ Un logon ke saath waqt bitao jo tumhe uplift karein.
✓ Inspiring books padho, motivational podcasts suno, right accounts ko followr karo. Yeh bohot underrated practices hai, inko seriously lo.

**Gratitude Practice Karo**
✓ Har din 3 cheezein likho jin ke liye tum grateful ho.
Yeh tumhare dimaag ko acchi cheezon pe focus karne ki aadat sikhaata hai. Aap woh sab dekhne lagoge jo accha hai instead of woh sab dekhna jo sahi nahi hai. Ye ek important skill hai.

**Apna Dhyaan Rakho (Self Care)**
✓ Exercise karo, sahi khana khao, achhi neend lo, groomed raho.
***Healthy body = Positive and Happy Mind***

**Positive Affirmations Bolna Start Karo**
✓ "Main strong hoon." "Main khush hoon"
✓ "Main koi bhi situation handle kar sakta hoon."
✓ "I am god's favorite child"
✓ "I am a magnet to money"
✓ "I attract good people in my life"
Tumhare shabd tumhari reality banate hain.

**Jo Control Me Hai, Uss Pe Focus Karo**
Har cheez tumhare control me nahi hoti, lekin tumhara reaction zaroor hota hai. Jo negative cheezein tumhare control se bahar hain, unhe chhodna seekho.
Positive soch seekhne wali cheez hai. Har din chhoti chhoti aadaton se tum apna dimaag positive rewire kar sakte ho.

## Positive Thinking in Action

### Jab Soch Badalti Hai, Zindagi Badalti Hai

**Scenario 1: Tumhari Job Chali Jaati Hai**

❌ Negative Response: “Ab mujhe kabhi job nahi milegi, koi mujhe ladki nahi dega”

✅ Positive Response: “Yeh moka hai kuch aur behtar dhoondhne ka.”

**Scenario 2: Tum Exam Me Fail Ho Jaate Ho**

❌ Negative Response: “Main bilkul bhi smart nahi hoon.”

✅ Positive Response: “Main aur mehnat karunga, agli baar behtar hoga.”

***Positive Thinking ek choice hai.***

Yeh har problem ka solution nahi hai, par har problem ko sambhalna zaroor aasan bana deta hai.

Apne dimaag ko accha dekhne ki aadat daalo, zindagi khud-ba-khud acchi lagne lagegi.

## Positive Mindset Activity: "Flip the Script"

**Objective:** Apni negative thoughts ko pakadna aur unhe positive, empowering beliefs me badalna jo tumhe aage le jaayein.

### Step 1: Apni Negative Thought Likho

Ek aisi negative thought likho jo tumhe pareshaan kar rahi ho.
Yeh tumhari ability, future, ya present situation ke baare me ho sakti hai.
✍ "Jo thought mujhe bother kar rahe hai wo hai ______________

______________________________________________

______________________________________________

### Step 2: Us Thought Ko Challenge Karo – Kya Yeh 100% Sahi Hai?

Apne aap se poochho:
"Kya yeh hamesha sach hota hai? Kya ek bhi aisa moment hai jab yeh galat tha?"
**Example**: Agar tum soch rahe ho "Main kuch sahi nahi kar sakta," toh ek moment yaad karo jab tum successful hue the.
✍ "Ek samay jab yeh thought galat tha wo tha________________

______________________________________________

______________________________________________"

### Step 3: Ab Usse Positive Thought Me Flip Karo

Ab is negative thought ko ek positive belief me badlo.
Yeh phrases use kar sakte ho:
✔ "Main seekh raha hoon ______________________________"
✔ "Main abhi tak nahi pahucha, par main better ho raha hoon

______________________________________________"
✔ "Main capable hoon ________________________________"
✍ "Mera naya positive thought hai __________________________"

**Step 4: Action Step Lo**
Apne naye belief ko support karne ke liye aaj ek chhota action lo.
**Example**: Agar tumhara naya belief hai "Main apni skills improve kar raha hoon," toh aaj se 10 minute kuch naya seekhne me lagao.
✍ "Aaj main 10 min book padhunga ya 10 min walk karunga"

**Positivity Diary Concept**
Ek jar ya notebook rakho jisme tum har din ek positive cheez likho —ek win, ek achha decision, ya koi chhoti khushi.
Chhoti chhoti wins milke self confidence build karti hai.

**Yeh Activity Kyun Kaam Karti Hai?**
Humara dimaag naturally negative cheezon pe focus karta hai, usko design hi aise kiya hai. Yeh tool tumhare dimaag ko train karta hai positive cheezein notice karne ke liye, confidence build karne aur action lene ke liye—jo ek successful mindset ki sabse important qualities hain.

Human mind ek bohot acha servant aur bohot bura master hai.
Agar aapne usey apne aap ko control karne diya toh aap pareshan rehne wale ho. *Train your brain to think positive in every situation.*
Ab kuch log bolte hai positive thinking se kuch nahi hota, sab bakwas hai.
Bolne do unko. Aap focus karo 'Positive Thinking' par.
Your life is what you make it.
Vichaar banaye zindagi. Remember?
Jaisa aap sochoge, believe karoge waisa hone lagega.

Agar aap sochoge ki ye kaam karta hai
Aap sahi ho
Agar aap sochoge ke ye kaam nahi karta
Aap sahi ho

Chapter 25

# WORST DAY OF MY LIFE

(Is chapter me death ke baare me baat hogi, raat me na padhein)

Vini aur main engaged the, Jaipur mein ek acchi zindagi chal rahi thi. Vini ek interior design firm me kaam karti thi, aur main apne businesses chala raha tha. Daily hamara milna hota tha, hum drives par jaate the, papa aur mumma Sunday ko Jaipur aate the Vini ke saath time spend karne aur papa apne haath se usey khana khilate the. Mujhe papa daily early morning uthate the ki Vini ko uske office chhod kar aa, bhale hi mujhe extra drive karna padta tha. Vini ke life me aane se papa bohot zyada khush the.
Best friends the ye dono —
Ek din, ek ajeeb si negativity ne mujhe gher liya.
Mujhe har cheez galat lagne lagi—mera kaam, Vini, mera future. Har cheez par doubt hone laga. Mera kisi bhi cheez me mann nahi lag raha tha. Aisa lag raha tha jaise sab kuch toot raha ho, jaise main iss relationship ko khatam karne ke edge par hoon.
Yeh darr, yeh bechaini, lagbhag ek mahine tak saath thi.

Ek din, bilkul lost feel karte hue, main bina destination ke meri car lekar drive par nikal gaya—sirf chale hi ja raha tha. Aur dheere dheere, main apne hometown ki taraf jaane laga.
Maine apne bhai ko call kiya aur kaha, "Kuch kapde le aa... main kishangarh ja raha hoon."
Woh sweetheart hai—bina kuch puchhe, le aaya.
Mujhe laga yeh negativity shayad COVID ke dino ka asar hai—log mar rahe the, businesses crash ho rahe the, hamare family mein bhi deaths hui thi.
Socha thoda time family ke saath spend karunga, mind fresh ho jaaye. Phir ek din, main bimaar pad gaya—5-6 din viral fever raha. Uske baad mere papa ko bhi same viral ho gaya.
Papa sabki madad karte the—even COVID me woh bohot logo ko serious condition me hospital lekar gaye the jab koi kisi ko touch bhi karne se darr raha tha.

Ek din woh poore din tak sote rahe. Kisi ne kuch zyada nahi socha. kyuki unhe free time mein sona pasand tha.
Shaam ko mera mann nahi lag raha tha toh main unke pairon ke paas baith kar apne laptop par kaam kar raha tha. Wo so rahe the.
Vini ka call aaya aur usne pucha 'papa kaha hain, baat karao ekbar'

Ab Vini aur papa ekdum friends jaise baat karte the, uss din papa ne phone lekar hello bola aur unko accha feel nahi hua toh woh bole baad me karunga.
Vini ne kaha koi baat nahi video call par sote huve hi dikha do papa ko ek baar mujhe.

Kuch der baar main bahar gaya aur phir jab lauta toh dekha, Anil chacha aur Nishank unse baat karne ki koshish kar rahe the —"Papa, theek ho? Kaisa feel ho raha hai?"
Phir unhone unka oxygen level check kiya—aur woh low tha.
Hum turant unhe hospital lekar gaye.
Ab uss time hospitals sabko admit bhi nahi kar paa rahe the kyuki hospitals me space hi nahi tha patient lene ka.
Somehow raat hone tak ek bed mila aur unhe humne admit kiya.
Doctors ne check-up kiya aur kaha, "Sab thik hai, hojata hai kabhi kabhi, kal inko discharge kar denge."

Agle din subah 8 baje humne dobaara pucha, and they reassured again, "He's fine. 12 baje tak discharge kardenge."
Vini ka mere paas call aaya aur Vini ro rahi thi, I asked kya hua toh she said 'mujhe sapna aaya ki papa nahi rahe'. I told her ki woh ekdum theek hai.

11 baje mere uncle ka mere paas call aaya aur unhone kaha jaldi se hospital ajao — main hamare gaanv wale mandir gaya huva tha.
Main kuch bhi ulta expect nahi kar raha tha, lekin ek dum se mujhe ajeeb sa lagne laga.
Main turant pohocha. Doctor ne kaha, "ICU mein jaao, unse mil lo."
Mere saare relatives jaante the kya hua hai, par kisi ne kuch nahi bola. Mujhe laga papa milne ke liye bula rahe honge andar.
Meri mumma baar-baar call kar rahi thi, puch rahi thi, "Kaha ho?"
ICU ke gate pe khade hoke maine bola, "Papa theek hain, unse milne jaa raha hoon, call back karta hu"
Main ICU main gaya—paanch doctors papa ke aas paas, CPR de rahe the. Main woh scene aaj bhi nahi bhool pata hoon, aur na kisi se discuss karta hu.
Main ekdum se ghabra gaya, pucha, "Kya ho raha hai?"
Ek doctor ne kaha, "Humne poori koshish ki, par bacha nahi paaye."

Maine kaha, "Kya bol rahe ho, dekho, woh saans le rahe hain."
Doctor ne bola, "Woh machine se horaha hai, body response nahi de rahi" Aur ye baat bolkar... sab doctors waha se chale gaye.

Main akela waha khada tha... papa ki dead body mere saamne thi.
Main paas main gaya aur unko touch karke bola 'Papa' 'Papa utho na' Ek second ke liye aisa laga ki koi movie chal rahi hai. Abhi koi bolega 'cut' aur papa uth jaenge. Lekin aisa kuch nahi hua.
Main waha khada tha aur ye soch raha tha ki ab life me main kya karunga. Aur ab next karna kya hota hai?
Pehle toh papa bata dete the ki ye kar. Ab papa ki dead body mere saamne hai uska kya karna hai ye papa se kaise puchoon?
Phir ekdum se dimag me aaya ki chhote bhai Chinu ko kya bolunga. Woh ICU ke bahar mera wait kar raha hai.
Mummy ko kya bolunga. Daadi puchegi toh kya jawaab dunga unko.

Main jaise hi ICU se bahar aaya Chinu ne mera face dekha aur woh samajh gaya ki papa nahi rahe. Utne me mera phone baja aur mumma ka call tha. Maine phone uthaya aur mumma ne pucha 'kaise hai abhi papa, milke aaya na tu'. Maine kaha, 'papa serious hai mumma, doctors bol rahe hai chances kamm hai bachne ke' aur mumma ne phone rakh diya.
Meri himmat nahi hui bolne ki 'papa nahi rahe ab'.
Mere cousins, chacha, hum sab ek dusre ko aansu bhari aankhon se dekh rahe the kyuki papa se sab bohot pyaar karte the.

Phone phir se baja—Vini ka call tha.
Maine phone cut kiya aur Vini ko message kiya 'we lost him'. So that waha se sab log aane ki preparation karlein.
Phir main aur Chinu Ajmer se Kishangarh ke liye nikle. Woh 30 minutes ki drive mere life ka sabse difficult hissa tha kyuki mujhe ye nahi samajh aa raha tha ki mumma ko ye news kaise dunga?

Maine apne close relatives ko inform kiya aur hum ghar pohoche.
Maa (daadi) ghar ke bahar khadi thi. Mujhe nahi samajh aaya ki unko kya kahu toh maine pucha mummy kaha hai aur unko andar bulaya.

Mummy bhagwan ke room me thi, beth kar pooja kar rahi thi.

Main paas gaya, unko piche se hug kiya aur bola 'mumma papa chale gaye'.
Meri mummy ne mujhe dekha aur bola 'aisa nahi ho sakta neenu, nahi ja sakte woh aise'.
Ye moment main pehli baar yaad kar raha hu kyunki yaha likhna hai. Isse pehle na mujhe ye sochne ki, na kisi se discuss karne ki himmat hui. Iss moment ne mujhe suddenly bada bana diya tha.
Ghar ka woh bada jise 4 logon ka aur agey aane wale parivar ka dhyaan rakhna hai.

- **Kya mujhe rakhna aata tha?** Bilkul nahi.
- **Kya mujhe rakhna padega?** Option hi nahi tha.

Meri mumma bohot zyada pooja paath, vrat karti thi, dukh mujhe is baat ka bhi tha ki ab woh bhagwan me kaise bharosa karegi.
Meri daadi already bohot kuch face kar chuki thi, kuch time pehle bhua ki aur ek cousin chacha ki death hui thi, woh ye toh deserve nahi karti yaar. Meri mumma ro nahi rahi thi kyuki woh ye baat ko accept hi nahi kar paa rahi thi ki papa ab nahi rahe hamare saath, ab woh nahi mil paegi unse.
Papa ko ghar laya gaya, covid ke kaaran body ko ambulance se bahar nahi nikala aur direct shamshaan lejaya gaya.

Mere papa ek charmer the, unko saj dhaj ke rehne ka bohot shauk tha. Toh hospital jaane wali subah woh uth kar shave karke soye the. Unko jab humne ambulance se nikala toh woh itne handsome lag rahe the ki mera mann kiya unko boldu ki ***'itna handsome lagne ka aapko koi haq nahi hai pitaji'.*** Lekin woh meri sunte nahi.
Hum ghar aaye aur main mummy ke saath betha. Tab jaake unko realize hua ki unki life me kya hua hai aur woh khoob royi.
Main aajtak ache se nahi ro paya kyuki mujhe lagta tha agar main toot gaya toh mere piche 5 log aur toot jaenge.

**Bhaiyo aur behno** - Agar aapke dono parents abhi bhi aapke sath haina, aap bohot lucky ho. Ladna jhagadna sab ek jagah hai, lekin koi bhi parent ko khona is duniya ka sabse painful moment hai.
Iss din se mere saare sapne mere parivaar se related hogaye. Kuch mere akele ka nahi raha. Kuch log mujhse puchte hai ki wapas Dubai kyu nahi jata. Jawab hai ki me akela nahi ja pata ab.

Pita is duniya ka sabse kamm aanka gaya (under rated) insaan hai. Mujhe yeh ehsaas tab hua jab main khud ek pita bana.
Ek din main apne do saal ke bete Vir ke saath khel raha tha. Tabhi meri mumma mujhe dekh kar muskurai aur boli, "Pata hai? Pehle jab joint families hoti thi, toh pita apne hi bachon ko sabke samne touch bhi nahi karte the. Aise pyar karna aur khilana toh door ki baat hai" --- Main hairan reh gaya. Aur tab mujhe samajh aaya—jo aadmi apne baccho ko pyaar jatane ke tareeke seekh hi nahi paya, wo kaise comfortable feel karega apne bacchon ko gale lagane me jab woh bade hogaye ho?
Main jab 24 saal ka hua tab papa ko pehli baar 'I love you' bola, ek mentor ke kehne par. aur mere papa soch rahe the ki ab kya bolu.
Unka jawab tha 'tu theek toh haina'
Ek pita poori zindagi apni feelings daba kar jeeta hai. Unhe bachpan se sikhaya jata hai ki "mard" ka matlab hota hai sakht rehna, apne emotions ko chhupa kar rakhna, aur hamesha mazboot dikhna.
Par sach yeh hai ki unki har koshish, har mehnat, har daant ke peeche pyaar aur care hoti hai aur ye intent hota hai ki unke bacche sahi raaste par chalein. Lekin baccha sirf ek hi emotion dekhta hai—unka gussa. Kyuki pyaar, lagaav, ya kamzori dikhana kabhi ek pita ke allowed emotions me tha hi nahi.
Aise hi dheere-dheere ek pita apne hi bacchon ki nazar me dushman ban jata hai. Phir bacche sirf tab unke paas aate hain jab unhe koi madad chahiye, paise, ya koi permission.

Aur ek pita, jo poori zindagi sirf deta rehta tha, ek pal ke liye ruk kar sochta hai— "Bachpan me jo bacche mujhe dekh kar khush hote the, ab sirf zaroorat padne par hi mere paas kyun aate hain?"

Agar tumhare pita aaj bhi khud ko express nahi kar pate, toh reason samjho. Kaash pehle mujhe yeh cheezein samajh aati, toh shayad unke saath kuch aur acche pal bita pata.
Agar woh aaj bhi aap ke sath hai toh aap bohot lucky ho. Woh aapko bina bataye kaise aapki zindagi aasan karne me lage hai aapko pata bhi nahi chalega. Aur aapko idea bhi nahi hai unki absence me life kitni zyada difficult hojaegi.
Kayi baar jo pyaar dikhai nahi deta, wo sabse gehra hota hai. 🖤

**Iss phase ne mujhe ek woh skill sikhai jo humein bohot pehle school me sikha deni chahiye thi.**

## Emotional Intelligence

Mere papa ka jaana... meri life ka sabse bura samay tha.
Uss din aisa laga ki sab kuch khatam hogaya. Sab kuch bura lagg raha tha, kuch samajh hi nahi aa raha tha, aur pehli baar... main bilkul helpless mehsoos kar raha tha.
Par waqt ke saath maine ek cheez samjhi—jo mujhe uss dard se bahar nikaal rahi thi, mujhe khud ko sambhalne ki taaqat de rahi thi... Woh thi Emotional Intelligence Skill.
Jiske baare mein kabhi kisine direct baat nahi ki thi.

### Emotional Intelligence hota kya hai? (EI)

Emotional Intelligence matlab apne aur dusro ke emotions ko samajhna aur unhe control (regulate) karna.
Sirf shaant rehna nahi, balki yeh samajhna ki tum kya mehsoos kar rahe ho, kyun kar rahe ho, aur kaise react karna chahiye.

**1. Apne Emotions Ko Samajhna**
Papa ke jaane ke din... shock, dard, gussa, darr, zimmedari—sab kuch mere upar ek saath agaya tha.
Agar maine unn feelings ko accept nahi kiya hota, toh shayad woh feelings mujhe tod deti.
EI ne mujhe yeh samjhaya ki emotions se bhaag mat, unhe samajh.

**2. Stress & Anxiety Ko Handle Karna**
Mujhe life ki sabse buri khabar apni maa aur dadi ko deni thi.
Uss moment pe mujhe unka sahara banna tha par mujhe usse pehle khud ko sambhalna tha.
Apne emotions par kaabu paa kar, unhe control karna—wahi toh real strength mujhe chahiye thi.

**3. Empathy – Dusron Ke Emotions Mehsoos Karna**
Waqt ke saath maine samjha ki kaun mere saath tha, kaun nahi. Emotional Intelligence ne mujhe dusron ke dard ko bhi feel karna sikhaya—sirf apna nahi.
Agar tum dusre ka dard samajh sako, toh tumhaari presence hi unke liye support ban jaati hai.

**4. Pressure Mein Decisions Lena**
Jab sab kuch haath se nikal raha ho, aur emotions control me nahi ho, tab sahi decision lena hi emotional intelligence hai.
Uss samay maine kaafi galat decisions liye. Samajh nahi thi itni.
Par agar mujhe EI ache se samajh aata toh uss waqt main sahi decisions leta— jo galtiyan kari woh nahi karta.

**5. Resilience – Gir ke Uthna**
Dard chala nahi jaata. Bas uska form change hota hai.
Emotional Intelligence ka matlab dard ko bhool jana nahi hota... uss dard se seekhna hota hai.
Life har kisi ko test karti hai—par tum kaise respond karte ho, wahin se tumhari real growth start hoti hai.
Aaj bhi main uss din ko bhool nahi paya hoon, aur shayad kabhi bhool bhi nahi paunga. Par maine itna zaroor seekh liya—
Life tumhe todne aayegi, par agar tum apne emotions ko control kar sakte ho, toh koi bhi situation tumhe khatam nahi kar sakti.

**Emotional Intelligence – dikhai nahi deta, par tumhe unbreakable bana deta hai.**

Aur ye bhi yaad rakhna, Grief, yaani gamm, har koi alag tareeke se handle karta hai. Koi rota hai, koi hasta hai, koi chup ho jaata hai, aur koi behosh tak ho jaata hai.
Aur inn sab mein koi bhi reaction galat nahi hota. Har kisi ka apna emotion process karne ka tareeka hota hai. Agar aap ro rahe ho, iska yeh matlab nahi ki aap hi sirf sahi ho aur jo nahi ro rahe woh galat hai. Kisi ka dard silent hota hai, kisi ka visible. Dono dard hote hain, dono real hote hain. Isiliye, grief mein comparison mat karo.
Bas ek doosre ke liye space banao.
Sabko heal karne ka apna waqt aur apna raasta hota hai.

## Why Everyone Should Work on Emotional Intelligence?

*Zindagi unpredictable hai.*

Kabhi kabhi life aise test karti hai ki lagta hai hum shayad handle hi nahi kar paayenge.
Par agar hum emotional intelligence develop kar lein, toh hum sirf survive nahi karte— Hum uss pain se grow karte hain.

**Kaise Start Kare Emotional Intelligence Build Karna?**

**1. Self-awareness (Apne emotions ko samajhna)**

Apne emotions ko bina judge kiye feel karo. Jab bhi gussa, dard, ya confusion ho— turant react mat karo. Ek moment lo, samjho ki tum kya feel kar rahe ho aur kyun.

**2. Self-regulation (Emotions ko manage karna)**

Emotions ko dabaana nahi hai, par unhe healthy tareeke se express karna seekhna hai.
Gussa aaya? Chillaane se behtar hai—gehri saans lo aur calmly baat karo. Easy nahi hai par ye seekh jana zaroori hai.
Aur agar chilla diya, toh jaao aur apologies karo. Agli baar chillane se pehle yaad rahega.

**3. Empathy (Dusron ko samajhna)**

Khud ke point of view se bahar niklo—samjho ki saamne wala kya feel kar raha hai.
Samajhne ke liye suno, na ki bas jawab dene ke liye.

**4. Effective Communication (Bina hurt kiye apne emotions bolna)**

Emotions ko control me rakh kar express karo—na zyada overwhelm, na kisi ko hurt karne wala.
Goli ke ghaav bhar jaate hai, boli ke nahi bharte.

**5. Mindfulness & Reflection (Emotions ko process karna)**
Emotion se bhaag mat jao. Usse face karo, samjho, aur heal karo. Yeh tumhare decisions ko better banata hai aur tumhe andar se strong.
Jab Tum Kisi Apne Ko Kho Dete Ho...
Duniya rukti nahi hai. Bass kuch samay ka break milta hai. Responsibilities waisi hi rehti hain. Log tumse waise hi expectations rakhte hain.

Tab Emotional Intelligence tumhari lifeline ban jaata hai.
Yeh tumhe help karta hai pain ko process karne mein... aur unn logon ke liye present rehne mein, jo tumhara saath chahte hain.

**Sabse Badi Baat?**
Yeh tumhe dard se heal karne mein help karta hai, dard ko bhulne ke liye nahi,
Uss dard ke saath jeena, uss dard se strength lena—that's real growth.

Life will test you, uss test ko tum kaise handle karte ho—wahi tumhe define karta hai.

## Activity: "The Emotion Journal"

Apne Emotions Ko Samajhne Ka Ek Simple Tareeka

**Step 1: Daily Emotion Check-in**

Har din raat ko, sirf 5 minute do aur likho:

Aaj ka main emotion kya tha?

(e.g., khushi, gussa, udaasi, tension, excitement)

- **Yeh emotion ka trigger kya tha?**

(Koi insaan, baat, ya incident?)

- **Maine kaise react kiya?**

(Shaanti se? Gusse se? Avoid kiya? Excited ho gaya?)

**Step 2: Reflection – Week Ke End Mein Socho**

Apne notes ko padhkar in sawaalon ke jawab do:

- Kaunse emotions baar-baar aaye is week?
- Kya koi specific trigger baar-baar aaya?
- Apne reaction se khush ho? Ya kuch aur tareeka behtar hota?

**Step 3: Action Plan**

Ek emotion choose karo jo negative tha aur baar-baar aaya:

**Write it here:** ____________________________________________

Next Week, Main Kya Karunga Jab Yeh Emotion Aaye:

________________________________________________________

**Example:**

**Emotion**: Frustration

**Action**: Jab frustrated feel karunga, ek minute rukunga, 3 deep breaths lunga, aur puchunga, "Kya yeh situation meri energy ke laayak hai?"

**Reminder**:

"Emotions tumhe control nahi karte—tum control karte ho apne reactions ko."

Chapter 26

# BRINGING NEW LIGHT TO OUR LIVES

## Shaadi ke Baad Ghar Me Khushi Wapas Aayi

Mere papa hamesha chahte the ki meri shaadi July mein ho.
Toh I ensured ki shaadi July mein hi ho —

**Iske piche 2 reasons the:**

1. Pehla, ghar mein new energy aaye. Shaadi ek bada celebration hota hai, aur main chahta tha ki itne andhere ke baad thodi roshni, thodi khushi ghar main wapas aaye.
2. Doosra, main chahta tha ki mummy ke paas ek nayi saathi ho — ek bahu, jisse wo baatein kar sakein, jiske saath woh waqt bita sakein, thoda akelapan kamm ho.

Lekin sab log yeh baat nahi samajh paaye. Kuch relatives ne mazaak banaya — kehne lage,
"Baap 3 mahine pehle guzra aur ab shaadi mein dance ho raha hai?" Yeh sunna chubha zarur, lekin dil se mujhe pata tha — papa meri jagah hote to woh bhi yahi karte.
Aur log galat bhi nahi the, meri soch unko nahi pata thi.
Shadi hote hi maine meri mummy ko muskurate hue dekha — kaafi time baad. Bhale hi woh hamari khushi ke liye ho.

Papa ka jana hamare liye ek bohot bada test tha. Woh dard, woh khhalipan — shabdon se bayaan nahi kar sakte. Lekin jab Vini ghar aayi, cheezein badalne lagi. Ghar mein baatein hone lagi, hansi gunjne lagi, zindagi wapas aayi.

Lekin mummy ke liye woh dard ab bhi zinda tha. Main aur Chinu mummy ko hamare saath rehne ke liye Jaipur le aaye the.
Lekin 30 saal ke rishte ka sudden end aasan nahi hota.
Hum samajhte the ki healing time leti hai.

Main ek cheez ke liye bohot thankful hoon — papa ke jane se 4 mahine pehle humne mummy-papa ki 30th anniversary surprise plan kiya tha. Unke sab doston ko bulaya, rishteydaar aaya, aur bohot accha celebration hua tha.

Uss celebration se pehle maine car li thi, Jaipur wala ghar decorate kiya tha toh kaafi paisa lag gaya tha. Ek baar toh andar se aaraha tha ki chhota celebration karlete hai, agli baar bada karlenge par phir bhi ek grand celebration kiya.
Ye main aapko isliye bata raha hu kyuki papa ke jaane ke baad meri life ko lekar kuch learnings hui. Usme se pehli thi ki....
Zyada paisa us time nahi tha lekin paisa toh baad me aagaya.
Agar woh celebration main nahi karta toh zindagi bhhar woh regret rehta. Unka anniversary celebration unke saath hi khatam hogaya.
Papa ke jaane ke baad ab main unke liye kuch nahi kar sakta lekin pehle unko expensive phone dilana, unke liye camera, expensive watch lane jaise decisions worth it rahe na. Bhale hi phone EMI par liya tha. Thank God maine woh uss samay karliya.
Aap bhi jitna best ho sakta hai apne parents ke liye karo.
Paisa wapas ajaega, lekin samay wapas nahi aega, woh wapas nahi aenge.

**Dusri learning -** Engagement hote hi papa ka mann kiya ki Vini ko lekar 3-4 din jaisalmer ghumne jane ka. Unko ghumna bohot pasand tha. Papa ne Vini ke ghar par bhi nahi bataya tha iske baare me, bola tha niklenge tab bata denge.
Logon ne hamare piche khoob batein kari ki 'sagai ke baad hi honeymoon par chale gaye', 'koi maryada nahi hai', etc.
Par agar aap ab iss baat ko samjho toh papa ne sirf wahi 3-4 din the jo Vini ke saath acche se guzare the. Uske alawa kabhi kabhi papa bass kuch ghanton ke liye Sundays par mille the lekin ye 3-4 din woh poore time Vini ke saath the. Ghume, khele, khana khaya, usey pehchana, laad kiye.
Agar log kya kahenge soch kar hum ghumne nahi jaate toh shayad papa apni bahu ke sath, jiska woh saalon se intezaar kar rahe the, kabhi time hi nahi bita paate.

Toh papa ye sikha ke gaye hai humein ki, tumhe jisme khushi milti hai, tum woh karo. Hoga jo baad me dekhenge.
Bass ye dhyaan rakhna ki kisi ko nuksaan na pohoche.

*Kuch toh log kahenge, logon ka kaam hai kehna.*
*Chhodo bekar ki baaton ko, kahi beet na jaaye raina.*

## Sirf Pyar Se Shaadi Nahi Chalti -

Hamare around koi is baare me baat nahi karta. Sharm aati hai, ajeeb lagta hai. Par hamein samajhna padega ki sirf pyaar se shaadi nahi chalti. Uske saath chahiye communication, efforts, understanding, respect aur self-awareness jaise tools.
Yeh kuch baatein hain jo ek strong relationship banane mein aur aapko ek acha partner banane me madad karti hain:

**1. Emotional Support Dena Zaroori Hai**
Zindagi hamesha smooth nahi hoti. Kabhi chhoti problems, kabhi bade challenges. Ek accha partner wo hota hai jo musibat ke waqt aapke saath khada rahe.
Vini ne mere tough time mein mujhe “theek” karne ki koshish nahi ki — sirf mera saath diya. Aur woh sab kuch tha.

**2. Communication = Dil Se Sunna Aur Samajhna**
Zyada bolne se nahi, sahi tarike se baat karne aur samne wale ki baat samajhne se relation strong banta hai.
Kya aap apni feelings openly express karte ho?
Bina judge kiye apne partner ko sunte ho? Ya purani baaton ko yaad karke sochte ho ‘ye toh aise hi karta/karti hai hamesha’.
React karne se pehle partner ke nazariye ko samajhte ho?

**3. Individuality Ka Respect Karna Sikho**
Shaadi se pehle aap dono alag-insaan the — aapke apne dreams the, habits aur nature tha.. Apne partner ko waisa hi accept karo. Ek accha partner dusre ko badalne ki koshish nahi karta — samajhne ki koshish karta hai aur zarurat padne par sahi raasta dikhata hai. Jab aap ek dusre ko support karte ho as individuals, tabhi relation strong banta hai.

**4. Jhagde? Honge. Lekin Maturity Zaroori Hai**
Disagreements to aayenge hi. Lekin uss waqt ka reaction hi aapke relation ko define karta hai.
"Main sahi hoon" prove karne se better hai yeh sochna — kya relation ke liye sahi hai?

Kabhi apologize karna padta hai, kabhi compromise.
Aur kabhi partner ke nazariye se cheezein dekhni padti hain.
Shaadi ek journey hai — roz seekhna padta hai, roz time, energy, emotions ko invest karna padta hai.
Aur jab aap dono ka focus ek dusre ko samajhne aur support karne par ho — tab pyaar bhi deepen hota hai, aur respect bhi.

Maine dekha hai ki agar aapka partner uss cheez par agree nahi kar raha jo aap bol rahe ho toh aap naraz hojate ho.
Nahi karna hai aisa, disagreement accept karna seekhna padega.
Agar aap disagreement ke liye ready nahi ho toh aap shaadi ke liye ready nahi ho. 2 log alag jagah se, alag pait se, alag culture se aakar jab saath rehte hai toh disagreement hona natural hai, fights, arguments hone hi hai.

Aapko bass seekhna hai ki argument aur ladai karni kaise hai.
Ek dusre ko behtar jaan bhi jaoge aur sath me khush bhi rahoge.

Aapko na best friends banna hai sabse pehle.

Kuch aur cheezein hai jo aapko jaan na chahiye...
Woh aagey padho...
Aur ekbar ye video dekhna, shadi ke pehle Vini and maine kya baatein ki thi.

## Intellectual Stimulation

"Intellectual stimulation" ka concept couples ke liye bahut important hai, aur agar dono partners is baat ko samajh jaayein, toh unka rishta sirf strong hi nahi, deep aur long-lasting bhi banta hai.

"Intellectual stimulation" ka matlab hai — aapas mein sirf pyaar ya attraction nahi, balki dimaag se bhi judna.
Jab aap kisi ke saath aise conversations karte ho jo sirf daily life ke kaam ya routine tak simit nahi hote, balki uske sochne ke tareeke, uski opinions, uske interests ko samajhne ki koshish karte ho — tab aap usse intellectually stimulate karte ho.
Yeh woh connection hota hai jo dimag aur dil dono ko jodta hai.

**Example for Couples -**
**Galat tarika:**
**Wife**: "Mujhe lagta hai kal mujhe woh workshop attend karni chahiye."
**Husband**: "Haan theek hai, dekh lena." (Bina interest ke)

**Behtar tarika (intellectual stimulation):**
**Wife**: "Mujhe lagta hai kal mujhe woh workshop attend karni chahiye."
**Husband**: "Woh wali jisme stress management ka session hai?
Kya cheez ne tumhe attract kiya usme? Main bhi soch raha tha ki emotional health par kuch seekhna chahiye."
Is second version mein husband sirf haan-bola nahi, usne genuinely interest dikhaya, conversation ko aage badhaya, aur wife ke thought process ko samjha.

**Ye kyu zaruri hai?**

- Jab partner aapke thoughts ko value karta hai, aap zyada respected feel karte ho
- Conversation interesting rehti hai, sirf roz wali baatein nahi hoti
- Rishta boring nahi lagta, har roz kuch naya discuss karne ko hota hai aur isse dono log grow karte hain — emotionally and mentally

**Jab main couple ko consult ya train karta hu toh ek common problem jo mere paas kaafi baar aati hai woh hai ki...**
Maan lo ek aadmi poora din kaam karke, meetings attend karke, stress handle karke ghar aata hai. Uska dimaag already bhara hua hota hai. Usne poora din socha, decide kiya, solve kiya, aur ab usse chahiye mental balance.
Par jaise hi woh ghar aata hai, uski wife wahi routine baatein karne lagti hai:
"Maid aaj late aayi thi... Neighbour ki shaadi mein jana hai... Ye kapde kaha rakh doon..." (jo ki galat nahi hai, kyuki uska mind inn cheezon me hi occupied hota hai)
Yeh sab baatein zaruri hain, par agar sirf yahi hoti rahe — toh aadmi emotionally aur mentally disconnect hone lagta hai. Kyunki uska dimaag already overloaded hai, aur usse chahiye ek rishta jo usse mentally bhi energize kare, soothe kare.

"Intellectual stimulation" ko samajhna aapko apne partner ke thoughts, interests, aur goals mein genuine interest lene me help karta hai. **Agar wife kabhi husband se puchhe:**
"Tumhare clients kya soch rahe the? Tumhe kya lagta hai us idea mein success hai?" Toh yeh sirf baat nahi, mental connection hai.
Jab koi aapse intellectually connect karta hai — aapka usme interest badhta hai, aap involved feel karte ho, aur rishta deep hota hai. Sirf routine baatein karte karte rishta sirf household management ban jaata hai.
Lekin jab partners ek dusre ke ideas, views, thoughts mein dilchaspi lete hain — toh rishta ek journey of growth ban jaata hai.

- Jab aadmi ghar aata hai, usse sirf information nahi chahiye — usse connection chahiye.
- Sirf "kya khana hai" ya "ye bill bharna hai" se uska mann nahi lagega.
- Jab aap usse mentally involve karte ho — uska stress kam hota hai, bonding badhti hai aur tab usey aapse partner wali feeling aati hai.

**Aap samajh pa rahe ho na main kya bol raha hu?**
Agey kya karna hai, agle page me maine woh bhi bataya hai.

**5 E's ke Magic ko samjho**

Kabhi-kabhi pyaar khatam nahi hota, bas growth match nahi karti. Jab ek partner apne upar kaam karta rahta hai — naye ideas, habits, learning ke saath grow karta hai — aur doosra partner wahi kaam, routine aur complaints mein atka rehta hai, toh ek be-aawaz doori shuru ho jaati hai. Uska solution? Dono ka milkar evolve karna.

**Ye 5 E's par focus karo**

**1. Education – Saath Seekhna**

Naye podcasts, documentaries, ya kisi topic pe discussion — jab dono seekhte hain, toh sirf dimaag nahi, dil bhi judta hai.

**2. Entertainment – Saath Hansna**

Routine se break lo. Comedy show dekho, game khelo, ya sirf masti karo — bina kisi stress ke.
Laughter is a great connector.

**3. Emotional Depth – Dil Se Judo**

"Tumhe sabse zyada darr kis cheez ka lagta hai?"
Aise sawaal dosti badhaate hain. Surface-level baatein chor kar andar ki feelings samjho.

**4. Engagement – Involved Raho**

Bas saath rehna kaafi nahi. Partner ke kaam, passion aur efforts mein interest lo.
Unhe lage — "Mujhe suna jaa raha hai."

**5. Evolution – Saath Grow Karo**

Har week pucho: "Tune is hafte kya naya seekha?"
Jab dono grow karte hain, tabhi rishta evolve karta hai.

Pyaar ko zinda rakhne ke liye sirf dil nahi, dimaag se bhi connection chahiye.
Sirf alag-alag grow mat karo — saath mein grow karo.
**Resources me ek '5 E's Weekly Challenge for Couples' diya hai**

## Understanding Love Language

Rishton Ki Gehraai Ka Raaz 🩶

Sab log pyaar ko ek jaise feel nahi karte.
Na sab usse ek jaise express karte hain.
Dr. Gary Chapman ne ek amazing concept diya — The 5 Love Languages (book).
Isse samajh aata hai ki hum aur humare partner kaise aur kab sabse zyada pyaar feel karte hain.

**Ek insaan 5 tareeke se pyaar ko feel karta hai.**

**1. Words of Affirmation – Jab Shabd Dil Chhoo Jaayein**
Kuch logon ko pyaar tab feel hota hai jab unhe appreciation aur encouragement milti hai.
Chhoti chhoti lines jaise: "I'm proud of you.", '"Tu meri best friend hai", "Tere bina adhura lagta hai." "You are very beautiful", Etc.
Yeh unka din banane ke liye kaafi hai.
(Meri wife toh emotional hojati hai thoda sa kuch bolte hi)

**2. Receiving Gift - Jab kuch unka pasandida unhe milta hai**
Gifts sirf cheezein nahi, thoughtfulness ka symbol hain.
Ek chhota surprise, handwritten note, ya koi meaningful gift — yeh unke liye pyaar ko receive karne ka tareeka hai.

**3. Quality Time – Sirf unke liye time nikalna**
Kuch logon ko tab pyaar feel hota hai jab aap unke saath poora waqt, bina distractions ke bitaate ho.

- Phone side mein rakho.
- Meaningful baatein karo.
- Saath waqt bitana = pyaar ko gehra karna.
- Unko jin topics me interest hai, unke baare me baat karna

(Meri love language yahi hai)

**4. Acts of Service – Unki madad karna**

Kisi ko acha lagta hai aap unke liye ya unke saath me kaam karein.

- Unke liye khana banana.
- Subah ki chai unko bed me dena
- Stressful kaam main madad karna.

Yeh sab unke liye sab kuch hota hai.

**5. Physical Touch – Jab Chhoone Se Tasalli Miley**

Kuch logon ko pyaar tab feel hota hai jab aap physical connection banate ho.

- Holding hands.
- Ek tight hug.
- Shoulder par reassuring tap.

Apne partner ki love language samajhne ki koshish karo, unko observe karo - harr action kuch kehta hai.
Kamm efforts me zyada khush rakh paoge. Aur apni love language bhi samjhane ki koshish karo.

**Toh Aapka Love Language Kya Hai?**
**Aur Aapke Partner Ka?**
**(Resources me aapko activity milegi 'Apna Love Language Discover Karo')**

## Shaadi Mein Love Language Kyun Zaroori Hai?

***Sabse common galti kya hoti hai relationships mein?***
Yeh soch lena ki jo tareeka aapko pyaar feel karata hai, wahi aapke partner ko bhi karayega.

**Example:**
Agar aapka love language hai Words of Affirmation (jaise "I love you" roz kehna), Aur aapke partner ka hai Acts of Service (kaam me madad karna),
Toh ho sakta hai ki aap roz bolte ho "I love you", Lekin jab tak aap unke liye unke hisaab se kuch kar nahi rahe ho, Woh feel hi nahi kar rahe ki aap unse pyaar karte ho.
**Example** - Aapke husband ko aaloo ka parantha pasand hai lekin aap roz unke liye subah uth kar ghanton mehnat karke bread pakoda bana rahe hai. Aur phir soch rahe ho ki main itna kuch karti hu, ye khush hi nahi hote.
Behen - Usko aaloo ka parantha pasand hai. Bass itna samajh lo.

**Love Language Samajhna = Sahi Se Pyaar Karna Seekhna**
Apne partner ka love language samajhna, pyaar karne ka ek naya tareeka seekhne jaisa hai —
Partner ki love language sikhna matlab unhe unke tareeke se pyaar karna. Jaisa unko pasand hai. Jaisa unko chahiye. Jo unhe khush kare. Iss se misunderstanding kamm hoti hai, aur connection deep ho jaata hai.

**Shaadi Ek Safar Hai, Destination Nahi.**
Log sochte hai shadi hogai.. bass ab kya efforts daalna.
**BIG Mistake**. Shaadi me apko roz grow karna hoga aur ek dusre ke liye better partner kaise banein, iss process par kaam karna hoga.

It's not about finding the perfect person.
It's about becoming the right person for each other.
Aur Jab Life me challenges aate hai...
Tab bhi pyaar mein woh power hai jo nayi roshni laa sakta hai.
Bas zaroorat hai samajhne ki – kaise pyaar ko feel kiya jaata hai, kaise express kiya jaata hai.

## Couple Connect:

"Hum Dono Ka Time" Activity

Pyaar, samajh aur connection ko deep karne ka ek beautiful tareeka.

**Step 1: Memory Lane – "Hamari Best Moments"**
Dono partners apne 3 favourite moments likho jo aapne saath bitaye ho.
Ek-ek karke share karo aur batao kyun wo moment special hai.

Example:
"Ek moment jo main kabhi nahi bhoolunga/bhoolungi wo tha jab hum __________ gaye the, kyunki uss din mujhe laga ki __________."

**Step 2: Dream Jar – "Hamare Sapne"**
Ek doosre ko 2 apne sapne aur 2 couple goals batao jo aap future mein achieve karna chahte ho.
Unhe likhkar ek jar mein daal do jiska naam ho "Hamare Sapno Ka Jar."
Example:

- **Personal Goal:** "Mujhe apna business start karna hai."
- **Couple Goal**: "Chalo Bali chalte hain next year!"

Har 6 mahine baad jar kholo, check karo kaunse sapne pure hue aur naye sapne add karo.

**Step 3: Appreciation Game – "Mujhe Tum Mein Ye Pasand Hai"**
Time lo aur 5 cheezein likho jo tumhe apne partner mein pasand hain ya appreciate karte ho.
Phir ek doosre ko pyaar se padh kar sunao.

**Specific bano!**
"Tu acchi hai" ke bajaye bolo, "Mujhe bahut achha lagta hai jab tu thake hone par bhi mere liye khana bana deti hai. Mera aur family ka itna dhyaan rakhti hai."

**Step 4: Love Language Ki Baat**
Pucho ek doosre se:
"Aisi ek chhoti si baat kya hai jo main iss week kar sakta/sakti hoon jisse tumhe zyada pyaar mehsoos ho?"
Usse likho aur agle 7 din ke andar wo zaroor karo.

**Couple Wali Photo**
Activity ke end mein ek cute selfie ya Polaroid picture lo, date ke saath save karo. Har mahine ek nayi yaad banane ka naya ritual.

**Reflection Time:**

- Aaj apne partner ke baare mein kya naya jaana?
- Kaisa feel hua ye activity kar ke?
- Aisi kaunsi ek baat hai jo tum apne relationship mein aur zyada karna chahoge/chahogi?

Ab na aap me se kuch logo ko lagega ki iski kya zarurat hai yaar!
Samjho pyaar na apne aap me magical cheez hai.. usme aap regular energy daal kar khush nahi ho sakte. Usme aapko thoda pagalpan, thoda mazak, romance and surprises jaisi cheezein daalti rehni padegi.

Aapki life me koi bhi cheez agar acchi hai toh woh isiliye hai kyunki aapne usme bohot efforts daalein hai. Be it your education, job, business, etc.
Lekin jab rishtey ki baat aati hai, tab hum sochte hai sab apne aap sahi hojayega. Ya phir samne wala efforts daalega.
Humne hamare ghar ya surrounding me bhi yahi dekha hai ki aadmi zyada express nahi karta.
Come on, hum ek partnership me hai aur partnership koi si bhi ho, dono ke efforts ke bina nahi chal sakti.
Aur ye sochna band karo ki ab kuch nahi ho sakta, humein toh 20 saal hogaye saath me, aise hi rehna hai sab boring sa.
Pray karo aur apni taraf se effort daalna chalu karo.

Trust me sab kuch badal sakta hai :)

## Ladne Ka Sahi Tareeka:

Strong Marriage Ka Secret

Mujhe aur meri wife ko social media pe bohot pyaar milta hai — **@viniandjai** hamara username hai.
Hum apni journey, apna pyaar, aur kabhi-kabhi apne struggles bhi share karte hain.

Sabse zyada pucha jaane wala sawaal?
"Aap log ladte ho kabhi?"
**Answer**: Haan, ladte hain. Aur isme koi galat baat nahi hai.
Ladna galat nahi hai, tareeka galat ho sakta hai.
Ladaai hona toh natural hai.
Bura tab hota hai jab hum ladte hain jeetne ke liye,
Na ki problem ko resolve ke liye.

**Jeetne Wale Fights vs. Problem-Solving Fights**
Har fight mein apne aap se ek simple sawaal puchho:
Main jeetne ki koshish kar raha hoon ya problem solve karne ki?
Agar goal hai "Main right hoon, tum wrong ho",
Toh fight khatam nahi hoti — sirf delay ho jaati hai. Isse hamesha dil bhara rehta hai aur aap kahi bhi bikhar sakte ho.

**Lekin agar goal hai:**
"Chalo milke samajhte hain, solution nikalte hain,"
Tab rishta strong banta hai aur aap dono khush rehte ho.

**Marriage Is a Team Game, Not a Tug-of-War**
*Fight ke beech mein yeh line yaad rakhna:*
"Hum dono ek dusre ke against nahi, problem ke against hain."
Mindset badlo, aur fights bhi pyaar ka zariya ban jaayengi.

Aur haan... ek baat yaad rakhna
**Happy Wife = Happy Life!**
(Trust me, life bohot easy ho jaati hai)

Chapter 27

# VIRU PAAJI KI ENTRY

March 2022 me Vini ne ek khushkhabri di — hum parents banne wale the.
Pehle toh samajh nahi aaya kaise react karu, par dil ke andar ek ajeeb si khushi thi — mere liye, meri maa ke liye, parivar ke liye, aur uss chhoti si jaan ke liye jo ab hamare beech aane wali thi.

Uss waqt, main Nishank ke baare mein bhi soch raha tha. Mujhe usko business start karwana tha aur kuch time me uski shadi bhi karwani thi. Family badh rahi thi, aur papa ke jaane ke baad ek father figure wali responsibility mehsoos ho rahi thi.

Vini ke tauji (bade papa) se mujhe rishton ke baare me bohot kuch seekhne ko milta hai.
Papa ke jaane ke baad ekbar main unse baat kar raha tha toh unhone mujhse kuch kaha. Unki ye baat me kabhi nahi bhulta aur usi par apna jeevan jeeta hu.
Woh log 3 bhai hai.
Unhone kaha ki beta mera kaam mere dono bhaiyon ka dhyaan rakhna hai. Unko koi taqleef nahi aaye, unke saare kaam hote rahe, woh dono saath aur khush rahe ye meri zimmedaari hai..
Baaki mere baccho ka dhyaan rakhna unki zimmedaari hai.
Agar maine mere bhaiyon ko achi zindagi aur soch dedi toh ghar ke baaki bacche apne aap set hojaenge aur khush rahenge.

Ye baat sunkar mujhe realize hua ki ek bada ghar acche se chalane ke liye aisi soch hi chahiye hoti hai. Selfless. Maine unko kabhi apne akele ke baare me sochte nahi dekha. Kabhi mujhe aisa nahi laga ki Vini unki bacchi nahi hai. Aisa lagta hai sab bacche inke hi toh hai.
Uss din maine uss soch ko apna liya aur pray karta hu aisa hi rahu.

Mere sasur ji mere go to person hai, mere dost, mere pitaji ki jagah ab wahi hai. Maze ki baat ye hai ki unka naam bhi **Mr. Vijay Pareek** hai, mere pitaji ki tarah. Mein bohot grateful hu ki mujhe woh mile, Vini ke through poora parivar mila aur ye value system dekhne ko mila. Vini ke ghar me 4 ladies hai aur aaj bhi chaaro ek hi plate me khana khaati hai.
**Unka maanna hai ki lad lo, lekin baatein band mat karo.**

## Chapter 28

# WE FINALLY BECAME A BUSINESS FAMILY

Ab main aapko ek cheez batane wala hu, isko please try mat karna. Ya karo toh apni risk par karna.
Nishank ke liye me koi business dekh raha tha, pareshan hogaya tha kuch samajh nahi aa raha tha.
Ekdin pareshan hokar maine bhagwan ko kaha ki bhagwan aap mujhe clarity de nahi rahe ho par aaj mujhe jawaab chahiye,
Main google search karunga 'best business in Jaipur', jo sabse upar aayega main wahi business start kardunga.
Agey aap sambhal lena.
Maine phone uthaya, search kiya aur samne aaya..
TumbleDry Laundry and Dryclean.

Main sab kuch Papa ji (sasur ji) se discuss karta hu kyuki woh experienced insaan hai aur khoob businesses build kiye hai unhone, Maine kaha Father sahab ye ek business hai, start karna hai Jaipur me. Unhone kaha theek hai meeting arrange karo, samajhte hai.
Meeting hui, sab acche se samjhaya team Tumbledry ne. Meeting ke baad Papa ji, Anshul (Vini's brother), Nishank hum sab ne connect kiya Zoom par. Kisi ne bola aur aisi brands se meeting karke samajhte hai. Maine kaha theek hai aur meeting end ki.
Maine Nishank ko dekha aur usse poocha, "Ready hai?"
Bina soche, usne kaha, "Jo teri iccha!"
Maine TumbleDry ke representative ko call karke bola 'ghar aao aur cheque leke jaao, business start kar rahe hai hum'.
Humare paas is business ka koi background nahi tha. Iska kya, kisi business ka background nahi tha, mere parents dono government jobs me the. Jo kiya woh Dubai me gir padke seekha tha.

Agle 4 mahine humne **TumbleDry, Bani Park, Jaipur** set up kiya, Finalizing location, store building, set up, business trainings, etc.
Kuch paisa mumma se liya, kuch mera aur kuch Nishank ka.
Vini ke tummy mein humara beta, Vir, grow kar raha tha.
Roz hum 8-9 ghante store set up kar rahe hote the. Pata hi nahi chala pregnancy kab nikal gai. Aur iss process me humne Garbh Vidhya padhi jisne humein parenting aur pregnancy ke baare me kaafi kuch sikhaya. Ab main pregnancy ke baare me pro bann chuka hu. Help chahiye toh batana :)
Kabhi kabhi lagta hai, papa is duniya se isliye gaye – taaki mujhe yeh sab sikha sakein, kyuki aise toh main unki sunta nahi tha kabhi.

Jab hamari store ready hui, uss din laga —finally family me ek "proper business" start ho gaya hai. Hum ab ek business family hai.

Pitaji bada khush hote ye sab dekh kar.
Ek naya era shuru ho chuka tha.

**FIRST MEETING KE BAAD TUMBLEDRY KO PEHLA CHEQUE DIYA**

Kuch din pehle ghar ki second car bhi aise hi aai thi.
Nishank ne ek din uth kar bola, bhai kal sapne main Polo GT chala raha tha.
Main, Nishank aur Vini kaam ke baad drive kar rahe hote the usually. Toh drive karte karte maine kaha le chal VolksWagon showroom dekhte hai teri Polo.
Hum waha gaye aur pucha ki Red Polo hai kya available.
Unhone kaha sir 6-12 months ki waiting hai.
Humne usse bye bola aur ghar jaane lage.
Jaise ki woh haa bolta toh hum khareed hi lete.

Usne piche se aawaz lagai aur bola ki sir ek car zaroor khadi hai, kisi ne mangwai thi lekin uska loan pass nahi hua toh woh le nahi paaya. Aap kaho toh dikha doon.

Woh car dekhi, koi kuch socche usse pehle maine token amount diya aur ek mahina baad Nishank ke birthday par woh car ghar le aaye.
**VolksWagon Polo GT, Automatic.**

**Secret Reason** - Main Nishank par thoda pressure daalna chahta tha EMI ka. Expense jab badhte hai toh income apne aap badh jaati hai. Aur jab gaadi aati hai toh laadi bhi aa jaati hai.

## Fixed Mindset vs. Growth Mindset

Hamari soch hi tay karti hai ki hum life mein kitna aage badh paayenge. Aur isi mein chhupi hai Fixed Mindset aur Growth Mindset ki kahaani.

**Fixed Mindset – Jab Soch Ruk Jaati Hai**
**Fixed mindset kehta hai:** "Talent aur ability ya toh hoti hai ya nahi hoti– seekhne se kuch farq nahi padta.
Zindagi bhar seekhte hi thodi rahenge. Hogai padhai."

**Log jinhe lagta hai:**

- "Mujhse nahi hoga."
- "Agar fail hua toh log kya kahenge?"
- "Main pehle bhi haar gaya tha, toh ab kyun try karu?"

**Inka focus hota hai:**

- Safe rehna - Galti se bachna,
- Dikhawa karna ki sab perfect hai.

Result? Growth ruk jaati hai.

**Growth Mindset – Jab Soch Aage Badhti Hai**
Ye mindset kehta hai:
"Skills aur talent seekh kar develop hote hain – main mehnat se improve kar sakta hoon."

**Log jinhe lagta hai:**

- "Main seekh sakta hoon."
- "Galtiyaan improvement ka part hain."
- "Agar mehnat ki, toh result milega."
- "Failure = Feedback."

**Inka focus hota hai:**

- Seekhna, experiment karna aur apne comfort zone se nikalna.

Result? Progress, confidence aur real success.

**Fixed Mindset**: "Main public speaking ke liye nahi bana."
**Growth Mindset**: "Abhi nahi aata, lekin practice se seekh jaunga."

**Real life example se samjho**
Socho, do log business shuru karna chahte hain, lekin dono ke paas zero experience hai:

**Person A – Fixed Mindset**
"Mujhe business ka kuch nahi pata... toh try karne ka kya faayda?"
**Result**? – Life wahi ki wahi. Sapne, sirf sapne reh jaate hain.

**Person B – Growth Mindset**
"Mujhe business ka abhi zyada nahi pata... lekin seekh sakta hoon. Research karunga, courses loonga, mentors se sikhoonga."
**Result**? – Skill build hoti hai, confidence aata hai, aur business chalu ho jaata hai!

**Difference? - Mindset Matters**
Talent nahi tha dono ke paas. Bas mindset alag tha.

**Growth Mindset Kaise Develop Karein?**
- Challenge se bhaago mat – usse grow karo
- "Main nahi kar sakta" → Replace it with → "Main seekh sakta hoon"
- Result pe mat atko – Progress ko celebrate karo

**Final Thought:**
Tumhara mindset hi tumhara future banata hai.
Career ho, relationships ho, ya personal growth – growth mindset hamesha aapko aage le kar jaega.
Talent aur luck mein mat faso – apne aap par believe karo, seekhte raho – aur dekho zindagi kaise badalti hai.

Jab hamne TumbleDry start kiya tha humko woh kaam nahi aata tha, par aaj woh ek successful business hai. Kyuki humne usko seekhne me jaan daal di thi. Kisi din business band hua toh iska reason hoga - ya toh efforts mein kami hogai humse business build karne me ya koi bada plan hai dimag me.
Waise chance kamm hai band hone ke because Chinu loves his business. Uska pehla business haina.

## Paise Se Rishta Sudharo – Zindagi Badal Jaayegi!

## Money mindset 2 types ke hote hai

Aap Kaunsa Follow Karte Ho?

**Scarcity Mindset (Kami ka Manasikta)**

- **Soch**: "Paisa kabhi enough nahi hota," "Mujhe hamesha paise ki kami rahegi."
- **Behaviour**: Har kharche pe hangama, risk lene se darna, naye mauke ko "paise barbaad honge" sochke avoid karna.
- **Focus**: "Kya hoga agar mere paas paisa khatam ho gaya toh?"
- **Natija**: Hamesha tension, opportunities miss karna, financial insecurity wali feeling me rahoge.

**Example**:
Salary milne ke baad bhi sochte ho, "Agla bill kaise bharunga?"

**Abundance Mindset (Samriddhi ka Manasikta)**

- **Soch**: "Paisa kamane ke anek raste hain," "Main aur kama sakta/ti hoon."
- **Behaviour**: Calculated risks lena, apni skill aur knowledge me invest karna, zaruratmandon ki madad karna.
- **Focus**: "Kaise aur opportunities grab karun? Kya naya seekhu"
- **Natija**: Growth, naye mauke seize karna, financial confidence.

**Example:**
Naya course kharidte time sochna, "Isse meri earning badhegi," na ki "Budget khatam ho jayega."

**Tip:**

- Roz gratitude likho ("Thank you universe for more money").
- Positive affirmations bolo ("Main paise attract kar raha/rahi hoon").
- Chhote steps me invest karo—jaise ek online skill course ya mutual fund.

## Common Beliefs Jo Aapko Roke Hue Hain:

**"Paisa kharab cheez hai." –**
Nahi! Paisa neutral hota hai – usko use kaise karte ho, woh sahi ya kharab result deta hai.

Meri ek mentor hamesha ek baat bolti thi ki log sochte hai zyada paisa jiske paas hota hai woh bura insaan hota hai.
Nahi. Paisa sirf ek magnifying tool hai.
Aap jaise bhi ho, paisa jab aapke paas aega, aapke character ko magnify kardega.
Aap agar acche insaan ho toh paisa aate hi aur acche hojaoge
Bure ho toh paisa aate hi aur bure.

People say - **Main paise manage nahi kar sakta.**
Bhai ye ek skill hai, talent nahi.
Budgeting, saving, investing – seekha jaa sakta hai.

Aap sochte ho, *"Zyada kamaunga tabhi save kar paunga."*
Galat! Kam paisa mein bhi saving ki aadat banao.

**"Rich log toh lucky hote hain."**
Majority ne mehnat, planning, aur patience se wealth banayi hai.
Unn logo ki nazar me aap bhi lucky ho jinke paas hath, pair, ghar, khana jaisi cheezein nahi hai.

## Mindset Shift Ka Formula:

- Scarcity → Abundance
- Guilt → Gratitude
- Fear → Action

**Reminder**:
Paisa kamaya jaa sakta hai – par pehle uska relation apne saath sudharo. Apne aap ko kaho - Main paisa deserve karta hoon, aur usse wisely grow kar sakta hoon.
I am a magnet to money, money likes me.
I attract money from all the directions.
Yeh affirmations roz bolna start karo and mean it when you say it.

Chapter 29

# DREAMS FOR FAMILY

## Sab sapno ka hi game hai

Mere do sapne the apne parivaar ke liye:

**1. Mere baad jitne bhi ghar me bacche hain, sabke paas apna apna iphone ho**

Jab me Dubai gaya tha, mere mann mein tha ki ek din mere saare chhote bhai-behen iPhone use karein, aur main unhe gift karu.
Ekbar Jaipur me kisiko apni family ke liye 4 iphones eksath kharidte huve dekh liya tha maine. Bass woh ek sapna bann gaya tha.

Aaj ghar me 10 se zyada iPhones hain. Jab naya leta tha, mera wala Chinu ke paas jata, uska wala Richa ke paas, phir Keshav, Cherry and so on.
Ab toh–

- 4 MacBooks
- 6 AirPods
- 5 Apple Watches (22 March 2025 tak)

Log soch sakte hain ki yeh sab materialistic hai. Par mere liye – yeh ek journey ka symbol hai. Kahan se chale the, aur aaj kahaan pahunche hain – uski nishani hai.
Aap ko lag raha hoga isme kya badi baat hai?
Haa mere liye bhi nahi hai ab toh.
Lekin woh purane wale Jai ke liye ye sapna tha. Main toh bass usko khush karne me laga hota hu mostly.
Usey acha lagta hai ye sab karna.

**2. Family me business**

Mere baad ki generation me sab business karein – yeh sapna tha.
Aaj Nishank aur Vini dono apne apne businesses kar rahe hai.
Cheezein behtar ho rahi hain. Woh sapne, jo sirf khayal the, aaj sach ban rahe hain. Main khush hoon.
Shukraguzaar hoon Kanha ka.

Aur haan – ab ek full bucket list taiyyar hai.
Sapne khatam nahi hue – next level par aa gaye hai.

Chapter 30

# THE PRESENT AND BEYOND

## From Dreams to Destiny – And the Journey Ahead

In 2022, I took a leap of faith and started my Soft Skills coaching business: '**Perform – The Soft Skills and Image School**'
Its doing well. Maine abhi tak hazaaron logon ko train kiya hai, helping them build confidence, communication, and their own personal brand. Ek book likhne ka mann tha, woh bhi ho gaya.

Nishank is married to our beautiful bahu Bhavika, bohot acche se apna business sambhal raha hai. Vini aur main, content creation karte hai, travel karte hai, laakhon logo ki ek digital family hai, jisko aur badha rahe hai. Harr mahine, 3-6 crore log humein dekhte hai —and honestly, it still amazes me. But now... there's a bigger dream on the horizon.
After 15 jobs, in 7 Industries, 6 businesses, working and traveling in 8 countries (and counting)— I've realized what I truly want.
I want to be healthy, wealthy and wise. Exactly jo school me sikha tha. Mujhe fit rehna hai, jo mann ho woh karna hai, logon ki madad karni hai, price tag dekhe bina shop karna hai, parivar ko ek life of choices deni hai, Vir ko is planet ki sabse cool cheez banana hai.

Is book me meri 30 saal tak ki journey hai.
Abhi tak me khushi ke liye, kick ke liye aur explore karne ke liye kaam karta tha, abhi iske saath saath me wealth & legacy par focus karna chahta hu.

Abhi toh shuruwaat hui hai. Agey main Spirituality me jana chahta hu, Yoga karna chahta hu, Travel karna chahta hu, nayi nayi cheezein seekhna chahta hu (acting, digital marketing, instruments, film making, skydiving, kite surfing, flying plane, sailing, jo bhi Vir sikhega woh aur bohot lambi list hai)

30 se aagey ki story ek dusri book me likhenge, aur behtar insaan bankar.
Tab tak ke liye aasha karta hu ye book aapke liye life changing ho
Aap apne liye aur apne parivar ke liye jeena seekhein.
Soft skills ko life ka ek important hissa banaye
Mazein karein, kisi se zyada expectations na rakhein
aur bohot zyada khush rahein.

Jab bhi aap ye book padho, acchi si energy bhej dena. Hope usko use karke main aapke liye kuch aur accha lekar aau future me.

**Before I say good bye to you**
2 actions me chahta hu aap instantly lein...

- Create a **Vision Board (Exercise)**
- Plan out your **Golder Hour**
  **- HEART ROUTINE**

Go to next page to learn how!

## Vision Board Activity

Create Your Vision Board

Turn your dreams into daily inspiration.

**Step 1: Gather Materials**

- Poster board or thick sheet of paper
- Scissors
- Magazines, newspapers, or printed pictures from the internet
- Markers, pens, or colors
- Glue or pins

**Step 2: Reflect & Choose Themes**

Spend 5–10 minutes quietly reflecting:

- Main zindagi mein sach mein kya chahta/chahti hoon?
- Mujhe sabse zyada kya khush karta hai?
- Kaunse achievements ka sapna dekhta/dekhti hoon?
- Kaunse experiences lena chahta/chahti hu?

**Choose 3–5 life themes to focus on: (themes chuno)**

- Career & Finances
- Health & Wellness
- Relationships & Family
- Travel & Experiences
- Personal Growth & Learning

**Step 3: Find & Cut Out Images (Images Dhundo & Cut Karo)**

Har theme ke liye aisi photos, quotes, symbols ya words talaasho jo tumhare dreams ko represent karte ho.

**Examples:**

- **Career**: Dream office setup, logo of your ideal company, stacks of books/certifications
- **Health**: Fit body, yoga, healthy food, morning routine
- **Travel**: Eiffel Tower, mountains, beaches, passport stamps

**Step 4: Apna Vision Board Setup Karo**

- Apni images ko is tarah arrange karo ki dekhte hi energy aur inspiration feel ho.
- Apne personal quotes ya mantras likho—colorful pens se style me likho.
- Yeh board tumhara personal vision hai—use bold, beautiful, aur bilkul "YOU" banao.

**Step 5: Roz Dekhne Wali Jagah Pe Lagao**

- Apna board us jagah rakho jo tum roz dekhte ho—apne room me, workspace me ya phone/laptop wallpaper ki tarah.

**Step 6: Roz 1–2 Minute Visualization**

- Har subah ya shaam apna vision board dekho.
- Khud ko woh zindagi jeete hue imagine karo.
- Jitna ho sake usse apni daily actions aur decisions ke liye motivation lo.

**"Tumhara vision board sirf sapney nahi; yeh unhe haqeeqat banane ka roadmap hai."**

## The Golden Hour - Morning Mastery

Start your day strong

Jis tareeke se aap apna din shuru karte hain, wahi tareeka poore din ko shape karta hai. Isi liye duniya ke successful log apne din ke pehli ghante ko Golden Hour kehte hain—aur is samay ka sahi se use karte hain.

**Golden Hour Kya Hai?**
Subah uthne ke baad ke pehle 60 minutes—jab aapka dimaag sabse fresh hota hai, energy high hoti hai, aur subconscious mind active hota hai. Aapne agar iss 1 ghante ko acche se invest kardiya toh ye aapke bachey huve 23 ghanton ka dhyaan rakh lega.

Yeh wahi waqt hota hai jab aap apne dimaag ko positive thoughts, clarity aur purpose de sakte hain.

**Kyun Zaroori Hai?**

- Din bhar focus aur productivity badhata hai
- Stress kam hota hai, aur self-control develop hota hai
- Aap apne goals ke saath better aligned hote hain
- Confidence aur mental strength banti hai
- Aapki energy sahi rehti hai

"Agar aapne apni subah jeet li, toh poora din jeet gaye.
Aur din jeet gaye, toh zindagi jeet gaye."

Toh kal subah sirf uthna nahi hai—
Rise. Apne din ko re-create kijiye. Apni zindagi ke master baniye.
Aapka samay golden hai—usse ek champion ki tarah jeeyein.

**1 Hour me karna kya hoga?**
Aapke liye maine ek concept banaya hai jo aapko life ke harr aspect me grow karne me help karega. Be it physical, mental, spiritual, financial or emotional. Iska concept ka naam hai **HEART Routine.**

# HEART ROUTINE

Zindagi sirf ek race nahi hai – yeh ek safar hai jisme har din thoda behtar banna, har pal mein khushi dhundhna aur apne sapno ki taraf steadily badhna zaroori hai. Ye framework aapki journey me ek dost ki tarah aapka saath dega.

**The HEART Routine**
Chaliye, samjhte hain HEART ka har letter aapki life ko kaise transform kar sakta hai.

**H – Health (Physical)**
Tandurusti hazaar niyaamat hai – Health is a thousand blessings aur health ke bina koi bhi success adhuri hai.

- **Exercise Regularly:** Gym ho, yoga ho, ya ghar ke workouts—jo bhi pasand ho, daily thoda movement zaroor karein.
- **Healthy Eating**: Apne meals plan karein aur nutritious khaana explore karein. Swasth aur swaad dono ka balance banayein.
- **Outdoor Fun**: Running, cycling, games, dance ya hiking—kuch bhi karein jo aapko active rakhe aur khushi de.
- **Self-care:** Relaxing bath lijiye, skincare karein ya kabhi-kabhi khud ko ek choti si massage dekar unwind karein.

**E – Education & Earning (Financial Growth)**
Padhai aur paisa dono ka balance zaroori hai. Gyaan aur income dono badhaiye.

- **Courses Join Karein:** Online ya offline koi bhi skill seekhne ka mauka kabhi chhodiye mat. Hamesha ek course me enroll raho.
- **Financial Goals Set Karein:** Short aur long term goals likhiye, track karein aur celebrate bhi karein.
- **Budgeting Habit Banaiye:** Paisa kaha jaa raha hai, iss par nazar rakhiye. Save aur invest karne ki aadat daaliye.
- **Side Hustle:** Apne passion ko income mein badaliye—freelance karein, coaching dein ya kuch bhi jo aap enjoy karein.
- **Finance Books Padhiye**: Paisa samajhna bhi ek kala hai—isse master kijiye.

### A – Affirmations & Gratitude (Emotional Strength)

Jo insaan har roz shukriya ada karta hai, uski zindagi mein aur zyada khushiyan aati hain.

- **Daily Gratitude**: Har din teen cheeze likhiye jinke liye aap thankful hain.
- **Affirmations:** "Main capable hoon", "Main successful hoon"—aise positive words roz repeat karke apni energy shift kijiye.
- **Apne Aap ko Compliment Karein:** Apni choti choti jeet ka celebration kijiye.
- **Love Notes to Self:** Khud ke liye pyare notes likhiye.
- **Emotional Check-ins:** Hafte mein ek baar, apne emotions ka review lijiye—kaisa mehsoos kar rahe hain, aur kya better ho sakta hai?

### R – Reflection (Mental Clarity)

Khud ke saath waqt bitaiye, aur dekhiye aap kitne zyada aware ho jaate hain.

- **Journaling**: Apne thoughts, dreams aur daily learnings likhiye. Agar aap woh insaan hai jo easily express nahi karta. Ek diary lijiye aur daily raat me jo mind me chal raha hai sab likh dijiye. Aapko accha mehsoos hoga.
- **Visualization**: Apne sapno ko aankhon ke saamne dekhiye—jaise sab kuch already sach ho chuka hai.
- **Meditation**: Daily 5-10 mins mind ko shant kijiye. Clarity aur focus dono milega.
- **Self-Assessment**: Apne strong aur weak points samajhiye, aur improve karne ka ek plan banaiye.
- **Daily Lesson:** Roz ek lesson likhiye jo zindagi ne sikhaya ho.

**T – Team Up with God (Spiritual Growth)**

Zindagi mein faith ho toh raste khud ban jaate hain.

- **Prayers**: Har din prayers karein – dil se. Chahe chhoti ho ya badi, har dua important hai. Kahi ek baat padhi thi - **Push yourself to pray, otherwise something else will push you not to.**
- **Spiritual Readings**: Aise books padhiye jo aapke soul ko shanti aur direction dein.
- **Workshops Attend Karein:** Kabhi spiritual retreats, seminars mein jaaiye—inner growth ko boost milega.
- **Morning & Night Rituals**: Din ki shuruaat aur ant kuch shaant palon ke saath kijiye.
- **Acts of Kindness:** Kisi ki madad kijiye—zaroori nahi paisa ho, ek muskaan bhi kaafi hai.

**HEART ko samjhein – Har Din Grow Karein**

Yeh routine ek perfect life ka promise nahi deta, lekin ek balanced aur purposeful life ki shuruaat zaroor deta hai. Har din HEART ka ek chhota step lijiye.

Dheere-dheere aap feel karenge ki kaise aapki zindagi transform ho rahi hai—andar se bhi aur bahar se bhi.

Ab aap mujhe kaafi acche se jaan chuke honge, aur samajh chuke honge ki growth kabhi rukti nahi— main aapko aage badhne mein poori tarah support karne ke liye yahan hoon.

**Main ye sab services provide karta hu:**

1. Customized 1:1 and group Trainings
2. Soft-skills boot camps (Communication, leadership, emotional intelligence, public speaking, etc)
3. Yearly Soft Skills curriculum for schools and colleges
4. Seminars, webinars & Keynote Talks
5. Sessions in India and Internationally—college festivals, corporate conclaves, industry events, private sessions.
6. Brand Collaborations & Partnerships
7. Co-created content - social media campaigns
8. Personal Growth Retreats and Events
9. Weekend workshops related to: vision boarding, goal-setting, mindset, soft skills, relationship.
10. Workshops for schools. colleges and corporate.

**Aap apne liye plan bhi customize kar sakte hain.**

Feel free to reach out to me,
**contact@jaivpareek.com**
**www.jaivpareek.com**

Let's turn your "what if" into "wow, I did it!" Together, we'll build The Better You— aap online, offline, India ya duniya ke kisi bhi kone me ho, we will figure out a way.

Ye book padhne ke baad apna review social media par zaroor share karein, aur **@Shutupandlevelup.book** account ke saath collaborate karein**. Use hashtag #shutupandlevelup** Zyada se zyada logon ki help karne ki koshish karte hai.

## Gratitude!

Log kehte hai unhone sab kuch akele kiya hai. Jhoot hai. Aap kabhi kuch akele nahi kar sakte. Na maine kuch akele kiya. Meri life ke har difficult mod par koi na koi aisa insaan aaya jisne mujhe agey ka rasta dikhaya.

Is book ke zariye un sab log ko shukriya kehna chahta hu jinhone meri life me value add ki hai aur difficult time me mujhe support kiya hai,
**My good time is for you.**
I want to start with my Daadi -
**Sri Mati Shaanti Devi Pareek**
and my whole family from Kishangarh, Indore, Dhamnod and Bhilwara.

Agness ma'am, Rohini Jain ma'am, Seema Lal ma'am, Sudesh Yadav ma'am, Kavita ma'am, Sanjay Chaturvedi sir, Kapil Charan sir, DK sir, Renu Sarawta ma'am, Aarti ma'am, Chetan, Seema chachi, Sarika maami, & my cousins who stood by me.
Anand Yadav sir, Tanya Bhushan in Jaipur
Mrs. Lubna, Mehreen Raj, Charou Shonek, Sharfun ma'am, Rashid bhai, Shakila bhabhi, Nadeem sir, Shriya, Sahil, Keval, Shubhi, Yadu in Dubai.
Rashi, Anjali, Akanksha, Fiza. Papa ji. Nishank. Akshay
(Richa, Ruchi, Sanskar for fixing spelling mistakes in this book)

My childhood friends for being useless yet important.
Anand, Divya, Ansh and Dhairya.

## Final Message from Your Elder Brother

Ye kitaab sirf shuruaat hai.
Ab baari hai tumhari—action lene ki.
Chhota shuru karo.
Learn. Improve. Grow. ( Seekho. Sudharo. Badho.)

Perfect time ka intezaar mat karo—woh nahi aega.
Jo hai, jaisa hai, jahan ho—bas wahi se shuru karo.
Aur yaad rakhna, zindagi tumhe jahan bhi le jaaye,
main yahin hoon—tumhare liye, tumhari har jeet par taali bajata hua.

Ek hi zindagi hai, bohot saare supplementation bharni hai upar jaake. Theek hai?

With love and belief in you!
Tumhara bhai
**From Bharat - For Bharat**

**Shut Up and Level Up**



First Edition: May 2025
ISBN: 9789334287288

For permissions or inquiries, contact:
contact@jaivpareek.com
www.jaivpareek.com